BLOOD WORK

He started with her wrist, but the jagged bow-saw wasn't doing the job.

Desperately, he scanned the cluttered tool and die shop. The electric band-saw? No, too messy.

He took a long swig from a pint of whiskey and tried to think. Something had to work.

Then he remembered: His machinist dad had once solved a tough job by using just a band-saw blade, wrapping one end in cloth to form a handle.

That would be perfect. He located a few of the finely serrated blades and returned to the body. He retched into a garbage pail from time to time, but the liquor helped.

When he finished cutting Tara Grant into fourteen pieces, the killer dialed the dismembered woman's cell phone number. He waited for the beep.

"Tara, pick up the phone!" he yelled. "Call your kids!"

LIMB
FROM LIMB

George Hunter
and
Melissa Preddy

PINNACLE BOOKS
Kensington Publishing Corp.

http://www.kensingtonbooks.com

Some names have been changed to protect the privacy of individuals connected to this story.

PINNACLE BOOKS are published by

Kensington Publishing Corp.
119 West 40th Street
New York, NY 10018

All Kensington Titles, Imprints, and Distributed Lines are available at special quantity discounts for bulk purchases for sales promotions, premiums, fund-raising, and educational or institutional use. Special book excerpts or customized printings can also be created to fit specific needs. For details, write or phone the office of the Kensington special sales manager: Kensington Publishing Corp., 119 West 40th Street, New York, NY 10018, attn: Special Sales Department, Phone: 1-800-221-2647.

Pinnacle and the P logo Reg. U.S. Pat. & TM Off.

ISBN-13: 978-0-7860-2029-4
ISBN-10: 0-7860-2029-6

First printing: October 2009

10 9 8 7 6 5 4 3 2 1

Printed in the United States of America

LIMB
FROM LIMB

PART I

1

St. Valentine's Day, 2007, started off as a frozen, chaotic mess in southeast Michigan. The first blizzard of the winter had swept through overnight, dumping up to eight inches of snow across the region. As the Wednesday-morning rush hour approached, temperatures suddenly dipped into the teens, while winds gusted up to thirty miles an hour. Road crews frantically spread salt on streets and freeways, attempting to melt the ice before Metro Detroit's hundreds of thousands of commuters hit the roads. But the gale defeated their efforts, blowing the salt away. Swirling snow drifts blinded drivers and obscured slippery patches of pavement, causing dozens of fender benders throughout the tri-county Detroit suburbs.

About twenty-five miles east of downtown Detroit, in the nineteenth-century mineral-bath resort town of Mount Clemens, Deputy William Hughes was among the crew manning the lobby at the Macomb County Sheriff's Office (MCSO) headquarters. Hughes, a twenty-year veteran, reported for work at 10:00 A.M. and was greeted by a leak in the ceiling of his small office, right over his desk.

Hughes had just finished moving his desk out of the drip's soggy path when a fellow deputy poked his head in and said someone in the lobby wanted to file a missing persons complaint. Hughes prepared to write his first report of the day.

The visitor, Stephen Grant, was alone. Hughes beckoned him into the cement-block cubicle, apologizing for the messy, wet office. Stephen said he didn't mind and took a seat. He then pulled out a notebook and consulted it for a moment before commencing his story.

In a jittery voice, the pale, dark-haired, wide-eyed visitor told Hughes he hadn't heard from his thirty-four-year-old wife, Tara, since the previous Friday night, when she stormed out of their Washington Township home following an argument.

Stephen explained that his wife was an executive with Washington Group International, a construction and engineering company with branches throughout the world. Tara worked in the company's San Juan, Puerto Rico, office and returned home weekends, her husband said.

The veteran cop took notice of a gash on Stephen's nose. The inch-long scabbed wound immediately aroused his instincts.

"I was concerned about the scratch—plus, he had waited five days to report his wife missing," Hughes said. "And he kept looking at his notebook, like he was trying to keep his story straight."

Macomb County over the past decade has gone from the sparsely populated, semirural home of Michigan's last remaining military base to one of Metro Detroit's most prosperous and fast-growing bedroom communities. Still, the missing persons there tend to be drug addicts who drop out for a few days, or ice fishermen who inadvertently float out toward Canada on giant Lake St. Clair—not prosperous businesswomen from the upscale enclave of Washington Township.

"Something wasn't right here," Hughes recalled.

2

The slim thirty-seven-year-old six-footer told Hughes he was a stay-at-home dad who labored a few hours a week in his father William Grant's small tool-and-die shop, making ball bearings, while his wife worked in Puerto Rico during the week. Stephen said he worked around the house most of the time and took care of the couple's two children—six-year-old Lindsey and four-year-old Ian. He did have help, he added, from a nineteen-year-old live-in German au pair.

Hughes didn't have to ask many questions; Stephen volunteered most of the necessary information without any prompting.

"He was rambling, and his eyes were really bugging out," Hughes said. "He was talking really fast. I just kept quiet and let him talk. I was listening real close to what this guy was saying."

Stephen freely admitted he was irked by his wife's long absences. He told Hughes an argument about her frequent travel had broken out the night of February 9 when Tara phoned from Newark International Airport to tell him her flight home was delayed because of a huge snowfall that had hammered the East Coast the previous day. Tara also announced she would be returning to Puerto Rico on Sunday, a day earlier than usual, to prepare for a presentation. That's what started the altercation, Stephen said.

"He said they argued about her travel schedule while she was in the Newark airport," Hughes said. "He said they kept arguing and hanging up on each other, and then calling each other back and arguing again, the whole time she was heading home.

"I figured he was pretty hot when she got home, and I figured some kind of fight must have happened, because of the scratch on his nose," Hughes said. "But I didn't want to confront him with the scratch just yet. I wanted to just sit back and let him talk."

Stephen obliged. He told the officer he had argued with his wife for about twenty minutes after she arrived home from Detroit Metropolitan Airport. Then, he said, Tara made a call from her cell phone before abruptly leaving the house and riding away in a black sedan.

Stephen said he heard his wife say, "I'll be out in a minute" before she walked away. He told Hughes the car that picked her up may have been from an airport limousine service, he claimed, she frequently hired.

According to Stephen, his wife's last words before walking out the door were a reminder that he needed to deliver her white 2002 Isuzu Trooper to the dealership Monday for a dent repair.

Less than ten minutes after Tara left, Stephen said, he heard someone enter the house. He told Hughes he thought it was his wife returning, and he hollered, "What the hell are you doing home? Get out!"

His angry shout startled the couple's au pair, Verena Dierkes, a slender teen with long blond hair who was letting herself into the kitchen through the garage after a night of dancing with friends.

Stephen said he explained to the German girl, who'd taken a job with the Grants in August, that he'd just had an argument with Tara. After a brief conversation, the au pair went directly to her room, Stephen told Hughes.

The sheriff's deputy voiced the question that would occur to dozens of investigators and observers over the ensuing weeks. "I asked why he waited five days to report his wife missing," Hughes said. "He said Tara's boss told him to wait."

Stephen told Hughes he left several messages on Tara's cell phone on Saturday and Sunday, but he got no response. On Monday morning, Stephen said, he contacted Tara's Washington Group boss, Lou Troendle, in Puerto Rico, but learned she hadn't reported for work. Stephen said Troendle then told him to hold off calling the police.

"He said they were supposed to have some big meeting with everyone before going to the police," Hughes said. "It didn't make sense."

That Tuesday, Stephen said, he telephoned Tara's sister, Alicia Standerfer, and her mother, Mary Destrampe, but he said neither woman in the close-knit family circle had heard from his wife. By now, Stephen said, he told his sister-in-law he was so frantic that *he would be happy to find out if Tara was with a guy in a motel,* according to Hughes's report. *Stephen further stated that he believes Lou and Tara's mother were not being truthful regarding Tara.*

"I asked him, 'Why didn't you call us to your house to report your wife missing? She was last seen at your house—instead of that, you come into the lobby,'" Hughes recalled.

Stephen explained that his sister had a friend, a Sterling Heights police officer, who had advised him to come into police headquarters to make the report. Stephen then earnestly pointed to his notebook and said, "If you want his name, here's his name right here."

"I'm thinking, 'Why is he trying to provide me with so many alibis from people he's spoken to, and showing me their phone numbers?'" Hughes said. "It sounded like a guy who was looking for a way out."

Stephen further aroused Hughes's suspicions when, less than ten minutes into the interview, he named himself as a suspect. "He said, 'I talked to my father, and he said the first person who is always suspected in these cases is the husband.' I thought that was a really strange thing to say," Hughes said. "He sounded like a guy who had done something wrong, and was trying to get out of it. But I had to hear his whole story. I wanted to try to stay neutral."

Stephen offered Hughes a bizarre theory about what may have happened to his wife. "He said Washington Group demilitarized chemical weapons, and he said her immediate boss was in charge of that," Hughes said. "He came in with the story that his wife was kidnapped by terrorists, and that she may have been exposed to nerve gas. I'm thinking to myself, 'This guy has been watching too much TV.'"

3

Hughes continued jotting notes for his report while Stephen meandered on with his tale, consulting his own spiral-bound ledger as he bounced from subject to subject. The veteran officer, who has been married for twenty-three years and has two sons, was surprised when Stephen began talking about Tara's alleged infidelities.

"He said his family thought his wife was having an affair with Lou, her boss," Hughes said. "He said they worked closely together, and that he was a little suspicious of that. But at first he didn't believe she was cheating."

Stephen later changed his story, telling Hughes he was concerned Tara was having an affair with Troendle, her group boss. Stephen also revealed that he and Tara had been to marriage counseling. "He said he felt she confided in Lou about their marital problems more than she did with him, because she was with her boss all the time, while he was at home with the children," Hughes said. "He said she was traveling so much, it was putting a strain on the marriage." Stephen also explained that he'd recently contacted an attorney and was considering a divorce.

Hughes said he decided to call Tara's boss in Puerto Rico, since Stephen willingly provided the phone number, one of many names and numbers that were recorded in the notebook he clutched. Troendle, the fifty-year-old executive who was in charge of Washington Group's

Puerto Rican operations, was at his San Juan office when Hughes called.

"I wanted to find out what was going on between Lou and Tara, since that was Stephen's concern," Hughes said. "When I talked to Lou, he seemed genuinely worried about Tara. He said he would assist us in any way we needed to find out what happened to her. He really seemed worried, because he said Tara would never leave without telling anyone. Right then and there, I got a sinking feeling in my stomach. I'm thinking, 'Oh boy, Stephen Grant is lying to me.' And he's sitting there smiling," Hughes said.

"After I got off the phone with Lou, [Stephen] asked if I wanted to call her parents, but I said, 'I'll leave that to the detective bureau.' Because after I talked to Lou, I was concerned Stephen was lying, and I figured I'd better leave any more phone calls up to the detectives. I got the feeling that this guy was playing me."

That feeling was reinforced when Stephen veered onto his next topic: the Grant family's live-in babysitter. "He started talking about the au pair," Hughes said. "I said, 'How old is she?' He said she was nineteen, and I asked him if he was having any kind of relationship with the au pair. He leaned back in his chair and smiled at me, and said, 'She'll never tell.'"

4

During the course of their conversation, Stephen disclosed that he knew of a warrant out for his arrest, based on unpaid traffic tickets. "I decided not to pursue that, because I thought the detectives might want to talk to him, and if they arrested him, he might not talk," Hughes said.

Hughes did, however, start asking tougher questions. "I asked him about the scratch on his nose, and I said he needed to tell me if there was a fight that night," Hughes said. "He started getting nervous, saying, 'No, no, no.'"

Stephen insisted it had only been a verbal spat, even though he admitted he'd had a few beers before Tara got home. He also mentioned that he kept a handgun in the house. "Then I asked him if we could send detectives to his house to ask further questions and look around, and he said we could," Hughes said. "Basically, I think he wanted to come in here and hit a home run with me, get the missing report down on paper, and exclude himself as a suspect. He seemed to feel good about the interview."

Hughes handed Stephen a preprinted witness statement form and asked him to recap his statement in writing. In a spidery, juvenile scrawl, the father of two poured out a story that filled two pages and spilled out of the lines provided into the document's margins: *I said it was not fair to the kids that they would only see her for one day,* he wrote of the argument he'd had with his wife. *She said "Tuff."*

Stephen stated that during the argument with Tara, he repeatedly said, *"The kids are going to be disappointed if you're not home Saturday,"* Hughes wrote in his report.

As Stephen told his story, Sergeant Brian Kozlowski was reporting for work. Striding through the sheriff's department lobby, he overheard Stephen relating his story to Hughes. Kozlowski later said one thing stuck in his craw: he had heard the man say his wife had been missing since Friday. The veteran detective wondered the same thing Hughes was wondering: why would anyone wait five days to report a missing spouse?

Finally, after more than an hour, Stephen's deluge of information trailed off. Hughes told Stephen that detectives would be in contact with him. The cop then typed out his report and submitted it to his supervisor, who turned the case over to the detective bureau as Case #0700003638. A description of Tara Grant—five feet, six inches tall, 120 pounds, brown hair, brown eyes—was entered into the nationwide Law Enforcement Intelligence Network (LEIN).

The most intense investigation in the history of the Macomb County Sheriff's Office was under way.

5

At the same time Stephen was spilling his story to Hughes in the lobby, the telephone rang in Lieutenant Elizabeth Darga's office, located just off the lobby. Darga, who oversees the day-to-day operations of the department's detective bureau, found the phone call peculiar.

"It was a woman who said she was a sergeant out of the Michigan State Police post in Lansing," said Darga, a twenty-year police veteran. "This woman said she knew the Grant family, and had been in contact with Tara's sister. She said that Stephen Grant was planning to come in to make a report, and that we should really look closely at this case because something was not right. She said there was no way Tara would have left like that."

Darga relayed the Michigan State Police (MSP) phone call to her boss, Captain Anthony Wickersham, who headed the detective bureau. "I said, 'You might want to hear this one. I just got off the phone with a female state police sergeant from Lansing,' and I told him what she said," Darga recounted.

Wickersham agreed that the case warranted a closer look. "It was obvious from the beginning, something wasn't right" he said.

Learning that Hughes had just concluded his meeting with Stephen Grant, Darga called Hughes into her office. "I asked, 'Did you just take a report about a missing woman?'" Darga recalled. Hughes said he had, and relayed to his boss what Stephen had told him.

"We immediately put a priority on this case," Darga said. "There are times when you get a missing persons report and there are factors that lead you to believe they took off for whatever reason, or there's some type of substance abuse. But in this case, there was none of that."

The first phone calls made in the investigation were to Tara's family. "Everyone said there was something wrong, because she would have never left her children," Darga said.

Darga assembled several detectives in her office at about 1:30 P.M. and explained the situation. "I told them about the information I'd gotten from the state police sergeant, and I directed everyone on what we needed to do," Darga said. "We had to start checking everything."

6

Macomb County sheriff Mark Hackel wasn't having a good month. It started heading downhill back on February 4, Super Bowl Sunday. What had begun as a relaxing evening at a friend's annual football party—watching the Indianapolis Colts get ready to square off against the Chicago Bears—soon turned to horror.

A few seconds after the Bears returned the game's opening kickoff for a touchdown, the sheriff's cell phone rang. The caller was one of his detectives, bearing news that disturbed, even sickened, the veteran lawman and his staff.

A woman named Jennifer Kukla had just been arrested for murdering her two young daughters inside their Macomb Township mobile home, the detective relayed.

Kukla, a thirty-year-old single mother who worked at a McDonald's restaurant near her small trailer, told arresting officers that voices in her head had told her to kill the girls, eight-year-old Alexandra and five-year-old Ashley. The killings would spare them from future pain, Kukla said.

She told deputies that she grabbed a butcher knife at about 7:30 A.M., and chased the dark-haired little girls through the trailer. She slashed her youngest daughter in the chest, and the bleeding five-year-old scurried to hide under the kitchen table. Ashley's older sister came to her defense, screaming, "Mommy, don't do it!"

Kukla wheeled and turned her attention to Alexandra, repeatedly stabbing the little girl in the throat, nearly severing her head. Then Kukla dragged Ashley from beneath the table and slaughtered her in the same manner.

In a bloody frenzy, Kukla proceeded to disembowel the family dog and its two puppies—to prevent them from eating her dead children, she later said. Finally the stringy-haired, ruddy-faced woman snatched her daughters' pet mouse from its glass cage and snapped its neck. Then she dragged her children into their bedroom and arranged their bodies, side by side, on the bed.

Kukla's sister, Lauren Russell, showed up at the narrow, dilapidated trailer more than ten hours later to take her sister to dinner. She found the trailer dark, though the front door swung ajar, despite the winter chill. As Russell ascended the trailer's front steps, she spotted Kukla through the open door. Her sibling was pacing the trailer's living room in circles.

Kukla met her sister at the door and told her she'd just killed her children. Russell, afraid for the safety of her own children, who were still waiting in the car, immediately ran back to her vehicle, drove away, and called police from her cell phone. "I think my sister may have harmed her children," Russell told the 911 dispatcher at 6:18 P.M. "She said she killed them. She said she was going to the deep ends of Hell."

Macomb sheriff's sergeant Lori Misch, who responded to the call, found Kukla sitting on her front porch, smoking a cigarette. Kukla told the sergeant she was waiting for a hearse made of bones to take her to Hades.

"That had to be the toughest case I've ever worked on," Hackel said. "I've seen some pretty bad things, but nothing prepares you for a case like that. As a human being, something like that can be difficult to deal with."

Two weeks after the Kukla atrocity, Hackel, a gaunt, media-friendly, second-generation lawman, would find his department embroiled in yet another bizarre domestic homicide case.

And within a year, the paths of Jennifer Kukla and Stephen Grant would cross in a perverse twist of fate that made headlines.

For the time being, though, Stephen was still just a suburban husband who claimed to be searching for his wife.

7

Stephen returned home from the police station that frigid Wednesday afternoon to the family's two-story Colonial in the Carriage Hills subdivision. With its taupe bricks, gray siding, green shutters, and general 1980s tract house design, the $242,000 property wasn't the fanciest setup in elite Washington Township. But the sweeping, snow-covered lawn was unbroken by any sidewalk and the rear lot was scenic with full-grown trees. The house also featured granite-topped kitchen counters, a fireplace-warmed den, and a wine cellar in the basement.

Washington Township, a onetime farming village, was on the northern fringe of Metropolitan Detroit's more prosperous suburbs. Nearby Romeo is the hometown of Bob Ritchie, a Ford dealer's son who gained fame as rapper Kid Rock; while a few miles to the west, Rochester Hills preened itself as the teen-years home of international pop icon Madonna.

Median household income in Washington Township was last figured in 2000 at a hefty $71,823. Its population had more than doubled since 1990 as professionals and executives became increasingly willing to trade longer commutes for a more pastoral home life. Unlike the grid-style layouts of Detroit's older suburbs, this ex-urban enclave was noteworthy for large lots, curvy roads, and the camouflage provided by mature trees and shrubs.

One of the community's greatest assets was nearby Stony Creek Metropark, a forty-four-hundred-acre nature preserve forever protected from developers. Residents and visitors enjoy hiking, skiing, and boating in the park, which is maintained by the Huron-Clinton Metroparks, a consortium of thirteen communities located along the namesake Huron and Clinton Rivers in southeastern Michigan.

It was a peaceful suburban existence that seemed farther than it really was from the crowds, crime, and decay of larger nearby cities. Tara and Stephen Grant had purchased their home on Westridge Street for $48,400 down and a $193,600 loan in 2001. It was their second house.

Now, on February 14, his errand at the police station finished, Stephen wheeled his Jeep Commander up the long driveway and into the two-car garage. Verena, the au pair, was home with Ian. Lindsey, a first grader, was still in school.

8

When Lieutenant Darga summoned her staff into her office to brief them about the case, she named Kozlowski lead detective. Kozlowski had a reputation as a tough, tenacious investigator. The hulking sergeant was an imposing presence whose size, shaved head, and bushy goatee gave him the air of a professional wrestler. He'd cut his teeth on the narcotics beat, after hiring on at the sheriff's office in 1990 as a corrections officer (CO) in the "Hackel Hilton"—otherwise known as the Macomb County Jail.

The Macomb County Sheriff's Office, which dates back to 1818, was growing as quickly as the county around it. Mark Hackel's father, William Hackel, had been sheriff from 1977 to 2000, when he was forced to resign after being charged with third-degree criminal sexual conduct.

A twenty-six-year-old woman told police the elder Hackel forced himself on her while she visited him in his room at the Soaring Eagle Casino and Resort in Mount Pleasant, during a Michigan Sheriffs' Association conference. Hackel, who maintained the sex was consensual, was convicted and served five years in prison before being released in 2005.

A three-person panel picked William Hackel's longtime friend and undersheriff Ronald Tuscany as the acting sheriff until the term was over. Mark Hackel, then an inspector, beat out eight candidates in the 2000 election for his father's former seat.

During his tenure, the younger Hackel had brought the department into the twenty-first century, implementing a cyber task force that investigated computer crimes, along with K-9 and motorcycle units to patrol the fast-growing county.

9

Darga decided she wanted two detectives on the Grant case full-time, so she appointed Sergeant Pam McLean as co–lead investigator. McLean, thirty-nine, was a seventeen-year veteran. The mother of three was working on several cases on February 14, including helping out with the Jennifer Kukla double filicide investigation.

Briefed by Hughes, Kozlowski and McLean made several phone calls that afternoon. Some of the calls were to Tara's Washington Group colleagues, including Lou Troendle. Tara's boss told police her itinerary called for her to leave Detroit Metropolitan Airport—about an hour's drive south of the Grant home—on Monday, February 12.

Kozlowski took note that Troendle's story called into question Stephen's claim that he'd argued with his wife because she said she was flying back to Puerto Rico on Sunday. Troendle also told Kozlowski he'd worked with Tara for ten years, knew her family and work habits, and felt it was "extremely unbelievable" that she'd disappear of her own volition. The articulate civil engineer told the detective he was very concerned about Tara.

Kozlowski and McLean also got in touch with the missing woman's family in Ohio, including her mother, Mary, and her only sibling, Alicia. As time wore on, Alicia—whose fair skin, high cheekbones, and wide smile resembled those of her missing sister—would emerge as the family spokeswoman and champion of her sister's children.

Alicia told police that Stephen had called her the previous day to tell her Tara was missing. He left a message on her phone saying, "Can you call me when you get a minute? It's no big deal."

When Alicia talked to Stephen a few minutes later, he sounded strangely calm, given the circumstances, she told police. During their conversation, Stephen said something about his wife that floored Alicia.

"He said, 'I wouldn't be surprised if she was shacked up in a motel with some guy somewhere.' I couldn't believe what I was hearing. How could he say something like that? I told him, 'My sister could be anywhere. She could be lying dead somewhere in the slums of Detroit, for all we know,'" Alicia recounted.

Tara's mother and sister both confirmed to investigators they hadn't heard from Tara since Friday, February 9.

Even more ominous: Washington Group security chief Joe Herrity came up empty when he tapped records for Tara's corporate e-mail, her company cell phone, and her American Express charge card account. *No activity was recorded on any of these since February 9,* Kozlowski wrote in his report.

"We talked to coworkers, neighbors—nobody had seen or heard from her," McLean said. "There's no phone calls, no e-mails. We're thinking, 'That's not good.'"

Already, the detectives were skeptical about Stephen's veracity. Protests by family members and friends that Tara wouldn't desert her children rang true. "I could not make [Stephen's] story work," Kozlowski said.

"A lot of red flags were going up," McLean agreed. "He waited five days to report her missing. He has a scratch on his nose, and you have a businesswoman with two small children who hasn't called home. Having small children myself, I know no matter what happens, you always call your kids."

It was time to talk to the husband in his natural setting.

10

Kozlowski was planning to call the missing woman's husband to set up an interview in his home when the phone in the detective bureau rang at about three that afternoon. Surprisingly, it was Stephen on the other end of the line, wanting to know how the case was going. Kozlowski explained he wanted to meet him at the house on Westridge Street, and Stephen agreed.

At about 5:00 P.M., the detectives slid into black Ford Taurus cruisers and swung out of the sheriff's department garage, heading north toward Washington Township. Because McLean had started work early that day, she planned to go straight home after the interview, while Kozlowski would be heading back to headquarters. They took separate vehicles.

They rode west on Hall Road, the county's perpetually jammed main east-west artery, then headed north on M-53. The northern end of the highway toward Washington Township was usually littered with dead raccoons and other small animals, which increasingly were forced out of their habitat by the rampant development in the area.

After making the seventeen-mile trek in about twenty minutes, the detectives pulled into the Carriage Hills subdivision and located the Westridge address. Stephen let them in and introduced the children and their nanny, Verena Dierkes.

McLean took Verena aside to the living room, while Kozlowski talked to Stephen in the kitchen. The kids were watching television. The au pair seemed in a rush to leave, McLean thought. "She was in a hurry to get out of there. She didn't want to talk to us. She said she had somewhere to go."

Verena, a tall, slender blonde who spoke in a soft German accent, had graduated from high school in her hometown of Aulhausen only eight months earlier. She still carried herself with an air of awkward innocence.

On the night of February 9, Verena told McLean, she'd gone out at about eight o'clock with a group of fellow au pairs to Mr. B's, a bar and grill in nearby Shelby Township.

Verena partied at the popular nightspot for a few hours and arrived home at about 11:30 P.M. She confirmed Stephen's account of a belligerent greeting when she walked through the door, adding that he told her he thought she was Tara. Stephen told her that the couple had been in an argument earlier in the evening, and Tara had left in a huff. The nanny said she and her employer stayed up and talked for a while and then retired to their respective bedrooms.

As Verena talked to McLean, she repeatedly told the detective she had to leave to meet friends. "The whole time, it was obvious she didn't want to have this conversation," McLean said. "I was suspicious of that from the beginning."

McLean was able to talk to Verena for about ten minutes before the young woman departed for her night out. "She said it was unusual for Tara not to call to check on the kids," McLean said. Verena also told the detective that it would have been odd for Tara to summon a cab or limousine service—which called into question Stephen's earlier story to Deputy Hughes that Tara often hired a car to take her to the airport. "She also said she had no knowledge of any marital problems," McLean said.

After Verena left the house, McLean talked to six-year-old Lindsey. "She gave me a tour of the house," the detective said. "Both the kids were hilarious—just great little kids. Lindsey is like a little mom. She's a really smart girl. She took me upstairs to show me their bedrooms, and then took me downstairs to show me the play area," McLean said.

As the girl showed off her home, the detective kept her eye open for clues.

11

Meanwhile, in the kitchen, Kozlowski noticed that Stephen's story was shifting. The mild-mannered "Mr. Mom" with the protruding green eyes told the deputy that Tara was going to leave for Puerto Rico on Monday, not Sunday as he had told Hughes earlier in the day.

Stephen elaborated on details of the previous Friday night: Tara had packed a larger suitcase, he said. She had said, "I'll be out in a minute" to a mystery caller on her cell phone before stepping out of the house, not to be heard from again.

At the detective's prompting, Stephen led him to the couple's bedroom upstairs, where he logged on to the couple's joint credit card account online, as well as to their LaSalle Bank checking account. Kozlowski noticed Stephen's hand was shaking as he touched the mouse. Like the American Express account, each was devoid of activity since before the previous Friday. Wherever Tara was, she wasn't charging anything or tapping the ATM machine.

Kozlowski then followed Stephen to the garage. He peered into Tara's white Isuzu Trooper and Stephen's Jeep, but he found nothing suspicious in either SUV—except the spiral-bound notebooks and folder lying on the backseat of Tara's vehicle. One, clearly, contained work-related "to do" lists. It struck the officer as odd she would've left that behind. With Stephen's permission, Kozlowski packed up the notebooks.

Stephen explained the scratch on his nose as an on-the-job injury—a piece of metal shaving had lodged under his safety glasses, he said, when he was doing some work at his dad's shop. He also showed Kozlowski a scratch on his hand and a bruise on his leg, and agreed when the detective asked if it would be OK to send over an evidence technician to take pictures of the injuries.

Kozlowski then asked Stephen if there was any infidelity in their marriage. Stephen pledged that he was faithful to the marriage, but Tara had been involved with someone in the past. However, he said, the affair was over now.

"I've interviewed hundreds of people, so you kind of get a sense of what to look for in these situations," Kozlowski said. "He appeared nervous, but he also was very forthcoming with information. At times he seemed to be overly helpful."

To the detective's trained ears, Stephen's words weren't ringing true. "I didn't believe his story from the start," Kozlowski said.

12

Lindsey led McLean into her mother's bedroom. The veteran detective immediately picked up on a few things that looked suspicious. "Her closet was immaculate," McLean said. "But nothing was missing. There were no spaces between the clothes to indicate she'd taken any clothes with her, and no shoes appeared to be missing, either."

McLean's gaze also was drawn to the three pairs of eyeglasses on the nightstand. "These are all things that you'd take with you if you were going somewhere," the detective said. Another anomaly: In the small master bathroom, with its contemporary fixtures, a dark stain marred the wooden floor. Stephen told the detectives his wife caused the discoloration by spilling hair dye.

Tara did often have her hair dyed, though she usually patronized a fancy beauty parlor. In fact, Stephen and Tara once had an epic argument over her $200 tab for a haircut and color at the ritzy Salon Moulin Rouge in Shelby Township, Stephen later recounted.

McLean allowed Lindsey to show her around the rest of the house, where the child proudly pointed out her favorite pictures and playthings. As she escorted

McLean, dark-haired Lindsey, a miniature version of Tara, confidently told the officer her mother was "at work in another country."

But, she told the detective, "my mom will be coming home soon."

13

After Lindsey's tour of the home, McLean went back downstairs to talk to Kozlowski and Stephen. The officer asked for permission to search through the bedroom more closely, and Stephen said it was OK.

"I went through the drawers, and I found envelopes full of cash, which I thought was kind of weird, but Stephen said they paid for everything with cash," McLean said. "And there were envelopes with 'phone bill' and 'electric bill' on them."

There were also several bags full of unsigned greeting cards. It turned out they were part of Tara's stockpile of cheerful messages for her children—she always left cards behind for the kids when she went on her business trips.

The more time McLean spent with Stephen, the more he got on her nerves. "He was really jittery, like he'd just drunk eight cups of coffee," she said. "He was just bouncing. I was like, 'Stop! Sit still and focus!' It was very hard to talk to him because he kept jumping from one subject to another."

As the detectives prepared to leave, Stephen's demeanor changed drastically, McLean noticed. "We asked if he would come down and talk to us some more," she recalled. "Then he said, 'Well, you don't think I did something to my wife, do you?'"

Kozlowski said he told Stephen, "If we thought you

were involved in the disappearance of your wife, we'd take you to jail right now."

Then Stephen surprised the detectives by breaking into tears. "He just broke down, sobbing like crazy," McLean said. "He wouldn't stop."

14

The two detectives again asked Stephen's permission to allow an evidence technician to stop by the house later to take some pictures. After he agreed, Kozlowski and McLean exited the house through the garage and walked toward their cars in the driveway.

"Once we were out of hearing range, we looked at each other and we go, 'He killed her.' We just don't know how he did it, or where she's at yet, but he killed her," McLean said. "Now we've just got to figure out what he did to her."

Deputy Adnan Durrani, Macomb sheriff's evidence technician, went to Stephen's house about two hours after the detectives. "He appeared to be nervous," Durrani said. "He was shaking. And he was very apologetic."

In addition to the small nose scratch, Durrani photographed a bruise on Stephen's left leg and an abrasion on his right hand. "He said he cut his nose on a piece of metal shaving at his father's shop," Durrani said. "As far as the hand goes, he said he cut it trying to start his snowblower." Stephen did not have an explanation for the leg bruise, Durrani said.

Durrani asked Stephen if he would come to the police station the next day to submit to a polygraph test. Stephen agreed.

15

Almost three hundred miles south, in Chillicothe, Ohio, Alicia was frantic over her older sister's disappearance. She kept calling her cell phone; no answer. She sent her sister e-mails, but there was no response.

Alicia called Lou, Tara's boss. He still hadn't heard from her, either. She felt she had to do something. So did her husband, Erik Standerfer.

The couple, in anguish over Tara's absence, and concerned for her children, began making arrangements for the care of their own kids and otherwise preparing for the long journey north. They would leave Saturday.

16

Within twenty-four hours after Stephen reported his wife missing, the Macomb County Sheriff's Office had created one of its standard missing persons flyers to be distributed to the media. The flyer described the petite 120-pound mom, including a photo of brown-eyed, curly-haired Tara smiling directly into the camera lens. The photo was from several that had been provided by Stephen when he reported her missing.

Tara was last seen leaving her home in Washington Township, MI 48094 in the evening hours of Feb 09 2007, the flyer said.

That was the official scenario, in the absence of evidence to the contrary. But that five-day gap between the Grants' argument and Stephen's police report didn't sit well with investigators.

Sheriff Hackel began polling his staff, asking for their hunches about Stephen based on experience, observation, and gut feelings. "Give me the percentage," he urged them. "Some were one hundred percent [sure] he did it," Hackel recalled. "Some said maybe fifty percent. Maybe she just didn't like the guy and wanted to get away."

The department didn't want to publicly name Stephen a suspect "and have him hiding in a hole," Hackel said. The sheriff was formulating other ideas.

Meanwhile, McLean began tracing Tara's telephone and credit card activity. She asked the telephone company for permission to obtain records covering all incoming and outgoing calls on Tara's Verizon cell phone from February 1 onward.

"You can get telephone records directly from the telephone company, but you have to have probable cause to search phone records," McLean noted. "Just the fact that someone is missing isn't enough. In this case, we were able to get the records based on exigent circumstances. That's where you [have] a situation that's above and beyond a normal situation. Stephen waited five days to report her missing. He showed signs of injuries. Tara didn't have a history of drug abuse or a history of leaving in the past. She had a great work history. If you take that all together, it's enough to search the records."

McLean later successfully petitioned 42nd District Court judge Denis LeDuc for search warrants for cell site locations, to determine where Tara was when she made the phone calls.

"We had to start checking everything," Lieutenant Elizabeth Darga said. "We had to check the airlines. Had she gone out of the country? Had she done any traveling within the U.S.? There was a lot to do."

While it's relatively simple to get access to telephone records, it's not as easy for police to obtain credit card information, Darga said. "But in this case, the last credit card Tara used was through her company. That was her main credit card. Thankfully, the Washington Group was very cooperative, and they provided us records of her credit card use."

Records showed the last time Tara used her company-issued American Express card was at 9:32 P.M. on February 9 when she paid for parking in the Detroit Metropolitan Airport parking structure.

Darga, who quarterbacked the detective team during the Grant investigation, said she and her crew brainstormed to come up with a checklist of what needed to be done during the first few days of the case. "Whoever could think of what we needed to do next, we would write it all down on paper, and when each thing got done, it would get checked off," Darga said.

A white board was hung in the detective room, to map out how the investigation was going. "We used the board to keep track of all the phone calls Stephen made the night of February ninth, and in the days after that," Darga said.

There were several possibilities to be considered, McLean said. "Who's to say she wasn't leaving her husband? Some people take a little downtime before they call and let their spouse know they're leaving them, so we had to look at that avenue," she said. "In a missing person case, even if you have suspicions, which we did, you have to consider all possibilities. So we went into this investigation with an open mind."

But even as the detectives considered all potential scenarios, their instincts told them Tara Grant was a murder victim, not a missing person. "We knew in the back of our minds that he killed her," Darga said. "And when we talked about it, we threw out all kinds of possibilities.

"We even wondered if he cut her up and disposed of the body that way," she said. "That was actually discussed, but we all came to the conclusion that this guy wouldn't have the guts to do that."

Investigators received a surprising fax Thursday morning. It appeared that Stephen Grant had hired himself a lawyer:

Because of the tone of your February 14, 2007 interrogation of Mr. Grant at his home . . . it is my humble opinion that it is necessary for me to provide a buffer between your department and Mr. Grant, wrote the sender of the fax, Detroit attorney David Griem. *Just as Mr. Grant answered all of your questions last night, he will continue to answer all of your questions in the future. I believe it is necessary, however, so there are no misunderstandings, that all of your future questions be submitted in writing which will, in turn, be immediately answered in writing.*

The message was another indication to investigators that something was amiss.

"We're trying to help this guy find his wife, and he lawyers up and says he'll only communicate with us by fax," Kozlowski said. "What kind of guy would do that if he really wanted us to find his wife?"

The white-haired, mustachioed David Griem was a well-known Metro Detroit lawyer. A former Macomb County prosecutor and U.S. attorney, he also was a veteran defender with high-profile cases to his credit.

In 2005, Griem defended prominent Macomb County real estate mogul Ralph Roberts, who was accused, along with state senator James Barcia, of funneling money to former Macomb County prosecutor Carl Marlinga's unsuccessful 2004 reelection campaign. In exchange, the prosecutor allegedly was to help two convicted rapists get new trials. The charges were eventually dropped against all parties.

Ironically, Griem also spearheaded the rape-conviction appeal of William Hackel, the county's former top lawman and father of the current sheriff. His roster of corporate clients included household names, such as Kmart, General Motors, and General Dynamics.

Griem was known for his poise before the cameras and often served as a legal commentator for local broadcasters, as well as in national venues like CourtTV and Geraldo Rivera's programs.

And he was about to get even more airtime.

17

Thursday afternoon, Stephen set out in his charcoal gray Jeep Commander with a $3,000-plus cash stash. One of his envelopes held $1,145; the other $1,912.

Motoring south along North Avenue in Mount Clemens, right near the sheriff's office, Stephen failed to signal as he turned east on Elizabeth Street. He was promptly pulled over by a deputy. It was 2:13 P.M.

The stop rattled Stephen, causing him to lose some of the cool demeanor that had perplexed the cops up till now. *"I know why [you're] pulling me over,"* he blurted, according to a later police report. *"It's because [of] my wife."*

The officer ran the usual check on Stephen's identification and found that he was driving on a suspended license. He was placed under arrest.

A closer look at Stephen's past revealed a terrible driving record, as well as a more serious brush with the law. Stephen was arrested in Clinton Township on October 28, 1989, for reckless driving and carrying a concealed weapon. He was stopped by Officer Mike Friese for driving seventy miles per hour in a 45mph zone. When Friese approached the car, he noticed a pouch near the brake pedal, and it held an unloaded Colt pistol. Stephen did not have a permit for the gun.

He was charged with reckless driving and carrying a concealed weapon. However, Stephen pleaded guilty to the lesser charges of careless driving and failure to obtain a permit for a handgun, and was fined $500.

Stephen's license was suspended three times in 2002 and 2003 for failing to pay speeding tickets in the Detroit suburbs of Allen Park, Rochester, and Troy. His latest two suspensions came in 2005 after he ran a red light in Mount Clemens and failed to pay fines in Clinton Township.

After Stephen's arrest, police also discovered that he had paid almost $900 in back traffic fines the day before reporting his wife missing. The fines stemmed from two moving violations and twelve parking tickets in several communities.

Accounts of the next several hours differ. Stephen claimed he was held against his will for six hours and interrogated at the Macomb County Jail.

The sheriff told a different story. Hackel said Stephen was detained for only a short time. "It's standard procedure—if someone is driving on two suspended licenses, we arrest them," Hackel said. "If my deputies let someone like that go free, and they later get into an accident and hurt someone, then what? So, of course, we arrested [him]. I would have questioned my officers if they hadn't."

If Stephen had been willing to submit to a polygraph exam, as he'd assured the evidence technician who had visited his house the night before, his jailhouse stay put him in a less cooperative frame of mind.

"Three police cars surrounded his car as he was driving home, and arrested him over an unpaid ticket for driving fifty-five miles per hour in a forty-five-mile-per-hour zone," Griem said. "Then they incarcerated him for six and a half hours and questioned him. Those are

Neanderthal tactics and demonstrated bad faith on the part of the police."

Stephen struck a macho pose when he discussed his February 15 police encounter with the *Detroit News*.

"I get why they stopped me—they thought I was going to be a little girl and go down there and cry and confess all my sins," he said. "But there's no sins, though. I'm a big boy and I can take care of myself."

Stephen said he was forced to retain an attorney. "It's not like I had Dave Griem on my speed dial. But do you blame me for getting a lawyer?"

18

Within two days of Stephen's initial missing persons report, Kozlowski had interviewed Sue Murasky, a counselor at Au Pair in America, the agency sponsoring the Grant children's nanny, Verena Dierkes.

Kozlowski told Murasky about the investigation into Tara Grant's disappearance, and they agreed the Grant home was not a fit environment for nineteen-year-old Verena. The young native of Aulhausen, a quaint, quiet village in Germany's vineyard-rich Rhine Valley, was on her first trip overseas, less than a year after graduating high school.

The French term *"au pair"* often is translated as "on par," meaning on par with family members, to distinguish the child-care providers from servants or other household staff. Generally, they are young women with an acceptable command of the English language who seek a year or two change of pace in the United States in exchange for working as a parents' helper.

Au pairs are placed through agencies with the blessing of U.S. Immigration officials. Classified as visitors, not workers, part of the bargain is that they are allowed time off to attend classes at local colleges and to socialize with friends, often other au pairs. Their sponsoring agencies generally provide nearby counselors who lend a listening ear to homesick teens, as well as organizing cultural, social, and educational activities for the young women.

Verena had been placed in the Grant home in August 2007 by Au Pair in America. She had been given a temporary assignment for a few weeks, and then she started working for the Grants. Verena attended Macomb Community College; she hoped to become a teacher.

Erik Standerfer said Stephen wanted Tara to hire a nanny to make his life easier. "They had an au pair in the house at his request from the moment their second child was born," Erik said.

Verena was the Grants' seventh nanny in five years. Most of them quit after only a few weeks.

Police contacted the couple's former au pairs in hopes of getting a clue to Tara's possible whereabouts. Some of the nannies said they were frightened in the Grant home, fearful of everything from someone snooping through their belongings to "tirades" from the master of the house.

One of the au pairs, a Ukrainian girl named Yana, said Stephen "gave her the creeps," Lieutenant Darga said.

"She said she never liked him," Darga said. "And she said she always got the feeling he was watching her. She said she left not long after she started getting that feeling."

The former au pairs also provided an insight into the Grants' relationship, Sergeant McLean said. "There were fights, but I don't think they had a relationship where they were screaming at each other all the time," she said. "It was a more subtle kind of manipulation, getting little digs in. It was a psychological kind of fighting."

Despite the qualms of the other au pairs, Verena told police she enjoyed her stay at the Grants' Westridge home. She joined the Grant family on an outing to a Detroit Tigers baseball game at Comerica Park in the summer of 2006 as the Tigers were fighting their way to a World Series berth.

In a photo taken that day, which would become iconic to followers of the case, Verena looked happy and relaxed as she posed beside Tara and the children in front of the ballpark. She was enjoying life in America.

But on February 16, that all ended.

Verena's counselor, Murasky, arrived that Friday, helped a reluctant Verena pack her bags, and wheeled them out of the Grant driveway.

This would not, however, be Verena's last visit to Macomb County.

19

That same Friday morning, February 16, John Cwikla, spokesman for the Macomb County Sheriff's Office, faxed flyers about the missing woman to the local media. He also sent a digital copy to the reporters on his e-mail list.

The next day, Saturday—eight days after Tara last was seen—a single paragraph headlined MISSING WOMAN REPORTED IN WASHINGTON TOWNSHIP was published inside the metro section of the *Detroit News*:

> *The Macomb County Sheriff's Department is investigating the disappearance of a 34-year-old Washington Township woman. Tara Lynn Grant was last seen at the family's home during the evening hours of February 9, according to sheriff's officials. The circumstances of her disappearance are unknown. Grant is white, 5-foot-6 and 120 pounds, with brown hair and brown eyes.*

A sheriff's office hotline number was printed below the brief.

Its dry, matter-of-fact prose didn't begin to hint at the dramatic events that eventually would unfold before Tara's whereabouts were discovered. But the notice did serve to spark the tinder of public interest. From this day forward, few editions of the local papers would fail to include a mention of what came to be known as "the Grant

Case," and few broadcasts would air without at least a snippet of Stephen Grant's increasingly histrionic pleas for his errant wife's safe return home.

Five hours to the south, the distraught Standerfers were packing their bags Saturday morning for the familiar trek up Interstate 75 to their home state of Michigan. Unlike their previous journeys from their adopted Ohio town, this trip seemed likely to forever shatter the happy, safe, upwardly mobile life they'd crafted for themselves.

Chillicothe, between Columbus, Ohio, and the northern Tennessee border, is a quaint riverside town whose roots stretch back to 1796. It served twice as the state capital, before its neighbor to the north, Columbus, permanently claimed that honor.

Families are attracted to the Main Street-USA flavor of Chillicothe's downtown, complete with its antique courthouse square and riverside parks.

When Erik Standerfer landed a high-paying managerial position at a paper mill in Chillicothe in 2002, he and Alicia moved into a three-bedroom ranch in the southwest side of the city. Alicia took a part-time job as a dental hygienist.

Chillicothe was twelve hours of freeway driving from their Northern Michigan roots, but the country values and neighborliness were familiar.

Two years later, Alicia's parents, Mary and Gerald "Dusty" Destrampe, moved into a small ranch in Chillicothe, less than two miles away from the Standerfers. Mary and Dusty had fallen on hard times. Dusty was incapacitated after a 2002 stroke. He no longer could work as a water treatment specialist at Fort McCoy, an army base in west-central Wisconsin. They decided to move close to Alicia and her husband.

In 2004, Alicia gave birth to a son, Alex. Daughter Payton was born the following year. But now, Alicia—

who knew her only sibling hadn't missed a day of work in ten years with Washington Group—fretted at the five-hour drive that separated her from the search for her older sister.

"We were frantic," Alicia said. "I knew there was no way Tara would stay out of touch that long. We knew we had to come up there and help find her."

Alicia said Tara hadn't mentioned returning early to San Juan when they last talked on the phone the previous Friday. It had been a forty-minute chat, while Tara waited at Newark International Airport for her delayed Detroit-bound flight—the same layover where Stephen claimed their phone fight had started.

"She said she was going to return to Puerto Rico on Monday," Alicia said.

Also on Saturday, Griem told reporters that Stephen had hired a former FBI agent, now a private detective, to trace Tara's whereabouts. After a few early vague mentions of the detective, the story faded away.

"Was there ever a private detective? I honestly don't know—but if there was, he never sought any help from us," Sheriff Hackel said. "We never heard from him."

Griem also said publicly that Stephen and Tara had argued over Tara's frequent business trips, and reiterated that Tara had left home via a dark-colored vehicle the night of February 9.

He also mentioned that Tara was in the process of laying off some fifty workers at her employer's San Juan, Puerto Rico, facility. "That's something to take into consideration," Griem said.

20

Alicia, Erik, and his sister, Jeannie, arrived in Metro Detroit Saturday afternoon and met with Kozlowski at the Macomb County Sheriff's Office. They talked for a while, and then Kozlowski provided dozens of copies of the handouts bearing Tara's picture. The Ohio trio then began peppering the area with the flyers.

After they'd hung the posters in gas stations and stores for miles along the southwest route to the airport, they headed back to Macomb County to visit Stephen. The plan was to order take-out pizza and brainstorm about what could have happened to Tara.

As Erik pulled his 2003 Saturn SUV into the long driveway, Stephen came outside to greet them. "I knew immediately as we walked up the driveway . . . that something was terribly wrong," Erik recalled.

Alicia agreed that something seemed amiss. Stephen tried to hug her, and she felt uncomfortable. She tried to pull away, but Stephen held her tight. "He just wasn't acting right," she said. "I got a really funny feeling right away."

Within minutes of greeting Stephen, Erik began fearing for his sister-in-law's safety. "It became immediately obvious that Stephen knew it was a waste of time to look for Tara," he said.

* * *

The days of the calendar's shortest month ticked on, a never-ending February for the Destrampes, the Standerfers, Tara's friends, and her coworkers as they waited, hoped, and prayed for Tara's safe return.

The other alternative was the dreaded message: Tara wouldn't be coming back.

The nonstop media reports, which soon would mesmerize Metro Detroit audiences—prompting them to snap up extra newspapers and dial radios or TVs to catch top-of-the-hour updates—hadn't yet escalated into the dozens-a-day volleys of information that would climax in a stunning on-the-air twist.

In fact, the metro final edition of Monday's *Detroit Free Press* referred to the case only in a brief posting headlined CONSTRUCTION EXECUTIVE STILL MISSING:

> *The whereabouts of a missing 34-year-old Washington Township woman remained a mystery Sunday, Macomb County Sheriff Mark Hackel said. . . . Police said the woman's cell phone was shut off, and she hasn't used her credit card.*

No solid information, no suspects, had emerged. No limousine service had stepped forward to identify itself as the one Tara hired the night of February 9. That nugget wasn't lost on Hackel.

"We realized early on there was no black car," Hackel later said. "We got no calls. Nobody came forward to say, 'Hey, that was me.'"

Hackel also knew that Griem made it a practice to polygraph prospective clients before signing on with them. The sheriff said he would have accepted those results if they cleared Stephen, who by then had formally declined through his attorney to submit to a police-administered lie detector test. But no results showing graphs indicating Stephen's guilt or innocence were proffered to investigators.

Hackel said Stephen pretended not to trust the police polygraph operator, "but that was just his way of getting out of taking the test," he said.

For a man supposedly hoping to get his lost spouse back at any cost, Stephen was keeping detectives at a distance. "Generally, we work in constant communication with family members," Hackel said. "We try to embrace them, but he would never get under our arm."

On Monday, Alicia and Erik were still putting up posters and providing investigators with more information about Tara. They'd spent the weekend taping the flyers—which featured a portrait of a beaming Tara in a softly draped scarf-neck sweater—from Detroit Metropolitan Airport to hotels and gas stations within a fifteen-mile radius from the missing woman's home.

Despite the dozens of posters and increasing publicity, "we don't have any leads," Alicia said. "Everything is a complete dead end. There hasn't been anything new."

Stephen—not posting flyers, but holed up in his Carriage Hills subdivision Colonial—ignored the ringing of the telephone and knocks on the door from TV, radio, and print reporters.

That, however, would change soon.

21

Hackel, the most high-profile law enforcement leader in Macomb County's 570 square miles, isn't your stereotypical "no comment, just the facts, ma'am" sheriff. The young lawman eschews what he calls "normal cop-think." Instead, he embraces modern tools and had been raising communication—with his constituents, his staff, the media—to something of an art form.

The son of his own predecessor, Mark Allen Hackel often pointed out that his teenage ambition was not to join the force but to own a 7-Eleven convenience store. After graduation from Sterling Heights High School in 1980, two and a half years working midnights as a sheriff's office dispatcher, changed all that.

At about 2:30 A.M. on July 16, 1981, Hackel took a 911 call from a man who said, "My neighbor just said someone killed his family."

"In the background, I can hear a guy crying—or pretending to cry," Hackel said.

The man Hackel heard sobbing was Robert Deroo. When detectives later got to his posh Macomb Township home, they went into an upstairs bedroom and found seventeen-month-old Jessica Deroo lying facedown in her crib. She had been suffocated.

They moved into the next bedroom and found five-year-old Nathaniel wearing blue pajamas and lying motionless on his back. He also had been suffocated.

In the master bedroom was the body of Deborah Deroo. The twenty-five-year-old housewife was spread-eagled on her bed. Her nightgown was pushed up around her shoulders, and her neck was heavily bruised. A can of Mace lay next to her outstretched arm. Investigators thought the placement of the Mace looked staged.

Another child, three-year-old Nicholas, lay motionless next to his mother on the bed. But despite the choke marks on his neck, Nicholas had survived.

Robert Deroo, a handsome cabinetmaker, was the prime suspect from the beginning, but prosecutors determined there wasn't enough evidence to bring charges against him. Upon reviewing the evidence two and a half years later, they changed their minds.

The sordid trial captivated the region. More than eighty witnesses were called over four weeks of testimony. It was revealed that Deborah Deroo was having an affair with her next-door neighbor. Another neighbor testified that on the night of the murders he heard a child shout repeatedly, "Don't, Daddy, don't!"

It took the jury only four hours to find Robert Deroo not guilty. Then, after a court battle with Deborah Deroo's parents, the acquitted suspect won custody of his son Nicholas.

Police—including Hackel—were furious. The case spurred Hackel to embark on his long career as a police officer.

"I recognized it was an important, exciting job," he said. "I didn't know I would fall in love with it."

So instead of becoming a 7-Eleven franchisee, Hackel stayed on the force. He attended the Police Academy at Macomb Community College. Despite being one of the youngest recruits, he came out number one in his class. He also scored first in the physical-fitness component.

He began his career as all deputies do, working in the Macomb County Jail as a CO. But he kept up with his schoolwork, too, pursuing a criminal justice degree, first at Macomb Community College, then at Detroit's Wayne State University. Juggling job and classes, Hackel took seven years to earn a bachelor's degree in criminal justice.

"I recognized how competitive it made me," Hackel said. Not just in terms of knowledge and promotions, either. The young deputy realized that an articulate, media-savvy, accessible lawman could be more effective than the traditional tight-lipped cop with an arm's-length, fortress mentality.

"You are a street corner politician," he said. "We can't put out literature . . . marketing our organization. We develop a reputation through the media."

Even in tough times, including his own father's legal woes, Hackel seldom wavered from his forthright, approachable demeanor. The strategy served him well; he swept his 2004 reelection run with 80 percent of the votes, and many have maintained he has a blockbuster future ahead as a politician outside of law enforcement.

"Sixties-era police were more brawn than brain," he said. "Now we need more business and people skills. We do not make anything, like a widget. We protect and we serve. The service part is harder, but more interesting."

More often clad in sport coat and tie—with a small gold sheriff's star on his lapel—than in one of his many cop uniforms, Hackel has spoken in twenty-first-century jargon of "marketing" the department. He has philosophized that law enforcement workers are simply "paid members of society doing what society should do for one another." His mantra for the sheriff's office has been "responsibility, accountability, availability, accessibility."

This sheriff has had his own Wikipedia entry, and his agency has operated snappy Internet pages. *(Welcome to your Web site,* reads the message from Hackel.) The site is complete with citizen-friendly features, such as a Kids Area, safety tips, a virtual tour of the county jail, and links to local newspaper sites. Residents heading out to vacation can fill out a house-watch request form and teens can learn about the department's Explorer program.

Hackel hosted a local cable-TV show, organized a senior-citizen greeter program at the sheriff's office, brought back the county's disbanded K-9 unit, and purchased a $150,000 thirty-foot "command center"— a custom RV with a sexy black paint job that is used in crisis situations and doubles as a roving police station.

But despite his attempt to make the sheriff's office a user-friendly organization, Hackel, fundamentally, has been a cop. And beneath the folksy, down-to-earth persona, that cop was becoming angry.

Hackel was fed up with Stephen Grant's coy cat-and-mouse tactics. It was time, he thought, to turn up the heat on Stephen, and the best way to do that was to lure him back out into the public eye.

And on February 20—eleven days into Tara's disappearance—a surprise source called the sheriff's office and provided the bait.

22

SEX, LIES, SPYING, trumpeted the front-page headline of the February 21 edition of the *Detroit News*.

The flashy scoop propelled the Grant story for all time from pathos to top-notch domestic drama. Quoting e-mails now in the custody of police detectives, the story documented Stephen Grant's flip, cavalier, and flirtatious correspondence with a former girlfriend. The e-mails also revealed that Stephen suspected Tara was cheating on him with her boss, Lou, who was referred to in the correspondence as "the Old Geezer."

In eight messages exchanged over an hour and a half at midday on January 25, 2007—when Tara was in London on another corporate trip—Stephen wrote to his ex that he considered marriage vows *like speed limits. Sometimes you have to break them and sometimes you get caught.*

So what are you going to do about the cheatin' wife? the woman wrote.

Don't know yet, Stephen replied. He bragged that he'd had a friend install a spying device on their home computer so he could monitor Tara's e-mails.

He rattled on, roguishly telling the nursing student—whose real name, Deena Hardy, was being withheld at the time—that he might *need a sponge bath* and that he was *all alone with no one to play with.*

I do want to see you naked, he wrote. *Naked women are always good to see. Especially if you haven't seen them in a while.*

Hardy also provided a copy of the e-mails to Captain Wickersham. "We were suspicious of Stephen even before those e-mails, but when we saw them, it made us even more suspicious," Wickersham said. "The e-mails made it obvious he thought his wife was cheating on him, which was very interesting to us. If there was foul play, now we had a possible motive."

The salacious e-mails revved up public interest in the case. CNN ran a report on Tara's disappearance. *Good Morning America* aired a taped interview with Hackel. The day the e-mail story ran in the *Detroit News,* chased by other local print and electronic reporters, Stephen Grant abruptly ended his cloister and granted numerous interviews.

"I hope Tara walks through that door," Stephen told Channel 7, sobbing dramatically, his eyes widening with every word. "God, please—call. Please. Call anyone."

Photos and video of Stephen—whose prominent, bulging eyes and breathless, melodramatic speech patterns undermined any attempt on his part for dignity and gravitas—were a dream come true for the investigative team. People who privately commented on the case agreed: Stephen simply *looked* guilty.

The term "bug-eyed" was fast becoming an adjective applied to Stephen Grant—not just as a physical descriptor but as shorthand for his increasingly flaky persona.

During interviews at Griem's Detroit office, Stephen told reporters that his wife had been out of contact before, but he said this was the first time he was "scared."

He raised the eyebrows of veteran reporters by blurting

out that he'd prefer that she be off with another man than in harm's way. "If she's with somebody else, OK. I can understand that," he said. "But I wish she would at least call home. Her kids are worried about her."

And while he steadfastly denied any involvement with her disappearance, Stephen repeatedly said that police had told him he was their number one suspect.

"I understand why I'm a suspect—I get it," Stephen said. "The police always look at the husband."

Hackel denied investigators were looking at Stephen as a suspect. "We haven't even established that a crime has taken place," the sheriff said.

Hackel also told reporters that Stephen, while granting wide-ranging media interviews as a distraught husband, was responding to investigators only via faxes to and from his lawyer's office. The sheriff also said his detectives had questioned Tara's coworkers, after a source told investigators there were rumors she was possibly having affairs at work. The subjects of the rumors denied the allegations, Hackel said.

Tara's family members were disgusted when Stephen's lascivious e-mail exchange was made public. "It sickened me," said Alicia, who by now had returned home to Ohio with her family. "I was flabbergasted."

Alicia and her mother, speaking to reporters, continued to contradict Stephen's assertion that Tara intended to head back early to Puerto Rico. Tara was tired from work and looking forward to an upcoming family getaway to Arizona, Mary said. And, she insisted, her daughter would never go two weeks without calling Lindsey and Ian.

"Her children are everything to her," Alicia added.

With Tara missing and Verena gone, Kelly Utykanski, Stephen's sister, was helping her brother care for Lindsey and Ian. Utykanski, thirty-nine, lived in nearby Sterling Heights with her husband, Chris. The squat, brassy redhead related to reporters how she had been helping distribute the missing persons posters and that Stephen was trying to shield the children from media reports. Ironically, a year later, it would be Kelly herself who contributed to some of the most sensational media coverage on the case.

For now, though, she was a concerned sister and aunt, looking out for the welfare of her brother's children. "They obviously know Mom is lost, and that police are looking for her," Utykanski said. "But we're trying to shelter them from this as much as we can."

23

Media interest in Tara Grant's disappearance was becoming so intense, Hackel decided to hold daily 11:00 A.M. press briefings in the conference room at police headquarters. Two large cardboard blowups of Tara's portrait were placed on easels on each side of the podium from where Hackel gave his daily updates. One of the photos was the picture that was originally released by police in the missing persons flyer, depicting Tara in a dressy sweater and scarf. The other photo was a shot of Tara leaning back slightly in a rocking chair and turning her head to smile at the camera.

"I figured having a press conference each day would allow me to pass information on to the media, and allow the media to ask me questions, without having to make a million phone calls every day," Hackel said. But each morning, the sheriff grimly reported the same thing: there was nothing new; there was still no sign of Tara.

Reporters, who crowded elbow to elbow at the large wooden table that dominated the narrow conference room, pressed Hackel: was Stephen a suspect?

Hackel maintained that Stephen Grant was not—although the sheriff continuously expressed frustration that Stephen refused to help with the investigation.

"It's become very clear at this point he doesn't want to cooperate with us," Hackel told reporters. "You would think he would be right there at our side, wanting to get all the information he could get from us. But he hasn't called us once. Think about that. He called us and said his wife is missing, but since then, he hasn't once called us to ask how the investigation is going, or if we have any new information," Hackel said.

"We're getting support from other family members, and from Tara's workplace," the sheriff said. "The only person who is not cooperating with us is Stephen Grant."

Detective Sergeant McLean was after another search warrant—an effort to trace Tara's whereabouts by the location of her personal/work cell phone. The warrant covered all incoming and outgoing calls from Tara's Cingular cell phone account from February 9 onward. The warrant also directed the Cingular National Subpoena Compliance Center to provide a list of *all recorded cell site locations activated by this number during this time frame.*

But like every other road pursued in the investigation so far, this one was a dead end.

Out of the public eye, Verena Dierkes quietly boarded a jet at Detroit Metropolitan Airport, bound for Frankfurt.

The young nanny was leaving Michigan behind, months earlier and under vastly different circumstances than she had planned. But her memories, and her secrets, soared toward Germany with her.

24

On Thursday, February 22, Hackel finally said aloud what he had been thinking all along: for the first time, the sheriff publicly characterized Tara's disappearance as the result of a possible crime.

"We're now focusing our investigation into the possibility of foul play," Hackel said. "This is day thirteen of her disappearance, so it makes you stop and think. If she's no longer alive, there's a concern about the body as evidence, and extracting evidence from the body. This is a difficult thing to discuss, but, unfortunately, in our business, it's something we have to consider."

Hackel then laid it on a little thicker, in phrases calculated to make Stephen sit up and take notice. He revealed that investigators planned to search undisclosed "wooded areas" for Tara's remains. "If there is a possibility that she is buried somewhere, there will be a thaw this weekend, so it will be easier to look," he said.

By design, Hackel later recounted, he only vaguely described the locale of the search. He was playing a bit of a psychological game with their chief witness. Over the past few days, he'd been reflecting on the number of times Stephen had mentioned Stony Creek Metropark, the four-thousand-acre preserve near the Grant home.

In fact, Hackel said, to his surprise, Stephen had actually described to a reporter for the *Macomb Daily* that he'd bumped into Hackel once on Stony Creek's bike trails—and noted that the sheriff hadn't been wearing a protective helmet.

"I thought, 'Great,'" Hackel recounted with a rueful smile. "'They're going to write a story about the sheriff not practicing good safety.'"

Also on Thursday, Hackel said that police were looking into "discrepancies" in Stephen's account of the case, which the sheriff described as "concerning." For one thing, he said, Stephen's immediate statement to Kozlowski and McLean when they showed up at his home the night of February 14 was that Tara had never disappeared before. "But then he told the news media she had disappeared twice before without calling him."

Stephen also had told detectives he heard Tara say, "I'll be right out" just before exiting the house. But no one had called her cell phone or her home phone after she arrived home that night.

Hackel also lamented the lack of practical assistance from Tara's husband. "We would like to get a look at her home computer, or get ahold of some of her clothes, so that dogs could try to track her," Hackel said. "But we don't have enough evidence for a search warrant, and Stephen Grant isn't letting us have access to the home."

Stephen was not cooperating with police, but he tried hard to be accommodating to the media. When reporters called for interviews, he rarely refused—and he often took the initiative to call the journalists to chat about the case. Investigators were tuned in to every word.

"We were living this case by watching the media," Hackel recalled. "That isn't a traditional way of doing an investigation, but since Stephen wasn't talking to us, we had to be very in tune to what he was saying to the media. I'd be in bed at night thinking about things he'd said to the media that day. I'd call people in the middle of the night, and they'd do the same with me. We were all trying to solve a puzzle. It's like watching a whodunit movie—you're trying to get a feel for the characters, and listening closely to everything they say.

"But unlike in a movie theater, where you can't play back what the characters say, with the Grant case, we *were* able to play it back. We taped every television interview, and we collected all the newspaper articles. Even if I was at a meeting, when the news came on TV, I'd have (sheriff's office spokesman John) Cwikla play it to me over the phone, so I could listen to it. We'd keep going back and listening to what was said, trying to piece it all together."

During Stephen's conversations with reporters, he seemed obsessed with trying to gauge his public image. "What are people saying about the case?" was a question he often asked.

Hackel disclosed to reporters at Thursday's press briefing the wooded area police planned to search: Stony Creek Metropark. The search would commence Saturday morning, he said. "This was just an absolute hunch," Hackel recalled. "Stephen had mentioned Stony Creek a few times in the media, so we decided to search the park."

The sheriff thought by announcing the search, and by inviting the media to cover it, Stephen might make some kind of move. "We really didn't have anything else," he said. "[Stephen] wasn't talking to us, and we weren't getting any real clues. Maybe if we searched the park, we might find something. And even if we didn't find anything, maybe it might force his hand somehow."

Hackel would later realize his instinct had been spot-on. But at the time, his decision to announce when and where his investigators would be searching was criticized—including by members of his own department.

"I knew some people were going to say we were pandering to the media, but I was also getting that criticism internally," he said. "Some people were giving me a hard time because I told the media about the search. They thought I was doing this to get attention. I told them I did want attention—it was a missing person case, and I was seeking the public's help."

On Friday, February 23, the polite sparring between Hackel and Stephen's surrogates escalated into blatant barbs. As anticipation of Saturday's search grew among law enforcement personnel, media members and the increasingly fascinated public, the sheriff abruptly preempted any chance of Stephen rehabilitating his public image as a grieving husband doggedly searching for his missing wife.

Stephen had told the *Detroit News* that he'd be an asset to searchers because of his familiarity with Stony Creek Metropark. "I know the area well," he boasted. "I mountain bike out there, and run out there all the time."

But Stephen, the sheriff said at his daily press conference, wasn't welcome at the search. "We don't need him there, unless he knows where she is," Hackel said. "Having him there might be a hindrance. His attorney told us in no uncertain terms that we can't talk to Mr. Grant except via fax. So it would be very difficult to have him there, if we couldn't talk to him."

Griem took umbrage and fired up his fax machine. *I'm bewitched, bothered and bewildered why the sheriff would say such a thing,* the lawyer wrote via facsimile to the sheriff's office. *Mr. Grant wanted to do anything and everything he can to help find Tara.* But now, Griem wrote, *I will fire him as a client if he participates.*

Hackel figuratively shrugged. His point had been made, loud and clear. "If he does show up or not, that's completely up to him," the sheriff said.

Goaded into action, Stephen dropped off two of Tara's laptops at the sheriff's office that afternoon. A Channel 7 television crew, which was at police headquarters on another story, spotted him entering the building. The station carried the story live on its noon newscast while Stephen was still inside. Within twenty minutes, the parking lot outside headquarters was crawling with reporters and cameramen waiting for Stephen to emerge.

When Stephen walked out a few minutes later, he seemed to welcome the attention. He told reporters he'd dropped off two computers: one was her current work computer, issued by Washington Group; the other was an old device that hadn't been used in two years.

Stephen explained he had just retrieved it from Comp-USA, where he'd taken it February 8 for repairs to the CD tray. "[Police] found out I picked it up . . . and they wanted it," Stephen said. "It's one of my wife's former laptops she used for work. The other one I gave them . . . if there are any clues, that would have something in it," he said. "I haven't touched that one. The [computer] she has now is the one she has with her. Her newest one is only a month old."

Kozlowski looked out his window and saw the group of reporters gathered around Stephen. The cop was disgusted. "He wouldn't talk to us, but I look outside and see him holding a press conference in the parking lot," he said.

The two laptops Stephen turned in were all well and good, investigators thought, but the computer they really wanted to inspect was the Grants' desktop machine—and that remained firmly off-limits.

"Unfortunately, it's been made clear we aren't going

to be allowed to look at that one," Hackel said. Later he called Stephen's appearance with the laptops "staged in front of the media."

"I had absolutely no use for [the laptops] whatsoever," the sheriff recalled. "We wanted the one in the house. But we didn't get that."

Such stonewalling by Stephen and his lawyer were among the behaviors that continued to raise questions among detectives and deputies working on the case. Wouldn't a truly innocent, distraught husband be demanding a polygraph, throwing open his whole life to investigators so they could eliminate him and move on to other possibilities? Wouldn't someone who wanted police to find his wife allow investigators a look at the home computer?

Still, if Stephen had committed foul play, he'd done a good job covering his tracks. Two weeks into Tara's disappearance, investigators had nothing they could take to a judge. Prosecutors were advising officers on the threshold of probable cause for searching the Grant's home. No one wanted to jump the gun and later have possible evidence thrown out as tainted by an unlawful search.

"We have to have an indication that Mr. Grant caused harm to her before we could get a search warrant," Hackel said. "But we don't have any information he did anything like that."

25

They started just after dawn. On foot, on horseback, and on all-terrain vehicles (ATVs), volunteer reserves and officers trudged through snowdrifts. They pulled up fallen tree limbs, scuffed up piles of dead leaves and literally beat the bushes. Overhead, observers in helicopters and airplanes patrolled the more desolate areas of Stony Creek Metropark's nature preserve.

"We decided to search near the main trail that was out there, Orchard Trail," Hackel said. "We searched near the areas where people would access the park. Usually, if someone takes a body and disposes of it, they do it near the main areas. They generally don't want to take too much time. They just want to dump the body and get out of there as fast as they can."

Hackel drew from a previous case he'd worked on before he was elected sheriff: the 1998 murder of Lisa Putnam, a Macomb Township state social worker who was beaten to death by twenty-eight-year-old Josephine Verellen and her twenty-two-year-old sister, Jacqueline, after Putnam removed Josephine's two children from their filthy home and reported the health hazard to the state. Both women were later convicted.

"In that case, they took her body to Leonard (in Northern Michigan), and dumped her body in the woods, just twenty yards from the road," Hackel said.

"We were thinking the same thing [in the Grant case]. If he did kill her and dump the body in Stony Creek, it would probably be within twenty to thirty yards of the main trail."

The mobile command RV was set up in the parking lot of nearby Powell Middle School, the spot also designated as the media staging area. The search area was off-limits to reporters, and Hackel instructed the rank and file not to discuss the details of the search with the press.

At home, local TV viewers followed the action on early-morning newscasts, then snapped off their sets and went about the business of the weekend—shopping, skating lessons, a day's work. But at Stony Creek Metropark, stomachs knotted and the shivers weren't all due to the February chill. Most of the 150 or so searchers dreaded what they might find, but even more, they feared another day, another weekend, another week, without answers.

Stephen's sister, Kelly, walked around the park a bit and met with investigators at the sheriff's mobile command center. Then she joined her brother and his children back in Washington Township, but she continued to take media calls on her cell phone. Stephen, she told the *Detroit News*, wasn't bitter about the sheriff's recent actions.

"He's doing OK, trying to remain hopeful that she will be found OK," Kelly said. "We know the sheriff is looking in to him. We just hope he is looking elsewhere as well."

Alicia, Erik, and Mary spent the day with the sheriff, lending moral support to the search crew. "I was taking them to various places in and around the park," Hackel said. "Wherever we went, Alicia was thanking the officers for helping. For the officers, I think it humanized the situation. When they saw her, I'm sure they thought, 'What if that was my sister?'"

* * *

A few hours into the search, a volunteer member of the sheriff's aviation unit radioed that he might have found something. While flying over a grassy area, he spotted what looked like a body.

"We thought for a minute, 'OK, that's it—we've found her,'" Hackel said. But the find turned out to be a false alarm.

"It was just a deer carcass," Hackel said. "I wasn't sure if I should feel happy or disappointed."

When the theme music trumpeted at noon for local radio and TV news broadcasts on the case, the search still was under way. But about a half hour later, a discouraged Hackel called it off.

"We decided to terminate the search, since we went to all the areas we'd planned to go into in the perimeters we'd set," Hackel said. The sheriff put out the call on his radio: "10-42"—police code for "out of service."

Alicia was obviously distraught when the search revealed no clues. "I have a completely empty feeling inside," she told reporters. "Now what?"

The postsearch mood was somber as the exhausted officers and reserves trudged to their cars in the school parking lot and drove away, Hackel said. "It was a lot of effort and work. I'm thinking, 'Now I have to face the media and tell them we didn't find anything, and face questions about whether it was really necessary.'"

But when Hackel met with reporters, he decided to keep Stephen guessing. "When the media asked if we were going to search other areas, I said we might," he said. "I wanted to keep [Stephen] off-balance, keep him wondering what we might be up to next."

During interviews he gave immediately after calling off the search, Hackel also made a plea to the public. "I asked people to keep their eyes open," he said. "I said,

'If you're out walking in a park and you see something that looks even a little suspicious, take an extra look.'"

It was a lawman's standard request for citizen assistance. Hackel had no idea how crucial it would turn out to be.

Around the time of the search, reporters began delving deeper into the backgrounds of Tara and Stephen Grant. So far, Tara had only been tersely described in most media accounts as an executive with the Washington Group, while Stephen was simply known as the husband, who was acting suspiciously, even if police weren't coming right out and saying it.

But on Friday, the *Detroit Free Press* ran a story about the next day's scheduled search of Stony Creek, which included a few paragraphs of biographical information about the Grants. The story explained that Tara had grown up on a farm in Perkins, a small town in Michigan's Upper Peninsula (UP). She met Stephen in 1994 while working toward a business degree at Michigan State University (MSU), readers were told. When they met, the story said, Stephen worked in the office of state senator Jack Faxon.

After their marriage, Tara Grant's career soared with the Washington Group while Grant said he readily played the role of Mr. Mom, the story said.

The next day, the *Detroit News* ran a front-page story under the headline WHO IS TARA GRANT? Interviews with Tara's childhood friends revealed her as ambitious and tough-minded, a girl who grew up in rural Michigan shooting her own .22 rifle and dreaming about bigger things.

The characters of this true-crime drama were beginning to take shape more clearly: Tara, the farm girl who grew up to become a beautiful jet-setting executive, and

Stephen, the jittery, bug-eyed stay-at-home husband, who many people thought was hiding something.

Free Press columnist Brian Dickerson summed up the situation succinctly in his February 23 column: *The mystery surrounding 34-year-old Tara's disappearance is as irresistible as any Lifetime Network original,* he wrote. *Stephen says he has no clue about what has become of his wife, but at water coolers across southeast Michigan, the lines already are being drawn between those who feel sorry for him and those who suspect him of being the next Scott Peterson.*

Stephen told the *Detroit News* he was well-aware that people were comparing him to Scott Peterson, the California man now convicted for the sensational murder of his pregnant wife, Laci.

Accounts of the Peterson case frequently analyzed Scott's demeanor during the time his wife was missing, and his lack of assistance during the frantic community-wide searches for her, or her body.

"I thought Scott Peterson was guilty, too," Stephen said. "So I get why everyone is looking at me as a suspect."

When Stephen was asked why he thought people suspected him, he said, "Because that's just how it is. You always look at the husband. Whether it's true or not, the husband always did it. But people who know me—even if they've only known me a short time—they know I didn't do anything wrong. They know it's not me. That guy is not me. When I first sat down and talked to my private investigator, he said, 'I can't believe the police are looking at you as a suspect, because you're not that guy.'

"He said, 'Someone who would harm his wife isn't the kind of guy who helps clean the house and cooks dinner. That guy is not you.'"

26

The day after the abortive metropark search, investigators regrouped and considered their next steps. "It was really getting frustrating," McLean said. "It's like we were trying to put together the pieces of a puzzle, but there were still a bunch of missing pieces. We were checking every angle we could think of, and we were coming up with very little."

By now, tips were pouring into the sheriff's hotline by the hundred, and each one had to be investigated. The leads were logged and checked out by all twelve men and women in the detective bureau. "We had to track down every tip," McLean said. "That, by itself, was a lot of work."

The tips ranged from the plausible—Tara was seen in a restaurant, or in Florida—to the absurd. One telephone tipster told the sheriff's office she'd just seen Tara on the syndicated game show *Wheel of Fortune*. Mediums and clairvoyants called in offering advice.

As far as the detectives were concerned, it didn't take a psychic to figure out what became of Tara. Though they couldn't say so publicly, most or all of the investigators on the case figured the circumstantial evidence pointed directly to Stephen.

"He's not a suspect, but his actions are suspect" was as far as Hackel was willing to go with his comments to the media.

* * *

More forces were marshaled. The Michigan State Police and the National Center for Missing Adults were enlisted. Any Jane Doe cadaver in any morgue within the United States was scrutinized, lest it be Tara.

Forensic investigators were tapping into the executive's laptops, but they still wanted to get a look at the family desktop computer, Hackel reiterated to reporters. "The two laptops we have are old ones that hadn't been used in a while," the sheriff said.

Griem provided an excuse: Stephen, he said, could not turn over the desktop computer because it held "information that would violate the attorney-client privilege." Further, he said, Tara "hardly touched" the home computer. He reiterated that Stephen had launched a private investigation into Tara's disappearance.

Stephen said his PI was working hard on the case. "He's making a lot of phone calls. He's looking into a lot of things. He calls me daily with new questions. The problem is the police won't give him any of their information," Stephen complained. "So he's in the dark about a lot of stuff. I don't understand why the police are doing that. It's not like the person we hired is a nobody—he's a former FBI agent."

Hackel disputed the claim that his detectives did not cooperate with the investigator Stephen had hired. "We never heard from any private investigator," the sheriff said.

The week wore on. Local editors and TV producers, desperate to keep the story at the top of broadcasts despite the lack of substantial new details, rehashed background material and replayed Stephen's tearful pleas. ABC's *Nightline,* Fox's *On the Record with Greta Van Susteren* and MSNBC had picked up on the case.

David Griem told the *Detroit Free Press* that national media were hounding him. "We had [CNN's] Nancy Grace show call us three times today and they told us that Sheriff Hackel is appearing, that Tara's sister is appearing, and, more or less, threatened us to appear," Griem told the newspaper. "We're not going to add to this media feeding frenzy."

The widespread media attention given to Tara's disappearance rankled some people who noted the relatively sparse press coverage given to another local missing persons case that was being investigated at the same time: the disappearance of Lizzie Mae Collier-Sweet.

Collier-Sweet, a forty-nine-year-old black woman from Brownstown Township, came up missing January 8, 2007—almost a month to the day before Tara's disappearance—after an arson fire destroyed the home the woman shared with her husband, Roger Sweet, who was white. Police found the missing woman's diary among the charred remains; it contained descriptions of the abuse inflicted by her husband over the years.

Collier-Sweet's diary also detailed a five-year-long affair her sixty-year-old husband was having with a mentally disabled relative, which began when the girl was thirteen years old. Police later discovered child pornography on Roger Sweet's computers, including images of sex acts with the teen.

After Roger Sweet was arrested, police took a closer look at the 1990 death of his first wife, Marlene Sweet. The death was initially ruled accidental when Sweet told police his wife slipped in the bathroom and hit her head on the concrete floor. But on January 19, police ruled Marlene Sweet's death a homicide. Roger Sweet eventually confessed to the murder of his first wife, but as of this writing, Lizzie Mae Collier-Sweet remains missing.

In the first month of Lizzie Mae Collier-Sweet's

disappearance, the local newspapers published only a handful of stories about the case. Television coverage was equally sparse, compared to the seemingly nonstop attention given to Tara's disappearance.

The discrepancy in coverage gave rise to charges of racism. E-mails to reporters and letters to the editors of local newspapers posed the question: why was Tara Grant's disappearance given so much more weight by the media than Collier-Sweet's case?

One reader wrote in an e-mail, *If Tara Grant was poor and black, nobody would care about her, just like nobody in the media cares about Lizzie Mae Collier-Sweet.*

The penchant for the media to highlight the disappearances of attractive, upper-class Caucasian women has been dubbed "missing white woman syndrome." But critics did not take into consideration one irrefutable truth that drove the amount of coverage given to the respective missing Metro Detroit women in the winter of 2007: the Tara Grant case sold newspapers and drew incredible television ratings, while stories about the Collier-Sweet disappearance did not.

27

As Hackel returned to his Mount Clemens office one day during the Grant investigation, he received an unexpected telephone message. "It was Chris Utykanski—Kelly's husband—asking me to call," he recollected. The sheriff hadn't realized that his former high-school classmate now was Stephen Grant's brother-in-law. "I thought, 'Oh, my gosh. I never put two and two together,'" he said.

Hackel forced himself to dial the phone. He realized that Chris Utykanski—now Kelly's fourth husband—was trying to smooth over the family's strained relationship with the sheriff's office. The two men talked for an hour and a half, warily circling some of the biggest unanswered questions in the case.

"I tried to be very diplomatic," Hackel recalled. "I said, 'There are some things in this case that we have to deal with.'"

When he finally hung up, the sheriff felt a stab of pity for his old pal. "He was a nice guy in high school," Hackel recalled. "I was pretty good friends with him, and knew him a long time. He was a real nice, easygoing guy. He always kept to himself, never argued with people, and never got into a fight. He was just a low-key guy who didn't bother anyone. I thought to myself, 'Boy, he has no idea what is really going on.'"

* * *

Meanwhile, Stephen continued giving interviews right and left. He now spoke to reporters with an easy familiarity, obviously pleased to be on a first-name basis with the men and women who were covering his wife's disappearance. The "Mr. Mom" appeared fascinated by his own notoriety.

"I want people to know me a little better," he said on Monday. "I think people have the wrong impression."

He began stopping in at the BP gas station across the street from the sheriff's office every day, purchasing copies of the *Detroit News,* the *Detroit Free Press,* and the *Macomb Daily,* along with his bottled water and Reese's Peanut Butter Cups.

"We could see him from our building going into the gas station every day," Hackel said. "We asked the gas station owner to let us look at his surveillance tape, and he was buying all three newspapers every day. It was obvious he wanted to know what was being said about him."

Also on Monday, Stephen told reporters that his private investigator, whom he again referred to as a former FBI agent, hadn't yet turned up any clues.

"I have to keep my faith that she's out there, and not ready to come home yet," he said. "It's really all I can hope for, that she's OK, but just not in a place mentally to come home.

"And if that's not the case . . . well, I'll deal with that when I have to. I can't imagine the other road. At the end of that road is two kids whose mother isn't coming back. And I can't get my brain around that."

He said his kids' lives had been turned inside out over the past two-and-a-half weeks. It was time, he said, that Lindsey and Ian returned to school—first grade for her and private preschool for the boy—after their winter break and a few days they were kept home due to illness.

Stephen admitted his earlier misgivings, that, because of extensive broadcast coverage, the kids' classmates would question them insensitively about their mother's fate.

"Kids hear things," he said. "My concern is, a lot of parents may have the news on while dinner is cooking and they may talk about things. People don't check what they're saying.

"I'm afraid that one of the kids in the school is going to walk up to [Lindsey] and say, 'Your daddy did something horrible to your mommy.' I understand that people are jumping to conclusions about me. I've done the same thing. But being on the other side of it, I'll think differently from now on."

Despite his fears, Stephen later said the kids' first day back in school—Tuesday, February 27—was normal. Meanwhile, he had come up with his own delicate way of relating the matter of their missing mother to the children: he likened it to when the family golden retriever wandered away for a few days about six months earlier.

"I told them, 'Remember when Bentley was lost for a while? Well, Mommy is lost like that,'" Stephen recalled.

28

On Wednesday, February 28, a crucial event took place below the media radar screen. As far as the public knew, the case of the missing executive was status quo, perhaps even waning a bit in interest as the days wore on. Newspaper articles were shorter and had moved off the front pages of the local dailies. Some papers even buried their "Tara updates" inside local sections, next to stories about city council meetings and road repair projects.

But at about twelve-thirty that afternoon, a local dental hygienist and nature enthusiast decided to take advantage of the 40-degree "warm spell" and go for a walk along Mt. Vernon Road and into Stony Creek Metropark. She hiked in a different part of the park than investigators had searched just four days earlier—a little-traveled, heavily wooded spot near some power lines, not far from the Macomb/Oakland County border.

Sheila Werner, an attractive thirty-four-year-old, wasn't accustomed to being a passive observer of her surroundings. She'd adopted a one-mile stretch of roadway near her Washington Township home—an undertaking usually reserved for civic groups and other large organizations—pledging to keep it litter free.

As she walked, her glance was attuned not only to the natural flora and fauna around her way, but to man-made debris and other items that didn't belong amid the woods and streams of Stony Creek.

"I knew about the Tara Grant investigation, and I knew the police had searched the park," she said. "And I remembered the police asking people to keep an eye out for anything that looked suspicious. So it was definitely in the back of my mind."

Perhaps that's why the Ziploc bag caught her eye. Tucked in a low cranny, where two gnarled tree branches met, just a few yards from the road, the bag's blood-soaked cargo stood out against the snow "like a sore thumb," she later said.

"I noticed blood pooling at the bottom of the bag," she said. The large bag also contained other plastic bags, a pair of rubber gloves, and some metal shavings.

Gingerly picking up the bag with her mitten, she retraced the path to her home and dropped the Baggie atop the freezer in her garage. Then she stepped inside and dialed the sheriff's office.

Deputy John Warn took the call. He immediately drove to Werner's house, and she showed him what she'd stumbled onto. "I asked her to take me to the area where she'd found the bag, and she did," Warn said. "Then I called the detective bureau and told them what was going on."

Not wanting to get up their hopes, some investigators surmised the Ziploc and its bloody contents were the detritus from poachers gutting prey in the woods. "The guys kept telling me, 'It's probably a deer bag,'" Lieutenant Darga said. "I'm like, 'What's a deer bag?' They said, 'It's a bag you use after you're finished cleaning a deer.'"

It was a plausible explanation. However, Darga kept coming back to the metal shrapnel in the bag—the kind of cast-off shavings found in tool and die shops that served Metro Detroit's auto-related manufacturing industries. That included USG Babbitt Inc.—the tiny family metal shop in Mount Clemens, where Stephen and his dad turned out ball bearings.

"There was also some animal hair in the bag that matched the color of [the Grants'] dog," Darga asserted. "I said, 'We need to get this to the lab right now.'"

Detectives sent the bag to the MSP Crime Laboratory in Sterling Heights. Serology expert Jennifer Smiatacz tested the blood in the bag. It was, indeed, human.

Turnaround time for forensic evidence in the state police crime lab can sometimes reach several months, but there was a priority put on the Ziploc bag, Darga said. "The lab got the results back to us the next day. They knew what kind of case we were working on, so they checked it out immediately."

The lab report inventoried the exact contents of the large Ziploc. Aside from the blood, shavings, and hair, the bag contained four clear plastic garbage bags, one pair of latex gloves, one 7-Eleven shopping bag, and an additional smaller Ziploc. All items had human blood on them.

"If you take it all together—human blood, the metal shavings, the hair—we were sure it was enough to get a search warrant," Detective Sergeant McLean said. "Before that, we'd been dying to ask the judge for a warrant, but we knew we didn't have enough. You never want to go to a judge when you're not one hundred percent sure your search will stand up in court."

The prosecutor's office concurred: the bloody plastic bag was enough to justify detectives' access to the Grants' house.

29

Friday, March 2, was a day that no one connected with the investigation ever would forget.

Finally, nearly three weeks since anyone last had spoken with Tara, authorities felt themselves gaining control of the investigation. And, over the next few days, the case would gyrate with one surreal twist after the other—more than making up for the previous weeks' maddening lack of progress.

McLean and Kozlowski drew up the search warrants for the Grant home and his father's tool and die shop. Judge Denis LeDuc, of 42-1 District Court, signed them.

At about noon on Friday, Stephen gave a shocking one-hundred-minute interview to the *Detroit News* in which he openly disparaged his wife and referred to her in the past tense.

"Everything is surreal, like I'm walking around in a dream," he began. "Nothing feels normal. It's just . . . weird."

He was asked to talk about his wife.

"Well, Tara looked completely different when we met," he drawled. "She was beautiful. It's hard to explain. She just looked a lot . . . different. She had the big hair, and it was a different look."

When he was asked to describe Tara as a mother, Stephen said, "She loves her kids. But, you know, most mothers don't travel five days a week. I've heard comments from people—'What kind of mother would leave her babies all week long?' She's gone five days a week. She's there on weekends, but it wasn't weird for her to come in and kiss the kids and leave again. Well, I'm sorry—is that a good mother? No, it's not. That's a bad mother.

"People think she was the perfect mother. I was a better mom than Tara was. There's no other way to put it. I was the mom in the house—she was gone all the time. If the kids needed someone to take them to swimming, or school, or soccer practice, I took them.

"Some of her family has said in the media how much she loved her kids, and how she would try to fly back in order to attend their functions," he said. "But that's not true. I can't recall one time when she did that. To be honest, as weird as it sounds for me to say this, I was the perfect mom—not Tara."

Stephen said he and Tara often had "power struggles. You know, both people trying to show who's boss, and who's going to run the household. It didn't need to be that way. In a lot of households, when there's an argument, that means fists are involved. But Tara and I never did that. It wouldn't come close to happening. I wouldn't do it."

Although Stephen said he had his suspicions about Tara's fidelity, he insisted he didn't think she'd ever had a physical relationship with another man—but he kept backtracking.

"Have I thought maybe there was something going on? Yes," he said. "Tara, over [the] past year, has been text messaging one of her old bosses. I told her it was a strange relationship. They text messaged in code. One day in the car, we were driving somewhere and she sent a text message—you could read it from across the car. It was a smiley face and it said, 'I'm peeing.' I asked her, 'What the hell does that mean? Why would you tell someone you're going to the bathroom?'

"She explained that it meant she was laughing so hard, she was peeing," Stephen said. "They text messaged like fourteen-year-old girls. This guy learned text from his fifteen-year-old-son, and he and Tara had all these little codes, the way the kids talk."

Stephen also discussed a racy e-mail he'd intercepted two years earlier, which, he said, Tara had written to an ex-boyfriend. "That was something I thought was physical with another man," he said. "It was a former boyfriend of Tara's. They'd been talking on the Internet. I saw one of the e-mails she'd sent, and it made me think there was something going on."

Stephen claimed he confronted Tara with the e-mail and that they had a bitter argument, followed by an all-night discussion about their deteriorating relationship. He said they agreed to see a marriage counselor. They attended counseling from February 2005, when he discovered the letter, until the summer of 2006, Stephen said.

"There were thirty sessions," he said. "We worked it out. It was mostly a lack of communication—we weren't talking, and she was getting that communication need fulfilled by this guy. But it never became physical, as far as I know, and I checked really hard.

"This was a former boyfriend from high school, and their relationship ended weird. There was no formal ending to it. But in the end, it ended up being nothing. I checked as hard as I could to make sure nothing had happened. This was in accordance to the rules set up by the counselor—that I have open access, and could question anything. The counselor used the term 'cheating'—even though it wasn't physical, she considered it cheating.

"It hurt really bad, but it wasn't like real cheating, like having a full-blown sexual affair. It was simply that she had an emotional thing with this guy. So the counselor said anytime I asked a question, Tara had to answer it. That was the rule, and it worked. She found out it wasn't the worst thing in the world for her to have to answer my questions and be open with me. We worked through it, but it was hard. It took a lot of long talks into the middle of the night.

"Were there still times when I had questions? Yeah? Did I ever demand she open her e-mail and have her show it to me? Yeah."

Stephen said he stopped questioning Tara shortly after they'd finished going to the marriage counselor. "I remember the last time I asked, 'Who are you on the phone with?' But I really wasn't worried about who she was talking to. The trust had come back."

Stephen became defensive when he was asked about Tara's high-paying job. "It's not like I don't make a lot of money myself," he said. "My job pays really well, too. I work for my dad. It's a family business—a major auto supplier. It's a small company, but I make a good salary. It's not like Tara supports me."

Then Stephen discussed the events of February 9.

"I was tired," he said. "I was just exasperated. By the time Tara left Friday night, I was tired. I was tired of the arguing. She walked out the garage door, and all I could do was close the garage door. I didn't want to have this discussion anymore. I was done. I was tired of bickering about it . . . the travel . . . and I gave up.

"My biggest concern that night was, I had to explain to the kids the next day why their mother wasn't going to be there, like she said she would," Stephen said. "Before she left, she used those words—'You can explain to the kids why I'm not going to be here tomorrow.'

"The last words she said to me were, 'Don't forget to take my truck in on Monday.' That really took the wind out of my sails. She was telling me that's all I was. It was like, 'You be the valet and take my car in.'"

At about 5:00 P.M., detectives and evidence experts descended on Washington Township. They were armed with ultraviolet lights and luminol to detect the presence of blood. They toted video cameras and other tools of the trade, as well as a sheaf of papers that allowed them legal access to the Grants' private home.

It was nearing dusk and an evening snowfall was getting under way. Stephen was just pulling into the subdivision in his gray Jeep Commander when police stopped him. Dressed in jeans, casual footwear, and a short dark jacket, Grant was patted down at the back of his vehicle and then led to a police cruiser.

As luck would have it, TV news cameras were rolling. While police had cordoned off the search area, a crew from WDIV Channel 4 already was on the scene, preparing for a previously scheduled interview between Stephen and Channel 4 reporter Hank Winchester.

Winchester later told the *Detroit Free Press* that he'd been getting as many as five phone calls a day from Stephen, who was obsessed with his own growing publicity.

The conversations had grown odder as the days of Tara's disappearance wore on, Winchester recounted to the *Free Press*. At one point, when the reporter asked Stephen for home video of Tara, such as holiday movies, Stephen jokingly alluded to "intimate movies" he and Tara had shot, and said, "Hank, I'm having guy talk with you. Don't take it the wrong way. That's the only thing I could think of off the top of my head."

The reporter said he still was haunted—to the point of nightmares—about Stephen's last request to him that

Friday, March 2: to tape an interview in the Grant home's garage.

"I think about the garage scenario and try to figure out why he wanted me in there," Winchester told *Free Press* reporter Jeff Seidel.

But Winchester's interview with Stephen never took place. Instead, the news crew was on hand for the most sensational twist yet in the Grant case.

"He's getting out of the car, he's getting out of the car," a newsman's voice excitedly ad-libbed as the crew unwittingly taped the scoop.

Captain Wickersham met Stephen as he exited his vehicle. "I told him we had a warrant to search his house. Our conversation was civil. He chatted with me like there was nothing out of the ordinary happening. He did ask if we were going to tear up his home searching for evidence.

"He said, 'You're not going to tear out the ceiling tiles, are you?' I assured him we would treat his home with respect."

After a conversation that lasted about twenty minutes, Stephen handed over his house key. He drove his Jeep into his driveway and let the police into his home.

"The first thing he did was call his attorney, and he put me on the phone with him," Wickersham said. "Griem asked me if we had an arrest warrant, and I told him we didn't. We only had a search warrant. He demanded we release his client, so we did."

Stephen leashed up the dog, Bentley, and headed down the street.

In a decision that would prove controversial, deputies decided not to follow him. "We had undercover officers watching him, but they were told to back off because the news crew was there," Hackel said. "We didn't want our undercover people on the TV news."

As Stephen walked away, a Channel 4 cameraman still had him in sight, but the waning daylight and blustery snowstorm camouflaged the suspect. Even as the videotape reels spun, Stephen and his dog disappeared from view.

By now, there were about fifteen police officers and evidence technicians milling around the Grant house. McLean was among them. "We were hoping maybe we'd find a clue on the home computer," McLean said. "I wasn't expecting to find much more than that."

Stephen trudged east through his subdivision with Bentley in tow. When he got out of sight of the police and news crews, he used his cell phone to call his friend Michael Zanlungo, who lived two miles away.

"He told me the police had executed a search warrant and had impounded his Jeep," Zanlungo said. "He asked me to pick him up at a crossroads near his house. I didn't understand why."

Zanlungo, also known as Mike, had been friends with Stephen since the Grants had arrived in Washington Township four years earlier. After the phone call, he got into the company car he'd brought home that night and met Stephen at the agreed-to location.

Stephen and his dog jumped into the car. Before Zanlungo had driven far, he noticed Stephen was acting strangely.

"He was very nervous," Zanlungo said. "He was sweating and looking over his shoulder. He asked, 'Are we being followed? That Taurus is following us.' I said, 'What's going on? You're not acting like an innocent person.'"

They drove east on 28 Mile Road, Stephen growing more paranoid by the minute. He said he wanted to see Lindsey and Ian, and Zanlungo offered to lend him his personal vehicle, a Dodge Dakota pickup.

"I was in a company car," he explained. "I didn't want

to loan him the company car because I knew he had a bad driving record."

Zanlungo said he drove back to his house and gave Stephen the keys to his yellow truck. "He put the dog in the truck and drove away."

30

As a team of five evidence technicians—two from the sheriff's office and three from the state police—searched the four-bedroom home, Kozlowski and McLean cooled their heels in the garage with a group of about eight other detectives.

"We were trying to stay out of the way of the evidence techs," Kozlowski said. "So we hung around the garage, just talking about the case. As I was standing there, my eye went to this green container—something about it seemed out of place." The container, which stood along the wall next to a bucket full of toys, was marked *Boys Clothes*.

"I walked over and tried to open the top, but it was hard to get open," Kozlowski said. "When I finally got the top open, there was a black garbage bag inside. I touched it. It was soft. It gave to my pressure. I almost closed the bag and dismissed it as a bag of salt or something, but I decided to tear open the bag."

When he ripped a hole in the plastic bag, he caught a glimpse of flesh and blood. His initial fleeting thought was *It's a deer carcass*. Then his gaze settled on a swatch of black fabric—a bra.

Kozlowski's coworkers were surprised to see the unflappable detective suddenly jump away from the container and yell, "What the fuck!"

The detectives gathered around the bin as Kozlowski peeled away the garbage bag to reveal a female torso—dismembered.

"It was weird, very surreal," McLean said. "We were almost in shock—we couldn't believe what we were looking at. By that time, we'd already come to the realization that Tara was gone, so that part of it wasn't that much of a surprise. But finding the torso . . . it was a huge shock."

Still, a surge of triumph tempered the horror inside the Rubbermaid tub. "There was also a sense of elation—we got him," McLean said. "We'd been working day and night. We'd sacrificed our personal lives. This is the kind of case that just takes over your life. All along, we knew he did it, but we weren't sure if we were ever going to be able to charge him. And when we found the torso, we're thinking, 'We got him! We got him!'"

The stunned detectives hollered for evidence techs to secure the garage. "Then we switched our focus to finding Stephen," McLean said.

Meanwhile, Hackel was busy fielding phone calls from reporters who saw Channel 4's live report on the search of the Grant home. The sheriff insisted that Stephen was not under arrest. "He's not even a suspect at this point," he told reporters.

It was a hectic evening, the sheriff recalled, but it was about to take a bizarre turn. "I'm in the office trying to do damage control with the media, thinking this night has become a nightmare already," Hackel said.

His cell phone rang again. This time it wasn't a reporter—it was the chief of staff, Captain Rick Kalm, calling from the Grant home.

"He said in a soft tone, 'We got her,'" Hackel said.

"I said, 'What do you mean?'

"He says, 'We found her in the house.'

"I said, 'Rick, you have got to be kidding me.' Then he told me, 'Actually, it's a woman's torso.'

"When he said that, I could feel the hair on the back of my neck standing up," Hackel recalled.

The sheriff hopped in his car and made the twenty-minute drive to the Westridge domicile.

"I looked inside the container and saw leaves and twigs, and I told Rick, 'He picked this body up from a wooded area and brought it back here. I'll bet it was Stony Creek.'" The sheriff ordered another search of the park. It would begin at daybreak.

Sergeant Mark Grammatico was asked to remove Tara's torso from the Grant home while detectives rushed to find Stephen. Grammatico ferried the plastic bin to the parking lot of a nearby shopping center, turning it over to Bill Robinette, of the Macomb County Medical Examiner's Office.

After peeling away four black plastic garbage bags and one clear bag, Robinette, a medical examiner (ME), inventoried the clothing left on the body: a black Gilligan & O'Malley bra, an extra-small gray or silver Ann Taylor shirt—torn, black Victoria's Secret v-string underwear, and the remnants of Isaac Mizrahi dress slacks, size 6.

Hackel called a press conference for nine o'clock Friday night, March 2, but he decided to hold off informing the media about the grisly discovery in the Grant garage. He merely confirmed that police had obtained a warrant to search the home, and didn't say much else.

"I didn't want Tara's family to hear about it on the news," he later said. "That would have been pretty gruesome. How would you like it if you were that person sitting at home and someone called you to tell you they heard on the news that your sister's torso had been found?"

With Stephen on the lam, Hackel was worried about the safety of Alicia and her family. He also was concerned about Deena Hardy, the ex-girlfriend who had provided the salacious e-mails. "We didn't know if he was going to try to get revenge on Deena for releasing those e-mails," Hackel said. "And there was also a possibility he might drive to Ohio and cause harm to Alicia or Mrs. Destrampe. We had no idea what his state of mind was at that point.

"I called and talked to Erik [Standerfer]," Hackel said. "I told him we had information to lead us to believe there was foul play, and that they needed to come up here as soon as possible. That's all I said. I didn't want to tell them what happened over the telephone. Erik pretty much knew at that point that Tara was dead, but he didn't have any of the details. This was about eleven-thirty at night. They immediately packed up the kids and drove up."

Hackel booked a room for the family at the Best Western ConCorde Inn in Clinton Township, three miles south of the sheriff's headquarters.

Meanwhile, Captain Wickersham phoned Deena and told her that Tara had likely met with foul play, and that Stephen was on the run. The captain suggested she spend the night elsewhere for her own safety. Deena went to the home of her friend Tom Gromak, the *Detroit News* staffer who had been instrumental in bringing the e-mails to light.

Hackel, who hadn't slept in two days, finally headed to his nearby home in Macomb Township to shower and change. But the night that seemingly never would end was about to get even crazier.

As the exhausted lawman pulled up to a deserted intersection, he saw a vehicle stopped in the middle of the road. It didn't take Hackel long to figure out why. *I can't believe I have to arrest a drunk driver in the middle of all this,* he thought, reaching to the dashboard of his unmarked car to flick on the red-and-blue flashers.

A high-speed chase ensued. "She wouldn't pull over for me," the sheriff recalled. "She was drunker than a skunk. Finally she ends up on somebody's lawn."

Hackel called for backup and turned his quarry over to deputies, then got home just in time to shower, change, and bolt back out for the Best Western to meet Tara's family and deliver the heartbreaking news.

As Alicia and her family approached Macomb County at about five-thirty Saturday morning, she called Hackel, who gave her directions to the Best Western. He met Tara's family in their hotel room and broke the horrifying news that detectives had found a dismembered torso inside the Grant garage.

"It was like your worst nightmare come to life," Alicia said. "We held out a glimmer of hope that she may still be alive, but we knew there was always a chance [that] something terrible had happened. But this was just the worst possible scenario. It's something you never would've imagined."

Breaking the news that a family member has been murdered is never an easy job, Hackel said. "It's one of the worst things we have to do as police officers. Especially in this case, where I'd spent so much time with the family, and this wasn't just telling someone that their loved one was dead. We had to tell them that she'd been dismembered. It was not easy."

31

At about 9:30 A.M., Saturday, a team of detectives, several dozen police reserves, and five K-9 units gathered at Stony Creek for a second search. In all, there were nearly one hundred people.

Sergeant Larry King, the Macomb administrative sergeant for the Macomb detective bureau, had spent a lot of time hiking in Stony Creek park as a child, and he was intimately familiar with the terrain. The twenty-one-year veteran led the group that conducted the second search of the park. This time they decided to check a wooded area not accessible to cars.

After about an hour and a half, Deputy Scott Lasky discovered a pink object lying on top of the snow near a tree. *The closer I got, the more I realized it was a body part,* Lasky later wrote in his report. The first piece of Tara to be located was one of her thighs.

"It was clean cut, and the skin near the cut had been pulled back," King said.

Shortly after the thigh was found, reserve officers Conrad Maday and Stephen Bonnell made an even more gruesome discovery: Tara's head, wedged beneath an upturned tree stump.

"You could see the hair and part of the neck," King said. "Once we found the thigh and the head, we backed the reserves out of there and secured the scene. Then we called in the medical examiner's office."

When technicians from the ME's office arrived, they photographed the two body parts, as they'd been found. "Then we removed the head from underneath the log," King said. "There was no doubt it was Tara. The head was well-preserved. [The weather] had been really cold, so it was pristine. The features were all there."

As detectives searched the park for more body parts, King was charged with carrying the bag containing Tara's head and other limbs. A right hand was found on top of the snow behind a bush. A large bone, thought to be a femur, was discovered nearby. "Animals had gotten to it and picked it clean," King said. A short time later, investigators found a left hand. "All that was left of it was bone and tendons," King said.

A foot was located in the snow. A lower leg was discovered in a hollowed-out log. "I'm walking through the woods and picking up pieces and putting them into a bag, thinking, 'This is screwed up,'" King said.

Every time he opened the bag to put another body part inside, King said, he could see Tara's head. Her eyes were still open. "It was like she was staring at me," he said. "In a situation like that, you've got to stop thinking about yourself and how you're feeling, and think about the family. If this had been my family member, I would want the police to recover her entire body. So we put ourselves in the mind-set that we were doing this to help Tara's family."

After several hours, the decision was made to halt the search, since dusk was approaching, and the cadaver dogs were becoming fatigued. King asked all available K-9 units to return to the park at nine the following morning. King gave the body parts to assistant medical examiner Sherry Huntley. A deputy was posted in the park overnight to keep the area secure.

* * *

About the same time police began their search of Stony Creek, Hackel held a press conference to announce the grisly find in the Grants' garage the previous evening. "The search today for a missing person has ended with a very tragic result," he said grimly, adding that a woman's dismembered torso had been found in the Grant home. "We believe the body to be that of Tara Grant," he said. "By no means did we expect to recover what we did."

Hackel said he was working with the Macomb County Prosecutor's Office to seek murder charges. "[Stephen] is the number one and, at this time, the only suspect in the murder of Tara Lynn Grant," he said.

Hackel said that Stephen was on the run, and erroneously reported that the suspect was believed to be driving a white pickup truck. Minutes later, Hackel fixed the error: Stephen was likely driving a yellow truck.

The suspect was to be considered armed and dangerous, the sheriff warned.

32

Meanwhile, Stephen was speeding north in the bright yellow Dodge Dakota Sport Quad pickup truck—seeking refuge in the rural expanses of Michigan that held memories of happier times.

Police later reconstructed his erratic path. He sneaked into his sister Kelly's house, hoping to find a gun. Instead, he pocketed a bottle of Vicodin; leaving his dog at his sister's house, he headed west to Lansing, near his childhood home. Along the way, he made three stops, purchasing items ranging from a Heath candy bar to a pint of Jack Daniel's to a toy cap gun—and a Magic Marker he used to color the pistol's red plastic tip a more believable black. The gun was to be brandished in hopes of committing "suicide by cop," should any lawman pull him over.

Thus fortified, Stephen bore down on the accelerator, his hot-dog-mustard-yellow getaway truck standing out on the highway that cut through Michigan's stark, leafless, snow-covered landscape. He was headed for the outer reaches of the state's lower peninsula, where he and Tara had taken their first romantic getaway together.

As the day wore on, Stephen called Kelly—a move that allowed police to use pinging, a method of measuring how far his phone's radio signal was from several cell phone towers, to narrow the search. His ATM withdrawal records already had created an electronic trail for investigators to follow.

Just when it seemed the day couldn't get any weirder, Kozlowski took an unexpected phone call in his cramped, cement block office at the sheriff's station. On the other end of the line was a sobbing Verena Dierkes, calling from Germany. She said Stephen had just rung her phone, waking her in the middle of the night. He confessed to killing Tara, saying it was an accident.

"Everything he said was a lie," cried the nanny. "Everything. And I believed everything. He said, 'She smacked me and she yelled at me and I pushed her back, and she banged her head and was dead.'"

Kozlowski hit the record button on his tape recorder and started taking notes.

That afternoon, medical examiner Dr. Daniel Spitz—another Macomb County son who followed in his father's footsteps—began an autopsy of the torso. Spitz was the offspring of the famous forensic pathologist Dr. Werner Spitz, whose résumé included work on cases ranging from the John F. Kennedy assassination to the unsolved murder of six-year-old JonBenet Ramsey.

Preliminary results showed that Tara Grant had been *strangled* to death.

33

Lawyer David Griem reported that Stephen had called him twice in the wee hours of Saturday morning from a hotel pay phone, sounding incoherent and suicidal. Griem couldn't persuade the murder suspect to surrender, but he did try to talk Stephen out of killing himself.

"He was increasingly emotionally distraught," Griem told the *Detroit Free Press*. "I was telling him all the reasons he needed to live—most especially, two main reasons— a little four-year-old and a little six-year-old." Later that day, though, he told reporters: "I am certain that Stephen Grant is dead."

However, after an early-morning pit stop to draw $500 from a LaSalle Bank ATM, Stephen still was barreling north, very much alive. At 12:20 P.M., on Saturday, a be-on-the-lookout (BOLO) alert was transmitted via the LEIN system. It told law enforcement personnel statewide that Stephen Christopher Grant was wanted on an open murder charge and may also be suicidal. The report gave Stephen's weight, height, and home address, as well as the license plate number of his escape truck. Pickup was available statewide, the bulletin said.

Thanks to cell phone technology and Stephen's own compulsive communications, the Macomb County Sheriff's Office was never very far behind the fleeing suspect.

* * *

As dusk approached, Stephen finally reached his destination: Northern Michigan's Wilderness State Park. He pulled the truck into the park, cut the ignition, and scrawled a good-bye to his children on a lined sheet of notebook paper.

At about 4:20 P.M., Stephen called his sister again and told her where he was. Fearing her brother was going to kill himself, Kelly called Detective Kozlowski and relayed the information. Kozlowski then told Lieutenant Darga about Kelly's phone call.

In turn, Darga called the Emmet County Sheriff's Office (ECSO) with a heads-up that Stephen could be somewhere in that agency's turf, some 260 miles north of Macomb County.

If the map of Michigan's lower peninsula looks like a mitten, Emmet County is roughly the left half of the middle finger's tip, right at the top of the mitt. Its sixty-eight miles of Lake Michigan shoreline and more than 10,000 acres of inland water attracted fur traders and trappers before Michigan was a state. Now the area's rich natural resources make it a mecca for outdoors enthusiasts, many of them among the 31,000 county residents.

Emmet County's primary business district is the resort town of Petoskey. An upscale bayside city, replete with historic bed-and-breakfast inns, and famous for its sunsets over Lake Michigan, Petoskey and its environs have drawn visitors from Chicago, Detroit, and points south for more than one hundred years. The city shares the moniker for the Petoskey stone—the speckled 350-million-year-old fossilized coral dubbed Michigan's state stone. Both are named for Chief Pet-O-Sega, an 1800s Ottawa Indian born to a noble French fur trader and a Native American princess.

Some 30 percent of Emmet County land is publicly owned, including Wilderness State Park, a thickly wooded preserve abundant in wintertime with coyote, beaver, muskrat, and mink. The forests of the park are dense with pine, fir, and ancient hardwood trees. Ponds and wetlands can be treacherous, and the State Parks Web site warns visitors: *It is easy to get lost, and everyone going into the forest is advised to carry a map and a compass.*

Stephen Grant had neither on Saturday night when he plunged into the park.

34

Earlier that day, Sergeant Timothy Rodwell, of the ECSO road patrol office, had torn the Stephen Grant BOLO message from the wire and posted it in the squad room. Rodwell, a Metro Detroit native, had moved away from the congestion of southeast Michigan after earning a bachelor's degree in criminal justice. In addition to serving in the sheriff's department, he was cross-deputized as a tribal officer, enabling him to handle problems on Native American land in the state.

"It was a typical Saturday," Rodwell recalled. "I came in for the two P.M. to two A.M. shift. I was the only supervisor, so I was checking paperwork and other things. It was cold—we were prepping for inclement weather, cars in ditches." Rodwell assigned a four-wheel-drive vehicle to the county's night patrol officer, instead of a regular cruiser, in anticipation of the snow and ice to come.

Later that afternoon, he said, "I happened to be walking by our office manager's phone and heard it ring. I generally don't pick it up, but this time I did. It was Lieutenant Darga." Stephen Grant, Darga said, was thought to be in Wilderness State Park, possibly headed for a cabin at Waugoshance Point, on the far western tip of the narrow, jagged land spit that stretched out into icy Lake Michigan.

Citing Stephen's call to his sister, Kelly, Darga related

that Stephen was thought to have swallowed pills and intended to end his own life. "She kept it simple. He was wanted on a homicide warrant and, I believe, dismemberment of a body," Rodwell said. "She said to really treat him as armed and dangerous."

Rodwell confirmed active arrest warrants out of Macomb County, as well as a federal warrant for Stephen's arrest. With a suspected killer on the loose in the peaceful community, Rodwell spared no options, setting into motion a broad array of emergency response tactics. "Then we grabbed some equipment and started heading to that area. It was thirty miles away and the roads were snow covered and ice covered," he said. "I had our central dispatch get ahold of an ambulance."

It took a while, however, for the nature of this chase to sink in to the guardians of peaceful, sparsely populated Emmet County, which hadn't experienced a homicide in nine years. "None of the news reports . . . from Metro Detroit had made it up here," Rodwell said. "We had no idea. But it was obvious toward the end of the night, when we saw the amount of newspeople gathered, that it was more than a regular homicide warrant."

Within roughly an hour, all available law enforcement agencies turned out for search or standby duty, including sheriff's deputies, the Michigan State Police, the Mackinaw City Police Department, the Little Traverse Bay Band police, and a Northern Michigan EMT team. The U.S. Coast Guard station in Traverse City provided a helicopter, its crew equipped with night-vision goggles. Officers at Emmet County headquarters in Harbor Springs logged a minute-by-minute account of the hunt for Stephen Grant.

A vacationing FBI officer driving a blue Ford Explorer, and armed with a long gun, headed to the scene; snowmobile units were dispatched and a K-9 officer was on call. Wilderness Park representatives were summoned to a makeshift staging area at the B&L general store, on Cecil Bay Road, near the park entrance.

Rodwell completed the thirty-mile drive to the scene, where officers were scouring parking lots for the yellow Dodge Dakota. "The park is huge. It's very rural, and there is only one road in and one road out," Rodwell said. "The snow was thick and we started realizing that this guy was not going to get very far with his vehicle."

Michigan state troopers were deployed to warn area residents of possible danger and to check darkened cabins for signs of trespassing. Rodwell, along with his colleague Lieutenant Mike Keiser, Sergeant Richard Rule, of the Michigan State Police, and Special Agent Joel Postma, of the FBI, organized a command post at a small redwood cabin that housed Wilderness State Park Office Headquarters.

The officials were worried about campers who had left their cars in lots and trekked by ski or snowshoe to seasonal cabins deep inside the park. "We were looking for the truck, but we also felt we had a responsibility to those people," Rodwell said. "I felt we needed to drive hard to get to the cabins. The last person they want to meet in the middle of the night is Mr. Grant."

Several officers grabbed shovels and cleared a path to the cross-country track, making way for a Department of Natural Resources truck with extra-wide tires. With its ability to ride atop the snow, the truck ferried campers out to their parked vehicles. "It was not mandatory to leave—but when you see five or six police officers with rifles and shotguns banging at your door, well, everyone was willing to go," Rodwell recalled. "Within two hours, we had the park evacuated."

Darkness had fallen, and the sharp lake-driven gales, snow showers, and deep snowdrifts combined to make misery for searchers. Around 7:00 P.M., the call went out for night-vision equipment. On-and-off snow squalls were driven by 20 to 25 mph winds off the lake, blowing drifts as deep as ten feet.

Finally, at 8:45 P.M., a break: Grant's getaway vehicle was spotted parked askew at the intersection of Lakeshore Road and Lakeshore Drive, near a footpath to the crescent-shaped sweep of Sturgeon Bay, south of Waugoshance Point. It was parked illegally at the junction of the two narrow, forested roads, its wheels sunk in the snow on the shoulder, blocking traffic.

Officers—who earlier had marveled among themselves at the fugitive's choice of a bright yellow escape truck—took a cautious approach. Stephen could be crouching in the truck's cab, or lying in wait in the woods a dozen yards away. Marksmen covered the vehicle from 360 degrees before officers approached and found it unmanned. They backed away, pending the arrival of a K-9 tracking dog.

During the lull, "it started sinking in that this was something really strange," Rodwell recalled. "It's cold, desolate. It leads to desperation. If this guy really has a handgun, we're in a bad position standing out here in the middle of the road."

Richard Rule, too, felt an eerie sensation. "He's in the woods—and we're not," the sergeant said. "You think 'Are you overreacting?' But you don't know. He's edgy, he supposedly has a gun. Who knows what he's going to do? We had to consider that."

Rodwell pondered the resources at hand. He checked the bulletproof vest in his car and determined how it could be split with another officer. Meanwhile, the winds kicked up to thirty-five miles per hour. Officers in their regular uniforms, plus parkas, hats, and gloves, were feeling frozen within minutes. "The dog couldn't locate any scent, so Lieutenant Keiser decided to dispatch a tactical team," Rodwell said. "We needed a different set of skills and equipment. We were looking for camouflage people who could last in that environment."

Representatives from other law enforcement bureaus converged on the park. Officers later let the air out of the Dakota's tires, so Stephen couldn't sneak back and take off in it. Macomb County was notified. Sergeant Kozlowski summoned Sergeant Jeffrey Budzynowski and Deputy Mark Berger, who left around 10:00 P.M. in patrol unit 112, headed for Petoskey.

Meanwhile, a local resident reported that earlier he'd seen Stephen leave the truck around 8:30 P.M.—the fugitive even threw the local a friendly wave. When the resident heard about the manhunt on the eleven o'clock news, he called the Emmet County Sheriff's Office.

Just after midnight, a dozen officers from various agencies, as far east as Alpena near Michigan's Lake Huron shore, started their search along the shore of Lake Michigan. They forged on, despite temperatures well below 20 degrees, made even more frigid by the windchill effect from the lake-borne winds.

Like a twisted fairy-tale character, Stephen had left a trail to mark the path of his flight. Officers first came across a watch, then the toy gun, the Jack Daniel's pint flask, a notebook, the candy bar, and a pair of pliers in a grocery bag from the Michigan-based Meijer supercenter chain.

Trackers had difficulty for a while distinguishing the marks of their suspect from trails left by innocent hunters and hikers. But eventually they followed tennis shoe imprints in the snow, prints that described a chaotic, frantic path that eventually veered into the forest. Due to the distance between the shoe marks, officers could tell someone was sprinting through the woods. But their quarry was running in circles, making no progress, senselessly doubling back and forth.

The searchers were trying to exacerbate Stephen's confusion by using the Coast Guard helicopter to flush him out. Emmet County deputy Scott Ford, who had hunted and fished in the area all his life, knew the park intimately and rode in the copter to guide pilots.

The aircraft flew low—about 150 feet from the ground—and its powerful searchlight swept the park. The chopper deliberately darted back and forth at high speeds, hovering over the water, then dashing for another run across the treetops. That was partly to disconcert their quarry and partly for their own safety. Officers still didn't know whether or not the suspected wife-killer was armed with a real gun.

"It would stop on a dime, search, and then get the heck out of there," Rodwell said. "They didn't want to be a low target for this guy. I figure they were pushing Stephen around and around. He was dodging the light. You'd have to be deaf or unconscious not to know the helicopter was there."

Ground searchers started finding footprints, and at 4:10 A.M., they found Stephen's wristwatch lying in the frozen snow. "There is a principle that when you have a hypothermic victim, they start stripping, they throw things off," under the illusion they are really hot, not cold, as their body's thermostat goes out of whack, Rodwell said. "That was one thought. Or maybe he's trying to shed anything a dog could track. Or maybe he's drunk or high." Either way, the officer thought, "he's not going to outrun a helicopter and eleven fit tactical guys."

Later they found the impression of a human body left in a snowdrift, as if Stephen had dropped down to rest.

35

At 6:37 A.M., a cluster of cops spotted Stephen curled up under a pine tree. The wanted man had spent his last few minutes of freedom barefoot, without a jacket, gloves, or hat, lying dazed on the frozen turf. Blood and cuts were visible on his coatless arms. Police radios crackled. "Contact!" an officer shouted. A few minutes later: "One in custody."

Officer Michael Parker, of the Petoskey Public Safety Department, shouted at Grant to put his hands in the air. His fellow officer, Larry Donovan, called out to the others when Stephen started to reach toward a suspicious lump under his clothing. Officer James Pettis, of the Charlevoix Police Department, flipped Grant onto his abdomen, while Donovan cuffed Stephen and told the half-frozen "Mr. Mom" that he was under arrest.

"Once we apprehended him, I almost wondered if he wasn't relieved that he'd been caught," Pettis recalled.

Then the mission shifted from tracking to rescue—"Because he is innocent until proven guilty," Rodwell said.

Stephen was able to identify himself to the arresting officers, but his speech was slurred and he had trouble controlling his limbs. The tree cover was too dense for an airlift so the officers hoisted Stephen to his feet and began walking him toward the shoreline and the rhythmic sound of the waiting Coast Guard helicopter.

While they walked, Officer Parker tried to talk with Stephen, who said he thought he was in Lansing, the state capital, two hundred miles to the south. Grant told Parker he'd ingested Adderall, a stimulant commonly used to treat attention-deficit/hyperactivity disorder (ADHD).

Stumbling along, the officers took turns half-carrying, half-dragging, Stephen through the snow and over obstacles, like fallen trees. Whoever wasn't hauling the frozen fugitive went ahead to tramp a trail through the underbrush, snowbanks, and low tree limbs. Stephen whined that he couldn't go on; the officers exhorted him with commands, "We've got to reach the helicopter" and "You are going to make it!"

Finally, after a more than a quarter-mile grueling trek through the challenging terrain, they reached the beach and the waiting rescue team, including EMT Larry Hansen. Stephen was towed on a sled behind a snowmobile to an open area, where one of the U.S. Coast Guard Air Station's HH65A "Dolphin" helicopters circled above.

Hansen took over, ascertaining that Stephen had no chest pain, then covering him with blankets and heat packs. Hansen first rode the rescue basket into the hovering chopper; then it was lowered to scoop up the prisoner.

Officers strapped Stephen in and handcuffed him to the basket; no words were exchanged due to the loud roar of the rotors overhead. A grainy Coast Guard video captured rescuers peering up from the ground as the winch turned and whisked Stephen skyward en route to emergency treatment.

36

When the helicopter touched down at Harbor Springs Airport, Hansen got Stephen into an ambulance and started an IV. Stephen complimented the paramedic on his skill with the intravenous needle. No one said anything else.

Health care professionals waited at the emergency entrance of Northern Michigan Hospital when the ambulance braked to a halt at 7:26 A.M. The most infamous patient they would treat that year was diagnosed with frostbite, hypothermia, and possible ingestion of narcotics. His internal temperature, measured by a rectal probe, was down to about 87.8 degrees Fahrenheit, ten or eleven crucial degrees below normal.

"It would not be compatible with life for very long," recalled Michael Johnson, M.D., a specialist in vascular surgery, who was summoned to the hospital to check out Stephen's severe frostbite.

Emergency room workers piled the patient with heated blankets, piped warm humidified oxygen into his lungs, and pumped warmed fluid in and out of Stephen's bladder through a catheter, the better to raise the temperature of his internal organs.

They moved Stephen to the intensive care unit (ICU), where Johnson conducted his examination. His patient was strapped to the bed by leather restraints at his wrists and ankles. A cardiac monitor kept tabs on his heart function. By that point, his body temperature had been brought up to near normal and Stephen was speaking lucidly, the doctor later recounted in testimony.

The surgeon checked to make sure the leather cuffs weren't impeding circulation or otherwise exacerbating injury to Stephen's frostbitten skin. While not yet medically sound—low body temperature can lead to delayed problems with kidney function and other issues—Stephen did not appear to be in imminent mortal danger.

Still, just in case, the lifesaving efforts continued. A nurse recalled placing warm towels on Stephen's head and folding them around his hands. A "bear hugger"— a full-body blanket that hovers above the patient's body blowing warm air up to 104 degrees—was draped the length of Stephen's bed. His feet and legs were mottled and red, even cut in some areas.

Stephen didn't ask for pain medication, his nurse noted. She observed that he seemed groggy and teary, with bloodshot eyes. He told her that while on the run, he had taken five of the Vicodin stolen from Kelly, along with sixteen Benadryl tablets.

Stephen became more emotional "in the afternoon as he started becoming more alert and oriented," recalled ICU nurse Michelle Geaudreau during a preliminary examination months later. "I remember we were talking about his children, and he got a little more teary-eyed."

The deputies from Macomb County had called their sheriff with the news of Stephen's capture. Deputy Mark Berger searched the Dodge Dakota, coming up with receipts from the ATM, Meijer, and McDonald's. They also found a piece of paper torn from a notebook, on which Stephen had scrawled a note of apology to his children. A second search, days later, also would turn up a five-pack of Meijer-brand razor blades and an eight-pack of BIC Ultra-Grip disposable shavers.

The deputies logged the evidence, pulled out of the command center, and started the hour-long drive toward the hospital in Petoskey.

Heading straight for the emergency entrance, they found Stephen lying on a treatment bed, surrounded by doctors, nurses, and three Emmet County sheriff's deputies. Once they had visually identified Stephen, they left to call Kozlowski. A helpful hospital staffer found an office where the Macomb County deputies, who had been up for more than twenty-four hours at this point, could use the phone, log onto a computer—and eat breakfast.

Around noon, they checked on a sleeping Stephen, now in the ICU, and relieved the Emmet County personnel from guard duty. At 1:30 P.M., Stephen awakened from his nap, and the Macomb officers introduced themselves.

"He was awake, alert. He seemed cordial—surprisingly cordial, to me," Budzynowski recalled in testimony. Budzynowski checked on Stephen's restraints. They talked about the view from the ICU room of Petoskey's beautiful scenery, watched a little hockey on TV, and discussed the players' salaries. They didn't talk about Tara. "Nothing concerning the whole ordeal," Budzynowski said. "I was satisfied that he was secured and he wasn't going anywhere. He seemed calm. His speech was fine. He was talking in complete sentences."

Stephen asked to watch the news; Budzynowski told him "that it would probably be better not to watch it, because it was a media circus concerning his situation."

Many sleepy Metro Detroiters were jolted awake early on the morning of Sunday, March 4, when they flicked on their TVs and radios to hear anchors excitedly relating "breaking news" alerts. The lead story—*the* story—of the day was unfolding in real time on the morning news shows.

Just after 6:30 A.M., a fugitive Stephen Grant had been found huddled barefoot under a tree in frigid Northern Michigan—practically across the Straits of Mackinac from his dead wife's childhood home, and about thirty-six hours after her headless, limbless torso was found in a Rubbermaid tub in the family garage.

37

The day held at least one more surprise for Metro Detroiters fascinated by the case. That afternoon, David Griem spoke to reporters outside his downtown Detroit office, announcing over the airwaves that he was dropping Stephen Grant as a client. He pledged to help Stephen find a new attorney, but he added that the two had "irreconcilable differences."

"I have to look at myself in the mirror in the morning," Griem said.

Months later, in pretrial testimony, Griem explained that he held the unorthodox curbside press conference because he knew of no other way to inform his on-the-lam client that he was withdrawing from the case.

Access to cameras was no problem; he'd been besieged by members of the media since Saturday morning, he said. The zealous reporters even followed him to his son's hockey game. Finally he seized the moment. He resigned on camera "to let Stephen know that I was no longer representing him and to let anybody who was watching or listening know that I was no longer representing him," Griem recalled. "There had been things that happened between Stephen Grant and myself in the past week that were driving me to this point, and I just feel that I can't give him one hundred ten percent."

* * *

Up in Petoskey, the afternoon wore on. Stephen, still trussed to his hospital bed, continued to make small talk with the deputies from Macomb County. At some point, he had a bite to eat.

Finally Deputy Budzynowski asked Stephen if he'd like to talk with lead detective Brian Kozlowski. Stephen said he'd rather speak to Griem. The deputy, forewarned, said he didn't believe Griem was working for Stephen anymore.

Stephen got "a blank look on his face, almost as if he was thinking about what he was going to say or how he was going to react," Budzynowski said. "Thinking about that issue that he may not have legal representation."

Budzynowski said that Stephen began asking questions, fishing for information. "Do you think I killed her?" he asked the deputies. "This was not premeditated." He also wanted to know if he'd get a "deal" for answering questions.

The officers repeatedly told Stephen not to make such statements to them; the lead detective was the proper person with whom to discuss the case. Budzynowski also cautioned Stephen not to summon Kozlowski on the four-hour drive just "to hear him say he wanted a lawyer."

Eventually, at the prisoner's request, they handed him the room phone and connected him with Kozlowski. "Come up, we'll talk," Stephen invited the detective. Then, before he drifted off to sleep, he thanked his guards for being "so cool."

PART II

38

A few dozen yards east of U.S. Route 2, buffered from the highway's nonstop traffic noise by a stand of towering, wind-bent pines, a vibrant flowering crab apple tree shelters several memorial plaques in the Gardens of Rest cemetery, just north of Escanaba.

Some of the graves, likely, have been there since before the leafy tree was planted, such as those of Joseph and Ellen Martineau, who were born in the late 1800s and died in 1960 and 1963, respectively, according to markers set flush to the ground in the breezy, expansive lawns.

Nearby, members of the Winker, Brazeau, and Derouin families rest almost within view of Lake Michigan's Little Bay de Noc. The dates of birth and death on the cemetery's six thousand or so grave markers mostly suggest lives long and full; many of the surnames echo those still proclaimed from the storefronts and marquees of Escanaba's nearby commercial strip, suggesting a continuity of family and purpose unique to such rural areas where upwardly mobile nineteenth-century immigrants came to seek hard but steady work in mines and lumber camps.

Shaded by an overhanging branch, a new and less weathered plaque marks the grave of a young woman who once showed the promise of matching and exceeding her hardy ancestors in strength, determination, perseverance, and success.

As a youngster, she calmly raised her rifle and felled her share of the deer and other wildlife that swarm Michigan's forests. By the time she was thirty, her passport carried stamps from overseas countries, such as England and Russia—when many of her old classmates still considered a trip to Lansing or Detroit an exotic journey.

A few years later, she was the primary breadwinner for a family of four, earning $168,000 a year—nearly five times the annual household income in her native Delta County—as a jet-setting manager for a global construction firm. She employed nannies from overseas, enrolled her two young children in foreign language courses, and deftly managed her weekly commute between suburban Detroit and a Caribbean job site. The future seemed packed with limitless possibility.

Now, though, she lies in pieces in a domed wooden casket—the daisies strewn atop it at her funeral no doubt withered or rotted or fallen to fragments. The oils from her friends' and family's fingertips imprint the surface of the glossy coffin lid, gestures made in a poignant last-minute attempt to keep her company as she was lowered into the earth.

Aboveground, the sod over the plot is worn to bare dirt in places, by contrast to the well-kept lawns elsewhere at the nearly seventy-year-old cemetery. Former coworkers, community members, the media, and the merely curious have trodden down the grass in order to gaze at the inscription on the rose-wreathed bronze plaque:

> *Loving Mother Daughter Sister*
> *Tara Lynn Grant*
> *nee Destrampe*
> *June 28 1972–Feb 9 2007*

Fake purple zinnias and white daisies fill the marker's small vase. More intimate tributes dangle from the crab apple limb above: a framed photo of Tara's children and their cousins, a hummingbird wind chime, tin horses. A childish pink-painted wooden heart says *I Love You*. The trinkets stir gently in the breeze, but even the ringing of the wind chime barely penetrates the eternal silence of Tara Grant's grave.

39

The baby girl destined for a life of both blazing success and searing tragedy was delivered at 3:57 P.M. on June 28, 1972. She was christened Tara Lynn Destrampe, her heritage an amalgam of several of the well-known dynasties of immigrant stock that dot Michigan's Upper Peninsula.

The infant's twenty-two-year-old father—a Vietnam veteran who had listed his occupation as "student" on his marriage license six months before—was Gerald Marcus Destrampe. A newlywed at age twenty-three, Tara's mother, Mary Destrampe, was a descendant of the Hynes and Champion families.

The couple lived on 6th Avenue South, in the lakeshore community of Escanaba, about two hours west of the Mackinac Bridge, which forms the gateway to the Lower Peninsula and the world beyond. Mary's marriage license listed her occupation as dental assistant, but she soon was to take on the role of motherhood as well.

For their daughter's birth, the young Destrampes chose nearby St. Francis Hospital, a venerable institution run by nuns since 1884. The delivery was attended by Dr. William LeMire III, who signed Tara's birth certificate two days later.

As described by her uncle by marriage, Thomas McLaughlin, Tara was a focal point for the hopes and expectations of the family. She was, he said, the first granddaughter, the first niece, his children's oldest cousin, and, later, a big sister. Many people's dreams for the future were embodied in this tiny infant girl.

Life in the Upper Peninsula shapes a child in ways that other, less assertive regions don't. Unlike the densely populated cities and suburbs downstate, people—fellow "Yoopers," as the denizens of the UP tend to call themselves—are relatively scarce, making lifelong family, neighbor, and school ties all the more precious. The remote peninsula and its fifteen counties make up 29 percent of Michigan's area—but house only 3 percent of its population. Distances are telescoped in these far-flung relationships—a one-hour drive to join friends for dinner or a ten-mile commute to elementary school is commonplace and unremarked. It's not unusual for middle-aged adults to work and socialize with playmates dating back to nursery-school days.

Nature and weather play a greater role, determining schedules, hobbies, and jobs. The beautiful yet rough terrain forges character: Kids grow up tramping through forests so dense that noontime resembles a moonlit midnight. They ski and skate; they sneak into old mines. They learn early how to drive and pilot a snowplow, and party in the dappled sunshine beside lazy rivers.

Water is ever present, in the nearness of the mighty, oceanlike Lake Michigan and Lake Superior, or quieter inland streams, rivers, and ponds. The year-round forecast is mostly "cool" and there is a notable absence of central air-conditioning in public places. Even in midsummer, an open window affords most of the necessary relief. Portable ACs sprout from some bars and offices, but keeping warm is of greater concern in the UP, where snowfall in some areas averages more than two hundred inches a year.

* * *

Mary Destrampe, her young daughter, and husband Gerald—known to most as Dusty—were natives of Delta County, in the UP's south central region. The local Chamber of Commerce touts Delta as the "Banana Belt" because of its temperate climate relative to nearby counties and its modest fifty-inch-a-year snowfall average—not much more than downstate cities, like Lansing and Ann Arbor.

Dusty had received an honorable discharge from the United States Army in March of 1971, after serving two years as an infantryman—including four months and twenty-seven days in Vietnam. During his army stint, Dusty advanced to the rank of specialist, fourth class. He earned his share of honors, including those for good conduct, Vietnam service, and the army commendation medal. As a marksman, he was awarded sharpshooter citations for the M-14 and M-16 rifles, and was rated as "expert" on the M-60 machine gun, which fires hundreds of rounds per minute.

Following his discharge, Dusty was transferred to the army reserves, obligated until 1975, but he was not recalled to service. Instead, according to family recollections, he eventually found work as a wastewater treatment operator at the now-defunct Sawyer Air Force Base in Gwinn, north of Escanaba.

In 1974, not long after Tara's second birthday, Dusty and Mary signed a contract for a homestead on Beaver Lane in Rock, Michigan, about halfway up state road M-35, between Escanaba and Dusty's job at the more northerly air force base.

If one turns away from the lake, northbound M-35 heads from Gladstone—a village of tourist motels, gas stations, and other commerce that flows gently from Escanaba's outskirts—toward Perkins and Rock, these are the tiny settlements that bracketed Tara's consolidated rural high school and formed the hub of her youth and young adulthood.

Driving along the straight two-lane road hemmed closely by fir and hardwood forests, parallel to railroad tracks, which have borne millions of board feet of timber south, it's easy to understand why a grown-up Tara later prized the Stony Creek Metropark near her Lower Peninsula home. A woman reared beneath unbroken blue skies and millions of trees would need the forested outlet to recharge from a routine of airline travel and subdivision home life.

A dozen or so miles north of Gladstone, downtown Perkins is a T-shaped intersection of crumbling asphalt sidewalks beneath a single blinking red traffic light. Lace-curtained twentieth-century trailer homes contrast with weathered, barely standing relics likely one hundred years their senior.

Wooden frame houses sit kitty-corner from the combination gas station-convenience store-post office that forms Perkins's one-stop-shopping commercial district. The village used to support two bars, but the Justin' Time tavern is shuttered and tempts entrepreneurs with an easy-financing offer in one of its curtained windows. Around the corner, the vintage Chum's is still going strong, a few yards down the street from St. Joseph's red-brick parish church.

Chum's, with its green-and-white-checkered linoleum, giant carved mahogany back bar, and Friday fish fry, caters takeout pizza to locals, offers respite to off-the-beaten-track tourists, and is as comfy as a second kitchen table for regulars who show up with custom-crocheted covers for their beer mugs.

40

The Destrampes paid $20,000 for about twenty acres previously owned by brothers Roger and Emmett Norden, members of a well-known dynasty that settled in the area when Beaver, Michigan, was a mainstay community along the Canadian northern lumber line. Now all that's left of the village is the road bearing its name.

"Beaver used to be a town with taverns and whorehouses—the whole works," said Charles "Chuck" Dedic, the fourth generation of his family to live in a rambling farmhouse just across the road from where Tara and Alicia grew up. "Once the depot was taken out, which was probably in the 1930s, everything else went away, too," said the retired schoolteacher, who has occupied his time with a commercial printing business and by documenting the history of the area and its people in books and pamphlets.

The Destrampe farmhouse started out as a Norden family log cabin, Dedic recalled, built by a character named "Little" Axel Carlson. At one time, the property hid an illegal moonshine still, and Dedic's own uncle did a bit of jail time with Little Axel after a local bar fight.

The Destrampes' tenure on the property was more wholesome. Dusty did extensive remodeling to accommodate his expanding family, which in March of 1974 had grown to include baby Alicia Ann.

The land and outbuildings on Beaver Lane, later de-

scribed by Alicia as a "hobby farm," are reached by a series
of twisting two-lane country roads well back from M-35 and
the parallel railroad track that for generations has run
freshly felled trees down to sawmills and paper factories.

Every so often along nearby lanes, the thick woods part
to reveal dwellings cobbled together from trailers and
sheds; cement block garages and modular homes inter-
spersed with well-tended ranch-style houses amid bright
flower beds and severely shaped evergreen shrubs. Many
homes feature a friendly gun dog or two gamboling
about the lawns.

"It's Podunk nowhere," Alicia told the *Detroit News*.
"Tara's roots are country bumpkin. You can't take that
away, no matter what you do."

Safe, isolated, surrounded by deep woods and sunny
wildflower-strewn meadows, just up the hill from a cattail-
ringed pond, the Destrampes' small farm setting seemed
idyllic for a country childhood.

Despite whatever additions Dusty made, the house looks
from outside to be a modest one-and-a-half-story shotgun-
style frame structure, with a narrow front porch and few
windows. The redwood paint on larger sheds and outbuildings contrasts with the house's no-frills white clapboard
siding, two chimneys, and weathered TV antenna. Apple
trees creep close to the graveled driveway, and a grove of
large pines gives some shade to the dooryard out back.

In a memoir typed up for the *Detroit Free Press*, and
later reprinted in Escanaba's small daily, Alicia recalled
growing up on the farm with her parents and big sister.
The girls became active members of the 4-H club, the
century-old "Head, Hearts, Hands, and Health" youth
leadership society sponsored by agricultural extension
services nationwide.

Alicia and Tara enjoyed riding lessons and cared for
Tara's Appaloosa, which bore the eccentric name RJ's

Broken Finger. They raised sheep, cows, chickens, pigs, and rabbits, some to show in the Upper Peninsula state fair at the Escanaba compound, only a five-minute drive from where Tara now lies buried.

An eighteen-year-old Tara eventually took the fair title for Grand Champion Market Hog. A photo shows her proudly posing with one hand on the plump pig, the other clutching an ornate trophy. She's an attractive, poised teenager with a winning grin and abundant curly brown hair.

Group activities also included hikes, backpacking trips, and—as part of her legacy from sharpshooter Dusty—marksmanship. Even as a preteen, Tara was at home with hunting guns, acquaintances say, and Alicia wrote that Tara once was part of a four-girl team that took home the state BB-gun championship.

From an early age, the girls were encouraged to bag game, especially at the family's traditional Christmas Eve rabbit hunt. Neighbors show off photos of the teenage Alicia with the six-point and eight-point bucks she shot. They remembered a youthful Tara's command of a .243 rifle during deer-hunting season.

Tara was the talkative one, Alicia recalled—so much so that teachers resorted to bribes and ruses, like the promise of a stick of gum, to keep her quiet during class time.

The girls were in and out of the nearby Dedic home frequently, Chuck Dedic said. His late wife, Annette, was a popular 4-H leader, and "Alicia was her right-hand man. The girls were very enjoyable."

Tara, he said, was a cute young woman who tended to speak her mind—"mouthy," he called it, but a little cooler and more distant than Alicia. "She wasn't as involved in 4-H as Alicia. She was more into the shooting sports—she killed a lot of deer.

"Tara was very up-front. She walked straight and confident. She was the kind of person who would make it."

41

Another family hobby was tapping the abundant nearby maple trees and boiling the sap down into succulent sugar. At first, the Destrampes tried the craft on the trees that ringed their farmhouse property. Eventually, in October of 1983, Dusty and Mary bought more forested acreage, just a few minutes' walk down the road. The sellers were again from a branch of the Norden clan, and they collected a flat $10,000 for the forty-four-and-a-half-acre plot.

The springtime syrup ritual grew greater in scope as the little compound known interchangeably as Dusty's Sugar Bush or Dusty's Sugar Shack swelled into three substantial redwood-painted buildings and an outhouse.

Experts say the "bush" refers to the stand of trees from which the sap is harvested; the shacks are the small structures used for boiling down the sap into the syrups and sugars that form the base of candy and other treats. The Canadian and New England tradition of "sugar shanties" and "sugar shacks" migrated into the UP generations ago, and now some are family-run commercial ventures selling products through Web sites and stores.

For fun or for profit, tapping maple trees is a labor-intensive project of the type that binds UP families. The tradition also typifies the outdoors-oriented, active recreation to which Yoopers gravitate with glee, even as their downstate counterparts cringe at the prospect of snowblowing a suburban driveway or dashing from heated cars to snug movie theaters and malls.

In a home video shared with Detroit's WDIV-TV station, and later posted on the independent Web site taralynngrant.com, a trim, T-shirted Tara smiles and waves a rubber-gloved hand at the camera as she scrubs the plastic tubs used to collect the sap. A man who looks like Stephen fills a long-necked bottle with a syrupy substance from a tap. "I got your butt," jokes someone off camera.

Then Tara narrates a brief tour of the snow-covered complex, noting expansions that the family had built over the years. Inside the pine-paneled structures, her smile seemingly audible in her nasal twang, she said: "My mom thought she'd be nice and put some decorations in there. Nice-smelling candles so it don't smell so bad."

The Destrampe family still owns Dusty's compound. Green gingham curtains ensure privacy at windows of the shanties. Rusting farm implements are fast becoming engulfed by thousands of seedling maples, and the five-gallon plastic buckets used to process sap dot the otherwise pristine forest. A faint unpleasant odor from the outhouse competes with the humid mossy smell of the woods.

Thistle, Queen Anne's Lace, black-eyed Susans and wild raspberries are slowly taking over the winding gravel drive that leads from Beaver Lane into the sugar shack complex. At the entrance, an engraved wooden sign reading simply *Dusty* is nailed over by a random board. At the foot of the same tree, a larger carved sign has fallen and is buried amid weeds. A shin-high iron chain warns passersby to keep out.

Two decades or more ago, the Destrampe girls would scamper along the trail after school, calling out to one another to announce the day's sap collection, Alicia recalled. She said it was a bonding experience for the girls, who seemed inseparable as they frolicked through an exemplary childhood of pets, wholesome activities, healthy outdoor exercise, and a loving family life.

42

Some recollections, though, hint at tension in Tara's childhood home. Neighbor Dedic figured he knew the Destrampes about as well as anyone in those parts—what with the girls joining his wife on 4-H outings and his frequent evenings with Dusty.

"We were rabid cribbage players," recalled Dedic, a white-bearded man whose cluttered farmhouse kitchen features a woodstove, early photographs of long-dead ancestors, stacks of research materials, and big glass jars of staples, like pasta and beans. "We were always playing."

Still, he said, these Destrampes were not part of the old guard of the Perkins community. "They were considered newcomers to the neighborhood," he recalled, even after a decade or more. "Most of their friends and connections were in Escanaba. 4-H and neighbors were their major contact."

Dusty, too, could be difficult, Dedic hinted delicately. The pressures of being the breadwinner for a young family, right after a stint in the Vietnam War, sometimes boiled over. "He had some real bad experiences, and sometimes that came out," Dedic said. "And he got a little bit difficult about things."

* * *

Tara may have been reflecting on similar problems when in adulthood she wrote a never-delivered letter to her parents as part of a leadership seminar workshop. The conference, held by LandmarkEducation, a global for-profit organizer of self-help curricula, encourages participants to improve their confidence, productivity, and relationships in part by confronting past problems and choices.

Tara attended the four-day $500 Landmark Forum introductory workshop in Phoenix, just about ninety days before she was killed. In a notebook filled with jottings ranging from travel itineraries to business goals, Tara wrote a frank letter addressed "Dear Mom and Dad," apparently as part of a workshop exercise. She spoke candidly of her love for her parents, but she also said she had been "inauthentic" with both, that term being a buzzword of the Landmark Forum.

She wrote to her father that she had not forgiven him for *how you treated mom throughout my entire childhood,* and said that she had, to a large extent, suppressed memories of strife and verbal abuse. She took her mother to task for *being passive and not standing up for yourself,* and wrote of her resentment of those family dynamics.

In the spirit of the conference, however, Tara went on to absolve her parents of their past conduct, and reiterated that she would stop making them "wrong," but rather would move on in hopes of a more honest and fulfilling relationship in the future. The letter, which was never torn from the spiral notebook, was signed "Your Daughter," with something scribbled out after those words.

While there are indications that the Destrampes weren't as harmonious a family as they were portrayed after Tara's death, the prevailing view to this day among neighbors and townsfolk is that Tara was a poised and confident "Daddy's girl," who pleased her father with her courage and marksmanship.

43

A notion crossed the minds of some of Tara's classmates, including Al LaCosse, a logger who attended school with Tara, and whose mom used to babysit the Destrampe girls when they were younger. "If Dustly hadn't been sick, he would've killed him," said LaCosse, tipping a few mugs of Budweiser at Herb's Bar in Rock, near the Mid-Peninsula K–12 school that most of the kids in the area attended.

Established in 1933, Herb's, which touts itself as the second-oldest family-run bar in the United States, is a time capsule of a joint, from the white-sided exterior and tiled linoleum floor to the vintage beer signs, chrome bar stools, and elaborate backlighted Art Deco center-piece, behind the barmaid, between mirrored shelves of liquor bottles. It has that comforting "old bar" smell missing from modern chain taverns, but in a nod to the twenty-first century, a large-screen TV blasts ESPN.

Regulars, many of whom casually enter through the kitchen instead of the front screen door, agreed that Tara—possibly the brightest star in her 1990 graduating class of forty-four pupils—seemed an unlikely murder victim. Classmates told the *Detroit Free Press* that she used to sign notes with nicknames like "Felix" and "Terrible." The paper reported that in her yearbook she declared her aim: *Make enough money to buy everything I want. Live in a big house with a Jaguar parked in the garage and some day get married and have a small family.*

Others remember Tara as a straight-A student, band member, and an enthusiastic cheerleader rooting on the Mid-Peninsula school's Wolverines in pleated red-and-white uniforms and 1980s "big hair." She played basketball and ran track.

"She was probably among the ten percent of the class who didn't party all the time." LaCosse grinned. "She was really smart. She went after everything. A go-getter."

According to Alicia's essay, a stint working at a local shoe store sparked Tara's love of business and particularly marketing. *With her knack for sales, she could likely sell you the shoes you were wearing,* Alicia wrote.

Still, university would have to wait. On their parents' advice, Alicia wrote, Tara completed a two-year associate's degree in business at the local Bay de Noc Community College.

Always industrious, Tara babysat for the young sons of Michaell Pepin, who moved to a house just across Beaver Lane in 1990. "She was real responsible for her age," Pepin recalled. "They were both good kids. They weren't obnoxious like some teenage girls can get."

Eventually, in 1992, Tara packed up and headed to her dream school several hundred miles south, to Michigan State University in East Lansing. She was familiar with the campus from attending 4-H camp there, family members said.

The university, established in 1855, is a city in itself, with about forty-five thousand undergraduate and postgraduate students, and more than ten thousand faculty and staff. That's about ten thousand more people than the entire population of the UP's Delta County—and doesn't even include the residents of East Lansing or the adjacent state capital of Lansing, with its 120,000 or so inhabitants, many of them government workers.

Some reports hint that Tara partied a little too much her first semester, and had to hustle to make up for it later. Alicia said that her older sibling was generous in inviting her down for the "full college experience," from football games and sitting in on classes to just hanging out in the dorm.

But again, Tara's own musings at the Landmark Forum hinted at a less-than-ideal sisterly relationship. She wrote about her feelings of competition with Alicia, of feeling that she could never be as outstanding in their parents' eyes as her younger sister. *I have always been striving for the attention/recognition I thought my sister was always getting,* Tara wrote.

Tara also admitted in her journal that she deliberately chose to go as far away to university as possible while still staying inside Michigan. While a few other schools were more distant than Michigan State from Perkins, her choice definitely took her light years away in terms of culture, sophistication, and intellectual challenge. *I think I was making a statement to my parents that I feel on my own, so I am going to go on my own,* she wrote.

She went further about her feelings of inadequacy in a separate letter to Alicia, one that, again, apparently stayed undelivered in the spiral ledger confiscated from her SUV by detectives.

Tara wrote that she had always given the illusion the two were close, but now admitted that was not accurate. She wrote of her deep resentment toward her sister, and acute feelings of competition going back for as long as she could remember. She said she had not fully allowed Alicia to be a part of her life, for fear of being similarly judged in return. The letter closed with a plea for a more open and "sharing" relationship, and was signed "Love, Your Big Sis."

44

While juggling art and business classes at Michigan State, Tara was introduced to Stephen Grant, a southeast Michigan native and college dropout who worked as an aide to then-state senator Jack Faxon, a Democrat from the affluent Detroit suburb of Farmington Hills.

Stephen didn't exactly sweep the confident Tara off her feet, but she was impressed by his political connections and seeming savoir faire, family members recalled. "It was the excitement of him knowing the area (Lansing)," her mom told the *Detroit News*. "He wined and dined her."

It's not clear what other romances Tara may have had before Stephen. In a Landmark forum exercise, she referred to having her "heart broke" by someone named Pete. It seemed she focused mostly on studies, with an eye to earning her Michigan State business degree. At any rate, she was in no hurry to get involved.

During an interview with the *Detroit News*, when Stephen described his courtship of Tara, he portrayed himself as a daring and chivalrous suitor. He said he was introduced to Tara at a party through a mutual friend. After chatting for a few minutes, they discovered they were neighbors in the Cedar Village Apartments, a sprawling complex a few blocks from the Michigan State campus, known for its wild parties. "We hung out, drinking, listening to my friend play guitar," he recalled. "The relationship was a slow evolution."

Their friendship was platonic for some months, he said, though not for lack of trying on his part. "I asked her out, and she turned me down," he said. "She said she kind of had a boyfriend from up north where she was from. I said, 'That's like kind of being pregnant—either he's your boyfriend or not.' But I respected that, and we were just friends at first."

Stephen tried to please Tara by showing her his world. He drove her the eighty miles south from East Lansing and introduced the art maven to Detroit's world-class art institute and museum. He sought to dispel her negative impressions of the "Motor City" with tours of ritzy suburbs, like Birmingham and Bloomfield Hills, where auto industry moguls dwelled in multimillion-dollar mansions; then he took her for a $2 hot dog at the city's famous Lafayette Coney Island. "That trip really opened her eyes," Stephen said. She opened up a little, divulging that she and her UP boyfriend were growing distant. "She told me she was planning on breaking up."

When Tara's grandmother Mary Jane Destrampe died in August of that year, Tara flew back north for the funeral in Escanaba. Before the service began, Tara's family received an unexpected visitor: Stephen Grant. "I felt the right thing to do was to come up and pay my respects to her grandmother," Stephen said. "So I drove up. It took all day. I called her and told her I was right there, and she said, 'What?' She was really surprised."

When they eventually met up, Tara had her boyfriend in tow. "The boyfriend figured she was home, and that she was his girlfriend again," Stephen said. "It was awkward. But it wasn't terrible."

Family members were taken aback that this stranger had driven five or six hours to Escanaba's Crawford funeral home for the services of a woman he'd never known, but Stephen said Dusty seemed pleased. "I apologized to Tara's dad," Stephen recounted. "I said, 'If I disrupted anything, I didn't mean to. I just had to come up to support your daughter.' He looked me in the eye and said, 'Son, you have to do what your heart tells you to do.'"

Stephen claimed Dusty invited him to join the family for dinner, and even to spend the night, but Stephen felt out of place and headed back downstate.

"The next day, Tara called me and told me she was in love with me."

45

According to Stephen, his impetuous trip to the funeral home had won Dusty's blessing, and opened both his own and Tara's hearts to their budding romantic bond. "[Dusty] thought it was chivalrous for a man to come up there for the woman he loved. That was the point where I realized I was in love with her," Stephen recalled. "So we started going out."

The couple dated for a few months before Tara moved into Stephen's apartment in small-town Okemos, a rural bedroom community for Lansing and East Lansing. But job hunt pressures soon forced them downstate to Auburn Hills, a suburb in Stephen's native southeast Michigan. "I couldn't find another political job," Stephen said. "That was right after 1994, the year the Democrats lost their shirts, and there were a lot of out-of-work Democrats."

Stephen worked for his dad, William "Al" Grant, at the elder Grant's tool and die shop in Mount Clemens. Working as a part-time helper making automotive bearings would be Stephen's on-again, off-again career throughout his adult life—though as usual, he often would tell much grander tales to acquaintances and friends. Lying and exaggerating were habits he had developed quite early in life.

46

Stephen Christopher Grant was born January 18, 1970, the second child and first son of Al Grant and his wife, the former Susan Payne. The young family lived in the eastern Detroit suburb of Sterling Heights. Sue was twenty-three and already a mom to three-year-old Kelly Kathleen Grant. Al Grant was twenty-eight.

Stephen had described his childhood home life as marred by the bickering between his parents. He told the *Detroit News* that his parents argued frequently and loudly as he was growing up, and that he was hurt by Al and Sue's eventual split.

Court documents show that the older Grants lived together from their marriage in January 1966 until September 1984, when Sue Grant filed for divorce. In spare legalese, the four-page filing stated that *the objects of matrimony have been destroyed and there remains no likelihood that the marriage can be preserved.*

The lawsuit also noted that Sue Grant, mother of fourteen-year-old Stephen and seventeen-year-old Kelly, *does love, cherish and wish to care for said children.*

Seven months later, in April 1985, Macomb County Circuit Court judge Raymond Cashen granted the divorce. The Grants were awarded joint custody of the kids, with Sue getting physical custody and the dependent tax exemption for Kelly and Stephen. Al was awarded "reasonable visitation" and ordered to pay health care costs and $51.50 a week cash per child, until each turned eighteen or graduated from high school.

Sue retained the right to live in the family's Riverland Drive house in Sterling Heights, though the couple was ordered to share any proceeds after a sale, as well as any repair costs of more than $100. She also got the 1984 Fiero convertible and ten shares of Detroit Edison utility stock. Al retained all ownership in his business—then called U.S. Grant Manufacturing Inc.—and a 1985 Chrysler.

Despite the custody order, Kelly chose to live with her dad after the divorce, while Stephen stayed with his mother on Riverland Drive. Sue remarried several times (and now lives in Arizona). She did not attend any of Stephen's legal proceedings, although she sent him some books while he was in the Macomb County Jail.

In the last interview before his capture, Stephen demonstrated his tendency to dramatize or change history in his recounting of his life story. He repeatedly claimed he was twelve when his parents divorced, though public documents indicated he was older. He described his father as an "engineer" and said his mother "did housework."

Stephen also portrayed himself as having been in the thick of a *Leave It to Beaver*–type loyal gang of buddies who developed lifelong ties. "There was a group in the neighborhood who all hung out. We're still friends, although we ended up all over the place."

But others recall Stephen as a rather lonely oddball who frequently failed in his frenetic efforts to impress. "He lived with his mom, but he never talked about her," recalled Paul Buss, who met Stephen as a freshman at Henry Ford II High School, and stated he was one of Stephen's closer friends. "He never talked about the divorce, or his father. I never met his dad . . . never saw his mom, even when I was at his house. I met her once, but it was kind of in passing. I don't remember his mom being home ever."

Paul said that Stephen was a high-strung, B-average student—smart, but not really trying hard. He didn't mix much or take part in extracurricular activities, a fact school records confirm. Stephen's manly interests in cars and weapons were at odds with his somewhat sissy appearance and demeanor, according to Buss.

"When we were in high school, he liked to shoot guns. There were some woods near his house and he'd go back there and shoot. He had some kind of machine gun, the kind where you'd pull the trigger and a bunch of shots would fire—an automatic," Buss recalled. "He'd always say, 'I went out and shot my gun last night.' But other than that, I never saw any kind of violent behavior.

"I never saw him get into a fight. To be honest, he seemed almost effeminate. It was the way he talked, and his overall mannerisms. He walks on his tiptoes. There was just something about him that seemed really effeminate to me. He'd talk really fast, and he'd get to sounding like a girl."

Buss said he never saw Stephen do drugs, date, make raunchy macho talk about girls, or really exert himself to do much of anything in high school—though you wouldn't know that to hear Stephen talk. "He did exaggerate a lot. It would be like fish stories. 'I caught one this big,' when you knew he'd only caught one five inches long," Buss said.

Like many people powerless to escape from an environment of strife, Stephen apparently coped by developing a powerful ability to reshape reality. Repeatedly, friends and acquaintances from childhood onward echo Buss in describing a penchant for twisting the truth, concocting schemes, or aggrandizing minor accomplishments.

Barbara Haney met Stephen when the two were working at a Chi-Chi's chain Mexican restaurant in Troy during their high-school years. Barbara was a student at nearby Waterford Mott; Stephen was a year ahead of her at his own high school in Sterling Heights. He invited her to his homecoming dance and she accepted. Since they attended different high schools, Stephen apparently thought he could impress his date with overblown tales of achievement.

"He has a vivid imagination," Haney recalled. "He tends to lie. He lives in a fantasy world. He told me a lot of things about himself when we went out that weren't true." For example, she said, Stephen claimed to be a basketball star.

"Well, my dad was the counselor at his school," Haney said. She told her father that she was dating a top athlete from Henry Ford II. "And he said Stephen wasn't even on the team, let alone being a star. After that one date, one of the guys we worked with asked why I don't want to date [Stephen]. I remember thinking, 'He lies. I can't trust him.'"

To get out of the awkward conversation, she simply told her coworker, "He's too skinny."

47

The courtship of Tara and Stephen continued, and the couple soon moved in together. Though their relationship blossomed, their careers weren't exactly taking off. Despite her newly minted business degree, Tara eventually took a job as a temporary through Kelly Services, the giant global staffing service based in nearby Troy, Michigan. Stephen continued to work for his dad.

Tara eventually landed another Kelly assignment, this time to a local office of Morrison-Knudsen, the onetime construction powerhouse that built landmarks ranging from the Hoover Dam to the Trans-Alaska pipeline. That company was in its death throes in the mid-1990s, however, and eventually was acquired by Washington Group International. It was there that Tara would spend the next decade in a determined and steady upward march.

In September 1995, Stephen engineered a romantic marriage proposal on a bench outside the imposing façade of the Detroit Institute of Arts, the museum which had so impressed Tara on one of their first dates. A year later, their nuptials took place on September 28, 1996, in a quaint country church near her childhood home.

The couple bought a house on Cardinal Street in Shelby Township, a fast-growing exurb, well north of Detroit. Stephen continued to work for his dad; Tara's responsibilities at Washington Group grew. Healthy, intelligent, seemingly in love, the Grants hadn't hit thirty yet, but they showed every prospect of enjoying the proverbial good life.

Paul Buss was surprised when Stephen renewed contact after a hiatus of several years. "We lost track of each other after I went into the service. Then one day, he just called me out of the blue, and we started hanging out again," Buss recalled. "This was after he got married to Tara. My wife, Becky, and I started hanging out as a couple. Becky went to Lindsey's baby shower. She used to say, 'God, they're such a perfect couple.' He and Tara really did seem like the perfect couple. They seemed happy together. I never saw them argue or anything."

Stephen was trying to become more cultured, developing sophisticated tastes in wine and food. "Stephen was a really good cook. I mean, a really good cook. He could make anything, and it was always really good. It was amazing. He made his own salad dressings. He'd just make stuff up as he went along."

And while Stephen seemed to be the more demanding spouse—perhaps to make up for his growing status as house husband to the rising executive Tara—neither Grant seemed to mind, Buss said. "He was always in control. He's the type who always wanted to be center stage," Buss said. "If he was there, you knew he was there. He was always the one who wanted the attention drawn toward him.

"Tara was really nice. She was just a great person. They seemed happy, but with Stephen, it was his way or no way. We'd get together and he'd already have everything planned out, and that's pretty much what we were going to do. He would say, 'Meet us for dinner. We'll eat dinner at this place, and then we'll go to this hockey game.' Tara never argued about it.

"She seemed like she really had things together. They say opposites attract—maybe that's why they got together.

He wasn't dumb, but he was reckless. If he wanted to do something, he'd do it without thinking. Maybe that's what attracted her to him. He never gave the impression he was jealous of Tara's success. In fact, he gloated about it. It didn't seem like it bothered him."

Not everyone had the same glowing impression of the Grant marriage. Alicia's husband, Erik, sized up Stephen as a bombastic control freak who ruined get-togethers and kept family members at a distance.

Alicia and Erik were married June 12, 1997, with Tara witnessing the marriage as her sister's bridesmaid. Erik, an engineer with expertise in the pulp and paper industries, is a self-contained man whose stoic demeanor contrasted sharply with the scathing commentary he eventually delivered on Stephen and the Grants' marriage.

"During family gatherings, Tara and I often discussed our professional lives, and I looked forward to those conversations," Erik said. "I could relate with Tara on this level at times much better than my own wife, and especially her husband, Stephen, who has almost never held what is generally accepted as a 'real job.'"

Regarding Stephen, he said, "I will tell you that I *never* liked or trusted this monster. I cannot begin to express how many times my family and I were betrayed or belittled by this man. Stephen Grant was the relative that everyone tolerated, only because he was married to Tara.

"The majority of any family functions in the thirteen years I have known Stephen have been extremely difficult due to his controlling presence. There were so many times during those years that Tara would ask us to do something together, such as go in for gifts, take family vacations, or come and visit when often we decided that we just could not, solely because of Stephen.

"Even on the day of her death, Tara was reaching out to our family to consider a vacation rental with them."

He and Alicia decided to nix the vacation, Erik said, "due to our extreme dislike and distrust of Stephen."

Tara maintained her loyalty, even in Stephen's most gauche moments, Erik said, implying that her need to cover Stephen's faults strained other family relationships. "Deep down, I know Tara was embarrassed of him . . . but she was too proud to say anything negative about Stephen aloud. I witnessed her come to Stephen's aid on more than one occasion—yet she would not allow others to help with her innermost struggles about how to remove herself and her children from the grip of Stephen Grant."

Alicia, too, recalled that Stephen caused stress at holidays and other family events. Alicia stated that she was "appalled by his worldly ways" from their first meeting, but that Tara seemed "captivated" by him. Stephen, Alicia said, reveled in causing controversy or making others feel discomfort.

There was even a huge family blowup in November 2006, at what would be Tara's last Thanksgiving meal, which Alicia and Erik were hosting. Alicia and Erik said they were afraid to pressure Tara to confront what they perceived as a dysfunctional situation, for fear of being shut out of her life.

Like many family members of murdered women, Alicia and Erik didn't consciously think of Tara as a victim while she was alive. But like the survivors of murdered women ranging from Nicole Brown Simpson to Laci Peterson—they felt that she was, indeed, on the receiving end of verbal, if not physical, abuse from Stephen. Now, Alicia said, she has realized that Tara and the children were victims of domestic violence throughout the Grants' marriage.

At one point, Alicia recounted, Stephen did something that created a chasm between the once-close siblings, although she declined to say what exactly happened. "[It] absolutely drove a wedge, and I can pinpoint that in the month and the year and the date when it happened," Alicia said. "She didn't talk about her personal life [after that]. From that moment forward, our conversations stemmed around her job, her kids.

"Never once did she delve into the personal aspects of her and Steve's relationship, and, you know, myself [and Erik] had a very hard decision to not push her, because we did not want her to be shut down completely, pushing further, but as everybody says, hindsight is twenty-twenty, and it's something I have to come to grips with."

48

In November 2000, Tara gave birth to daughter Lindsey. The little girl turned out to be a curly-headed miniature of her proud mom, and Tara's high energy and strong work ethic helped her learn to balance the demands of motherhood and career.

Stephen, not working full-time, was available to pitch in. For a time, everything seemed to be working out. Then, in early 2002, the Grants learned they were expecting another baby. In an interview after Tara's death, Stephen claimed the pregnancy was unintended.

"Tara had gotten what she thought was a [birth control] shot, but they gave her a flu shot instead," he claimed. "It was a surprise. At first, it was tough, because we weren't ready for that mentally—we thought it was going to be just one kid. But then he was born, and he was as perfect as his sister was."

Baby Ian was born in November, and while he was welcomed as a beloved addition, the extra work of watching both an infant and toddler proved too much for Stephen. By then, the couple had moved from Shelby Township to the more upscale Westridge Drive house. And Tara's job was starting to require more frequent travel.

Friends and family maintain that Stephen demanded household help, and the couple opted to hire live-in au pairs rather than use off-site day care or other options.

Stephen always helped to choose the au pairs, insisting on attractive ones, Alicia recalled. The foreign workers had exotic names like Samonique, Yana, and Londy. Tara, who had high expectations for her children, was more interested in the cultural opportunities presented by hiring foreign nannies.

One former neighbor, Dave Scheuer, lived across Westridge from the Grants, and felt that Tara was a demanding, if loving, mother. "Tara was constantly pushing her kids. That was her personality," Scheuer said. "She was really driven herself. She'd demand that Stephen take the kids to certain events, like ballet, when she was gone. Several times, she complained to my wife about how elementary schools don't offer Spanish. She had the kids tutored at an early age. One of the au pairs was Spanish, and she was teaching them while she was there. Then they had a tutor come into the home. Lindsey was pretty grown-up—that was because of all the tutoring."

As the children grew, Tara relished planning activities and parties for them, taking advantage of her kids' dual November birthdays to plan his-and-her celebrations, like the cowboy/cowgirl theme that Alicia recalled in her memorial essay.

The kids were the love of Tara's life, and most of her family and friends have said that she went to extreme lengths to make up for her work-related absence through phone calls, notes, and quality time when she was at home.

Tara—the hardworking, driven, energetic worker-mom-sister-wife—also seemed aware at some level that she had become a strict taskmaster to her beloved offspring. In her musing at the Landmark Forum, she wrote a list of personal goals, including *to realize that I have two beautiful, smart, loving children . . . that are ONLY CHILDREN*. Stop being critical, she admonished herself in the notebook. Twice she wrote, *Stop worrying about looking good.*

But on another page of the notebook, Tara struck a more upbeat tone, charting a list of potential Christmas gifts under the heading "Holiday Ideas." She planned to get an ornament for Alicia and Erik, a talking Elmo for her nephew Alex, and a VHS/DVD player for her mom and dad. For herself, she wished a video camera for her laptop and golf lessons.

The lists for her children were the longest and reflected Tara's motherly mix of indulgence and practicality: a scooter, dance lessons, and the *Cinderella* movie for Lindsey; and for Ian, another movie, hockey lessons, and a Hot Wheels track.

For her husband, she planned the grandest gift of all: a trip to California's Napa Valley, the upscale wine region known for its lavish vineyards and luxurious hotels. The never-realized trip was to have been a combination birthday and Christmas present, her note indicated.

It appeared that Tara, whatever her misgivings, was willing to try to make her marriage to Stephen a success. As with the letters to her parents and sister that were part of the seminar homework, she wrote another—the longest and most heartfelt—to her husband.

Tara apologized to Stephen for "invalidating" him, dominating him, *always needing to make you wrong* and *not really loving you at all*. She wrote of having her heart broken by someone named Pete, and that she needed to *get complete with Pete* so that she would no longer push away Stephen, whom she describes as *the one person who has fully committed to me to love me unconditionally*.

Later in the letter, Tara again promised to stop *making you wrong* and asked to renew their wedding vows so that she could *have a clear mind and an open heart to fully love you for the incredible human being that you are*.

As far as is known, this letter went unread until homicide detectives found the notebook after Tara was reported missing.

49

The last few years of the Grants' marriage were strained by any measure—two young children kept busy with lessons and play, Tara's nonstop travel, pressures to keep up with the Joneses, a succession of foreign nannies occupying the bedroom down the hall.

Then there were the special pressures of the Grants' relationship. Stephen didn't seem entirely comfortable with his status as a part-time machinist earning $18,900 in 2006—less than his wife's $28,000 bonus, let alone Tara's six-figure salary. He made a few stabs at doing more with his life. He registered two business names—Precision Centerless Products and Grant Bearing Specialists—but neither project ever got off the ground.

Stephen's eccentricities had strained relationships with Tara's family members and now he was working on the neighbors—borrowing tools one minute, but the next getting peeved about little things, like how the people next door mowed their lawn.

"He did have a temper, and he'd hold a grudge," said Dave Scheuer, who also witnessed a few arguments between the Grants. "I remember one argument they had outside on their lawn. They were going on vacation. He was in the car with the kids, ready to go, and she was inside. They started arguing because she wasn't ready to go. He didn't back down to her, and she didn't back down, either. She was pretty strong-willed."

Still, Scheuer didn't see any major tragedies brewing, even if the Grants were a bit standoffish. "I'd say he was [a] pretty good dad. They kind of kept to themselves. Their kids weren't out playing with the other kids in the neighborhood, which was kind of odd," Scheuer said. "They kind of looked down on other people, like they were better than everyone else.

"Our kids and their kids never played until they went to school together. It was just push, push, push, as far as the training goes. They were an example of those parents who pushed their kids hard. She insisted Stephen do the same thing when she was gone."

Everyone agrees that Stephen was getting increasingly riled by Tara's frequent travel, especially since she'd taken the Puerto Rico assignment the previous year. He complained to neighbors, to strangers, to anyone in his limited circle of adult contact who was willing to listen.

Stephen was a regular at the Buffalo Wild Wings bar and restaurant about a mile down the road from his dad's machine shop. Dawn Stanek met Stephen on her first day of work there: August 25, 2003. He came in a few times a week, she said—always for boneless wings with a side of blue cheese, he was "addicted" to them— and emerged as a sort of Jekyll and Hyde character.

The decent Stephen would sip an Oberon Ale, speaking lovingly of his kids and regaling servers with cute anecdotes. He'd pick up the tab—anonymously—for tables of military members nearby, and leave generous tips for the staff.

The fun-loving Stephen would beat everyone at the bar on the electronic trivia game, while boasting of trail riding at Stony Creek on his $2,500 mountain bike, and rooting for his alma mater, Michigan State, by decorating his entire house in the Spartans' green and white. (After Tara's death, the Standerfers found a bag of supplies from Kinko's, and realized that Stephen had faked an MSU diploma by cutting and pasting and photocopying parts of real ones. He never graduated from any college.)

The self-pitying Stephen would complain about his dad, saying they never saw eye to eye. He'd rail against Tara's relatives, saying how much he hated having to attend family gatherings.

But sometimes the weird Stephen would emerge, and things would get creepy. He told the women he wasn't really a tool and die worker, but a covert operative for Tara's employer, Washington Group. He couldn't divulge his exact title or duties, however.

"He said he worked for Tara. He said she was his boss," Stanek recalled. "He said, 'I work under Tara'—that's how he'd put it. 'Under Tara.' But he would never tell me what he did. He said it was top secret. He said he'd have to kill me if he told me."

Stephen would imply, with a straight face, that he, too, was traveling the globe on dangerous and important work. "He'd say, 'I'm going undercover on this big mission out of the United States for the Washington Group.' He said he had bodyguards. He acted all mysterious, and said he couldn't tell me where he was going," Stanek said. "I'd say, 'Bullshit,' but he'd tell me he was dead serious. He always tried to leave the impression that he was with the CIA or something that involved top secret security."

They didn't believe him, though Stanek was concerned enough to run out from behind the bar and hug him once when he'd reappeared after a four-month absence. For the most part, the staff all liked him and tolerated his eccentricities—though for some, his salacious conversations about his nannies, and his angry screaming at them by phone, were more than a bit off-putting.

"The au pairs he had were beautiful," Stanek said. "He

used to say he'd pick them out personally. He had one au pair who got involved with a young man, and so he said he sent her back. That was exactly how he'd say it— 'I sent her back.'"

Fellow patrons would tease Stephen—"You and your au pairs," they'd say—but he persisted in telling tales that implied the girls were wild with desire for their "Mr. Mom" employer. One night, Stephen said, he was in his backyard and the light in an upstairs bedroom came on. He said the au pair started undressing; he said she was doing it for him. And he said she would wear skimpy outfits to try to entice him.

The vindictive Stephen didn't try to hide his petty tirades against the young women who were thousands of miles from home, working in an unfamiliar household, while he sat at the bar sipping his beer.

"He'd get really mad at the au pairs," Stanek said. "I'd hear him screaming at them over the phone when he was in the bar. One time one of the au pairs broke the dishwasher, and he was yelling at her. Then he told me, 'None of these girls are any good.'"

Another time, she said, one of the Grant kids was sick and Stephen was exasperatedly trying to describe how much medicine to give the child. "He started yelling at her, saying, 'You're so stupid.' After something like that would happen, he'd send them back," she said.

Then Verena entered the picture and Stephen started showing his cell phone pictures of her around the bar, saying, "Look how beautiful she is."

"He talked about her all the time," recalled Stanek. "But about three or four weeks before the murder— that's when he really started talking about her."

50

The staff at Buffalo Wild Wings liked Stephen, for the most part, though they thought he was kind of flirty for a married man. He'd rib them about their lack of interest in current events, asking, "Don't you know what's going on in the world? Don't you pay attention?"

He'd tell two female waitresses that he could picture them "together" and boast about his own sexual conquests. Sometimes his conversations had an eerie echo of Scott Peterson's, the California man eventually convicted of killing his spouse, Laci, after telling a new paramour that his wife had recently died.

One time, Stephen told Stanek, he tried to pick up a girl at a Michigan State game, and he told her that his wife was dead. "I asked how he could do something like that, and he said, 'I'm going to Hell anyway,'" the barmaid recalled. "He used to always say that. He would say he was an atheist, and he didn't believe in anything. When you'd ask why he did something like cheat on his wife, he'd say, 'I'm going to Hell anyway. I'm an atheist. I don't believe in God.' He always said he was going to Hell."

Stephen said he didn't like it when Tara accompanied him to MSU games—that he didn't have any fun with her there. Once, he boasted, he went alone and had a casual tryst after the game.

"He said something about having to walk to the motel for several miles, and that they did it in the motel," Stanek said.

51

For all Stephen's casual admission of his own roving eye, he went ballistic at the thought of Tara being unfaithful. Though family and investigators are close-lipped about the details, one story has it that Stephen found a Christmas card Tara had written to another man; Tara explained in the note that she wouldn't be able to get away during the holidays to meet him.

A source close to Tara's homicide investigation said a letter was found in the home indicating she had recently been tested for sexually transmitted diseases; her motives for obtaining the tests remain unclear. Was she worried about catching something from Stephen, or the other way around?

52

On February 1, 2007, eight days before he murdered his wife, Stephen sent her an apologetic letter in which he discussed another e-mail she'd supposedly written to her ex-boyfriend.

I am sorry, he wrote in an e-mail. *I keep fucking up and don't know why. I love you Tara and I was hurt by what I read. I know we have gone through this already, but I was not expecting to read what I read.*

Stephen promised never to bring up Tara's e-mail again—or the man to whom she'd sent it. He then wrote about the troubles they were having with her job: *I know you have to travel for work. I get that, and I am proud of you for all you have done and earned in this job. But you are on the road a lot . . . and you do drink, sometimes too much when you go out. When people drink . . . they sometimes forget who they are for a time and do things they might not otherwise do. Do I think that you have . . . I do not know. I am being honest but in reality I can never really know except in my heart. And there I answer no!*

The lonely, jealous husband freely impugned his wife's reputation to others, from his "Old Geezer" comments to Deena about Tara and Lou Troendle to his outbursts at the bar.

He even impersonated Tara in her own e-mail accounts. Stanek recalled: "He came in one day and said, 'I've got to talk to you about something. I think my wife is having an affair.' He said it was an old boyfriend of hers from up north. He said he went through her computer and looked at her e-mails. Then he said [he] got her boyfriend's e-mail address and sent e-mails to this other guy, pretending to be Tara. He was trying to trick this guy into saying something that would show Tara was cheating. Somehow Steve threatened to hurt this guy. He sent him an e-mail saying he was going to hurt him. That's what he told me anyway," Stanek recalled.

The dreary winter wore on, until one Friday lunch hour when Stephen waltzed into Buffalo Wild Wings. He was sporting a red-and-white-checked shirt. He was in a jaunty mood, ignoring his snack. "He started showing me some text messages that Verena had sent to his cell phone," Stanek said. "He didn't eat. He just kept talking about these text messages, and showing them to me, over and over.

"I said, 'Eat.' But he didn't listen. He was like, 'Look at this message. Look at this one. Look at this one.' They were pretty hot messages, and it sounded like she wanted to have sex with him."

The barmaid admonished Stephen to leave the teenager alone and think about the consequences. "I said, 'You have a wife and two beautiful children at home. What if someone is in the background watching you do anything.'"

For a few days, Stephen was too busy to make it in for his regular meal. But about a week after Tara went missing, a coworker told Stanek that Stephen had been in for his wings and cheese.

"She said he had scratches on his hands. He told her his cat did it," Stanek recalled. "I said, 'He doesn't have a cat.'"

PART III

53

Kozlowski and McLean, who had barreled up I-75 to Petoskey after receiving Stephen's summons, had been listening to their suspect's hospital room confession for about an hour, Sunday, March 4, when, back in Mount Clemens, Alicia and Erik approached the podium in Hackel's briefing room.

The couple peered solemnly at the pack of reporters, cameramen, and photographers who were covering the evening press conference. Alicia's quavering voice could barely be heard above the relentless clacking of shutters as she began reading from a prepared statement:

"My family and I would like to take this opportunity to express how deeply saddened we are at the loss of Tara, a genuinely beautiful mother, daughter, sister and wife, whose life was needlessly and abruptly ended the night of February 9th.

"As Tara's only sibling, I feel passionately about maintaining my sister's voice since it's become impossible for her to speak herself. Tara loved her children, her two beautiful children, with all her heart and did everything in her power to provide for her family. Those truly close to Tara remained confident throughout this whole ordeal as she would never desert her children or her employer.

"While this outcome represents the worst possible scenario imaginable to anyone, we take comfort in the fact that Tara is now in a better place.

"*We are filled with grief and are horrified at the manner which Tara's life was needlessly taken and are filled with many, many unanswered questions. We hope and believe that Tara's murderer will ultimately be brought to justice. Tara's death leaves behind two beautiful children whose lives are going to be forever affected by this gruesome act. Her children will certainly need your continued support.*"

Alicia broke into tears, and the cameras clicked with renewed intensity.

A steady flow of reporters arrived at the Utykanskis' Sterling Heights home Sunday seeking interviews, only to find a handwritten sign taped to the front door: *Do not knock on door or ring doorbell. Children sleeping.*

54

The sun rose at 7:02 A.M. on Monday, March 5. The tragic, exhausting weekend was finally over—but the frenzy was just getting started. Hackel and Macomb County prosecutor Eric Smith held a joint 9:00 A.M. press conference in the sheriff's headquarters. Hackel said Stephen had confessed to Tara's murder.

"He gave a very lengthy confession, laying out exactly what took place," Hackel told reporters. "I think he felt the need to get it off his chest. This was something he initiated. He voiced interest in wanting to discuss this with our people. He said he wanted to clear his mind.

"He was very detailed in his description," Hackel said. "He indicated the method in which he took her life, and how he dismembered her body. Tara died of strangulation." Stephen dismembered Tara in his father's shop, Hackel said.

A reporter asked if Lindsey and Ian were home during the murder. "The kids were at the house," Hackel said. "But they were asleep."

Hackel was asked if his detectives were questioning Verena. "We've had lengthy conversations with the au pair," he confirmed.

Was Verena a suspect? "As we've indicated, Stephen Grant is the only suspect," Hackel answered. "The au pair has been cooperative."

Did Stephen have a history of abusing Tara? "There's been talk that there was a lot of arguing, but nothing to indicate there was physical abuse," Hackel said.

Hackel said Stephen was housed in the jail's medical unit. "He will be closely monitored," he said.

The sheriff then yielded the podium to Smith.

With Stephen now safely in police custody, the focus would soon shift from the sheriff to another youthful, second-generation lawman. Soft-spoken and handsome, Eric Smith also had deep Macomb County roots. His father was Clinton Township police chief Robert Smith, who held the post for twenty-four years before he died in 2000. His brother Robert Smith Jr. was a Clinton Township firefighter for twenty-two years, who also served as the city's fire marshal.

"My father set a great example for us," Eric Smith said.

After graduating from Chippewa Valley High School in Clinton Township, Smith earned his law degree from the Detroit College of Law. In 1993, he joined Macomb County prosecutor Carl Marlinga's office as an assistant prosecutor. After prosecuting a variety of cases the first few years, Smith was assigned to the sex crimes unit, where he handled child abuse cases. He spent eight years in the unit.

Marlinga, who served as prosecutor for twenty years, decided not to seek reelection in 2004 after he was indicted by the U.S. Department of Justice (DOJ) on charges of conspiring with state senator Jim Barcia, of Bay City, Michigan, and real estate broker Ralph Roberts to help rape suspects get a new trial in exchange for a $34,000 donation to Marlinga's failed 2002 congressional campaign. (A Macomb County jury acquitted Marlinga, and the feds dropped their case against Roberts and Barcia, thanks in large part to the work of defense attorney David Griem.)

Marlinga's decision to not seek reelection left the prosecutor's seat open for the first time in forty-four years. The election pitted Smith, a Democrat, against Republican David Viviano, who ran a private Mount Clemens law firm. Viviano's father, Antonio Viviano, was a longtime Macomb County Circuit Court judge who recently had been appointed chief judge, a position he would assume the following year. As chief judge, Antonio Viviano would render a crucial, controversial decision in the Grant case.

The 2004 prosecutor's race was close and contentious. Smith and Viviano exchanged barbs throughout the campaign. Smith said his opponent had too little trial experience to make an effective prosecutor. Viviano countered that the Macomb County Prosecutor's Office needed change, and that the thirty-eight-year-old Smith, who had spent eleven years working for the former prosecutor, represented more of the same.

Four hours after the polls closed on November 2, the race was still too close to call. Smith finally was declared the winner early the next morning. He had garnered 53.4 percent of the votes.

Prosecutor-elect Smith hardly had time to savor his victory before he was caught up in a controversial case that drew national attention. Less than three weeks after the election, on November 16, a seventeen-year-old boy and his fifteen-year-old girlfriend were arrested when a tipster told police the youthful couple had induced a miscarriage by having the boy repeatedly hit the girl, who was six months pregnant, in the abdomen with a souvenir baseball bat over a period of several weeks.

Smith charged the boy with intentional conduct against a pregnant individual resulting in miscarriage or stillbirth, a fifteen-year felony. The decision was widely criticized. Detractors insisted the boy's actions did not constitute assault, because his girlfriend had agreed to the scheme. Smith argued that the boy didn't have a right to hit a pregnant girl in the stomach with a bat, whether she consented or not.

"It's not OK to commit a crime against someone just because they give permission," Smith argued. Legal experts compared the case to that of Jack Kevorkian, the Detroit-area doctor known as "Dr. Death," who was sent to prison after granting an elderly woman's request to help her commit suicide.

The case also fanned the abortion debate, along with the question of whether a fetus should be considered a human being. Some people also said the boy should have been charged with murder, for murdering the unborn baby. Others insisted the girl should have also been charged, not treated as a victim.

In the end, the boy pleaded no contest to the charge and was given eighteen months of probation and two hundred hours of community service.

Smith formally took over the reins as prosecutor on January 3, 2005. He implemented several new policies his first day on the job. He banned plea bargaining by assistant prosecutors in life felony cases, such as first-degree murder. He created a senior crimes prosecutor position to handle crimes against the elderly, such as assault and fraud.

He also established a "Teen Court" in area high schools, in which students judged other students and meted out punishment on misdemeanor cases. The program aimed to educate students about the law, Smith said.

In another first-day move, Smith appointed Therese Tobin, an old friend from law school, as chief trial attorney. She was the first woman to hold that position, making her the highest-ranking female in the history of the Macomb County Prosecutor's Office.

* * *

Therese Tobin has a friendly, low-key personality when she isn't cross-examining a witness. In court, Smith's chief trial attorney displays the same kind of aggression that earned her a place in the St. John Fisher College Athletic Hall of Fame. Tobin, who tops six feet, was captain of the Rochester, New York, school's women's basketball team, which in 1988 advanced, to the Division III Finals of the NCAA Tournament. She was a classmate of Smith's at the Detroit College of Law, where she earned her law degree in 1991.

Also working on the Grant homicide case with Tobin and Smith would be William "Bill" Cataldo, assistant prosecutor. During some twenty-one years as a defense attorney, his clients had ranged from a transsexual who killed an uncle to get money for a sex change operation to a landlord who tried to hire a hit man to assassinate two judges who had jailed him for failing to fix up his properties.

Cataldo, who is called "Shaggy" because of his shoulder-length gray hair, plays guitar in the rock group Hung Jury. Ben Liston, chief of staff for the prosecutor's office, is the band's lead singer. Cataldo, Smith's chief of homicide, also worked as a radio producer and teacher.

Early in Smith's first term, he brought first-degree murder charges against Patrick Selepak and Samantha Bachynski, a couple whose Bonnie and Clyde–style crime spree across Michigan culminated in three murders, including the grisly torture and slaying of a pregnant woman and her husband. It was another Macomb County case that garnered national attention.

Selepak, twenty-seven, had served ten years in prison for armed robbery before being paroled in May 2005. He was sent back to the penitentiary six months later after he violently attacked his girlfriend, stuffing sand in her mouth to muffle her screams. Corrections officials wanted to keep him in prison, but they thought they were compelled to release him because they hadn't held a parole revocation hearing within forty-five days of his return, as department rules had required in the past. The rule had since been rescinded, although the officials in charge of his case didn't know it. On January 10, 2006, Selepak was mistakenly released on parole.

Selepak, described by family members as a "charmer," began dating Samantha Bachynski, a dim, heavyset nineteen-year-old girl he met through a mutual friend. Just a few weeks after being released from prison, Selepak convinced her to help him commit several armed robberies. Selepak also began a relationship with a married woman, Melissa Berels, through a telephone chat line. Selepak said the phone flirtation quickly developed into a sexual affair, although police and Melissa's relatives dispute the claim.

On the afternoon of February 15, 2006, Selepak had Bachynski drop him off at the Berelses' home. He was hoping to find Melissa alone. He took a duffel bag containing two rifles out of Bachynski's car, and she drove off to run some errands. No one was home, so Selepak broke in through a back door and waited. He was surprised when Melissa's husband, Scott, came home early from his job at a small machine shop. They hung out for a few hours playing video games until it was time to pick up Melissa from her job at a nearby grocery store. By the time they got back to New Baltimore, Bachynski had returned from her errands and was waiting in her car.

Once they were all inside the house, Selepak's demeanor suddenly changed. He forced Scott into the bathroom, tied his wrists with duct tape, and repeatedly struck him in the head with a rifle butt. Melissa screamed and said she was going to call the police. Selepak told

Bachynski to guard Scott, and then he stormed into the kitchen to confront Melissa.

"Melissa's last words were 'I'm pregnant. I want to call my mom,'" Smith said.

Selepak strangled her to death, then returned to the bathroom and again bludgeoned Scott with the butt of the rifle. But he wouldn't die. Selepak then came up with the idea of injecting their victim with bleach using a hypodermic needle. He sent Bachynski to a local drugstore to purchase a box of needles.

When Bachynski returned, she and her partner approached the victim. Scott informed them he was afraid of needles. The deranged couple taunted him with the needle for several minutes before finally injecting the bleach into his veins. In agony, Scott still did not die. Selepak eventually suffocated him, and he finally stopped breathing.

Selepak and Bachynski wrapped the two bodies in plastic, threw them into a spare bedroom, covered them with some debris left over from a home improvement project, and fled. They drove about seventy miles north to the Flint area, where they met fifty-two-year-old Winfield Johnson in a gay bar. They stayed at Johnson's home for a few days; Selepak slept in their host's boudoir, while a jealous Bachynski fumed alone in the guest bedroom.

During their third day in Johnson's home, a television news report named Selepak and Bachynski as suspects in the Berels murders. Johnson announced he was going to call the police. As he walked out of his house, Selepak shot him in the back. He then dragged his body back inside, wrapped it in cellophane, and threw it into the back of Johnson's pickup truck.

Later that day, Selepak and Bachynski drove Johnson's truck to the home of a friend, Tara Beacham, to give her a lift to a nearby hotel, where she had a job interview. Selepak and Bachynski told her they would wait outside the hotel. Beacham, who also had seen news reports about the Berels murders, went into the hotel and called police. Selepak and Bachynski were arrested as they sat in the parking lot. Police found Johnson's body in the back of the truck.

There were two separate trials: one for the Berels murders, the other for Johnson's killing. During both trials, Selepak often smirked at the victims' relatives as he strutted into the courtroom. He openly taunted court officials. Eventually, claiming he was tired of sitting in court, he pleaded guilty to all three murders.

Bachynski whined constantly throughout her two trials, claiming Selepak had forced her to participate in the murders. Jurors didn't buy it—she was convicted of first-degree murder in both cases.

"Patrick Selepak is the kind of killer who has no conscience whatsoever," Smith said. "He's the kind of guy who just chills you to the bone."

Smith's first term as prosecutor had been eventful, but it was just a warm-up for what he was about to tackle.

55

"This case is probably the biggest case in the country right now," Smith told reporters after he replaced Hackel at the podium during the Monday-morning press conference. "A lot of people have been glued to their TV sets."

Smith announced that the open murder charge against Stephen had been upped to first-degree murder. He explained that defendants are often charged with open murder early in a case, which allows prosecutors the flexibility to alter the charge if more evidence comes to light. "People don't generally plead guilty to first-degree murder, so we're anticipating this will go to trial," Smith said.

He said he was bringing a first-degree murder charge because Stephen had plenty of time to consider his actions while he was choking Tara. "Manual strangulation takes as long as five minutes before death," he said. "Premeditated murder is an opportunity to take a second look, or a moment to reflect on your actions. So, case law says that you can use manual strangulation as evidence in premeditated murder."

When asked if Stephen had offered a motive, Smith replied that he hadn't. "Evil rarely explains itself," he declared. But the prosecutor stressed he wouldn't need to establish a motive in order to get a conviction. "To us, it's not an element we have to prove. We just have to establish that a crime was committed, and that it's the defendant who committed it."

Smith was asked: would Stephen's confession hold up in court? "I'm sure his new attorney, whoever it is, will try to challenge it, but I doubt anything will come of it," he said. "The detectives interviewed the defendant at his request. It was all recorded on tape. He is recorded waiving his Miranda rights. That's pretty cut-and-dried. These detectives are experts in their field."

A reporter wondered whether a judge might grant a change of venue, given the publicity the case had received. "I've been with the prosecutor's office for fifteen years and I've never seen a motion for change of venue granted," Smith said. "The issue isn't whether people have heard about this case—it's about whether or not they have heard about it and can still make an informed opinion as to guilt or innocence. Mr. Grant was a willing participant in the investigation and we intend to use any statements he made against him, including those made to the media."

Painstaking efforts had been made to ensure the case was airtight, Smith promised. "This was the most thorough search warrant I've ever seen," he said. "Our chief of appellate was involved, along with seven or eight prosecutors. We made sure we not only met but exceeded the probable cause standard. We're building a very strong case."

Harkel again fielded a few questions. He was asked to summarize the events of the past few weeks. He sighed. "It's been tough," the lawman admitted. "Not only the emotional toll this has taken, but the difficulty of the investigation itself.

"This has been a difficult year. This case came on the heels of . . . a mother who killed her children," he said,

referring to Jennifer Kukla, the woman who murdered
her two girls inside their Macomb Township trailer.

"We have to make sure Stephen Grant's rights are not
violated," Hackel added. "But Tara Lynn Grant had
rights, too."

Smith was asked if Verena would be called as a witness
during the trial. "The au pair is someone we definitely
want to talk to, but it's a logistical nightmare," Smith
said. "It's very difficult to subpoena someone who is a citizen of another country. She's not charged with a crime.
We'd just like to talk to her, and potentially call her as a
witness. But that could take months of negotiating with
the authorities in Germany. It's not an easy thing to do."

Smith said Stephen would be arraigned at 1:00 P.M.
the following day. The proceeding, which normally
would be held in 42-I District Court in Romeo, near
Washington Township, would instead take place in the
42-II District courtroom inside the county jail. The
change was due to security reasons, Smith said.

56

Monday was a busy day for everyone connected to the case. Medical Examiner Daniel Spitz confirmed at a press conference that the official cause of Tara's death was strangulation. "There was visible bruising on the neck, and injuries to the cartilage of the neck, which indicate manual strangulation," he said.

Tara, likely, fought with her husband the last few minutes of her life, Spitz said. "The body showed signs of an altercation," he added. "A struggle, likely, took place. There were other injuries to her head and body."

Spitz said authorities were going through the formality of conducting a DNA test to confirm the identity of the remains.

Tara's body parts, which were exposed to the elements for three weeks, were well-preserved, Spitz said, because of the cold temperatures. However, he said, some of the limbs showed signs of animal activity.

Dr. John Bednar, an emergency room physician at Northern Michigan Hospital, addressed the reporters who had been staking out the facility since Sunday. Stephen had fully recovered from his hypothermia, and there was little chance he'd be permanently injured, the doctor said at a noon press briefing.

"He's awake, alert, calm, and cooperative," Bednar said of his infamous patient.

It was also revealed that police would be transporting Stephen back to the Macomb County Jail within a few hours.

At about 1:30 P.M., Monday, Macomb deputy Phillip Neumeyer and his German shepherd partner, Bullet, conducted a third search of Stony Creek Metropark. The dog sniffed out a blue rag underneath a fallen tree, and a black shoe nearby. That was all Bullet found.

Only eleven of Tara's fourteen body parts had been accounted for. Her right arm from the elbow to the wrist, her left lower leg, and her right foot would never be recovered.

State social service workers removed Lindsey and Ian from Kelly's Sterling Heights home Monday afternoon and placed them in the care of the Standerfers.

"Whatever's best for the kids," Kelly said when reached by phone. "I'm not going to make this a huge custody battle."

She wouldn't talk about the murder, though. "We're still trying to sort this all out, so it's best not to say anything about that right now," she said. "Obviously, it's horrific, and it's hit the family hard."

As deputies prepared to drive Stephen back to Mount Clemens, he asked to speak to Northern Michigan Hospital's chaplain, Dan Thompson. The request was granted, and deputies stepped out of Stephen's room for a moment to allow the brief, private discussion.

The hospital's automatic glass doors slid open at 1:43 P.M. and a deputy appeared pushing Stephen in a wheelchair. The killer wore a black-and-white-striped inmate's uniform, which was a dramatic departure from the blue or green jumpsuits usually issued to Macomb County prisoners. He also wore a pair of huge white cloth boots designed to keep his frostbitten feet warm.

Channel 4 reporter Hank Winchester had made the trek from Detroit to Petoskey. He fired questions at the wheelchair-bound prisoner: "Stephen, did you kill your wife? Stephen, do you have any statement to make at all?"

Stephen kept his eyes forward and said nothing as the deputy wheeled him past the media corps toward a sheriff's department black SUV. The battery of reporters, photographers, and cameramen were joined by a few curious locals, who brought along their cameras and snapped pictures of the event. Stephen grimaced in apparent pain as he was helped into the SUV. The vehicle pulled out of the hospital lot followed by two Macomb County sheriff's cruisers.

Back in Metro Detroit, television stations carried the perp walk live, and as the three black vehicles headed south toward the Macomb County Jail, a news helicopter followed them, broadcasting a live aerial view of the convoy.

Hackel later revealed that the black-and-white-striped prison uniform Stephen wore was in reality the sheriff's Halloween costume. "I knew the media was all going to be there, waiting to take his picture, and I thought it wasn't right for him to get sympathy from people because he was in a hospital gown," he said.

There were no other prison uniforms available, Hackel explained. "The only available prison uniform was a size fourX, which was huge," he said. "So I drove to my office and found a black-and-white prison costume I had for a Halloween party. Stephen Grant was a prisoner, and I wanted to reflect that. Plus, if he escaped, I wanted him to be wearing something visible."

Stephen arrived at the Macomb County Jail at 5:40 P.M. The SUV in which he was riding disappeared into the jailhouse through a garage door at the rear of the facility. Stephen was then escorted to the jail's medical unit, where he was given a solitary cell in a high observation area. He was put on suicide watch.

Later that night, Griem went to the jail to see his former client. Stephen refused the visit.

On Monday, Channel 4 reported that they'd spoken with some of the Grants' former au pairs, who painted a dark picture of life at the Westridge home. One of the au pairs said she locked her bedroom door because Stephen scared her with his frequent tirades. She said Stephen was verbally abusive to his children, and that there was always a lot of screaming going on in the Grant household.

Another nanny told the station that Stephen would spy on her through a peephole into her room—a report that was later confirmed by Lieutenant Elizabeth Darga, head of the Macomb County Sheriff's detective bureau. "During the investigation, we talked with the au pairs who had lived with the Grants," Darga said. "They're very difficult to interview because . . . sometimes there's a language barrier. But we got some interesting information from them."

Yana, a former au pair from Ukraine, who spent only three weeks working in the Grant home before asking to be reassigned, told detectives that Stephen was "weird," Darga said. "She said she never liked [Stephen]," Darga said. "And she said she always got the feeling he was watching her. She told us he had a peephole set up in his closet so he could see right into the au pair's room. She said she knew he was watching her, and she left not long after she started getting that feeling."

When police later searched the Grant home, they found the peephole, Darga said. "It was in his closet, just like the au pair said. He had tried to cover it up with plaster, but it was easy to spot."

57

Stephen spent a quiet first night in jail, Hackel said at his morning press conference on Tuesday. "He's very subdued," he said. "He's been cooperative."

"He's being closely monitored because of his condition," he said. When Stephen was ready to leave the medical unit, sheriff's officials would decide whether to put him into the jail's general population or in a unit where he could be put on suicide watch, Hackel said.

The sheriff was asked what it was like to have such a high-profile prisoner in his jail. "He's no different than anybody else," Hackel said. "We are treating him like any other prisoner."

"How are you holding up?" a reporter asked.

"It's been crazy. Today was the first chance I've had all week to get some time on the treadmill," said the fitness-buff sheriff. "And even then, I was still getting calls on my cell phone from the media. So I'm on the treadmill doing interviews."

A vendor on eBay tried to cash in on the Grant mania. He put up for auction a black-and-white-striped shirt with *Prisoner, Macomb County Jail* stenciled in red letters across the back. A picture of the shirt was displayed under the misspelled headline STEPHEN GRANT MURDER—

JAIL JERSEY—MACOMB COUNTY. *Barely used Macomb County Jail Collectors Shirt,* the ad proclaimed. *Genuine Stephen Grant Macomb County Jersey. Only one available . . . all messages welcome.*

The vendor, whose screen name was curiosity 137, set the minimum bid at ninety-nine cents. Within a few hours, the bidding had reached $15.

"It's a hoax," Hackel said.

The eBay account of curiosity 137 disappeared within a few days. It was never determined whether someone had bought the shirt.

Tara (left) and Alicia Destrampe posed in their cheerleader uniforms for the Mid-Peninsula High School yearbook. Growing up on a small farm in rural Michigan, the outgoing sisters were exceptionally close. *(Yearbook photo)*

On Valentine's Day, 2007, Stephen Grant showed up at the local sheriff's office to report his wife Tara missing. *(Courtesy of The Detroit News)*

Stephen told police he last saw his wife leaving the garage of their Washington Township home the night of February 9. *(Courtesy of The Detroit News)*

Stephen reported that the last time he saw Tara, the couple argued about her business travel as she repacked her suitcase in their master bedroom. *(Courtesy of the Macomb County Sheriff's Office)*

Stephen told police he wasn't just a "Mr. Mom" who stayed home while his wife traveled; he boasted of working in the family tool-and-die business owned by his father. Later, even veteran detectives were shocked by what happened in the shop. *(Courtesy of the Macomb County Sheriff's Office)*

A *Detroit News* scoop revealed salacious emails Stephen sent to his ex-girlfriend Deena Hardy about two weeks before Tara disappeared. *(Courtesy of The Detroit News)*

Tara's mother, Mary Destrampe, and Alicia worked closely with investigators, and tried to keep hope alive as the weeks of Tara's disappearance wore on. *(Courtesy of The Detroit News)*

Notations on an investigators' white board reflect their doubts about Stephen's story. *(Courtesy of the Macomb County Sheriff's Office)*

Macomb County Sheriff Mark Hackel held daily press conferences, complete with enlarged photo of Tara, to satisfy intense public interest in the case. *(Courtesy of The Detroit News)*

Sheila Werner loved Stony Creek Metropark and the surrounding area. Her observation during a stroll in the snowy nature reserve provided a key break for investigators. *(Courtesy of The Detroit News)*

When police got a search warrant for the Grant home, twenty-two days after Tara went missing, Detective Brian Kozlowski was drawn to this green tub in the garage, marked "Boys' Clothes." *(Courtesy of the Macomb County Sheriff's Office)*

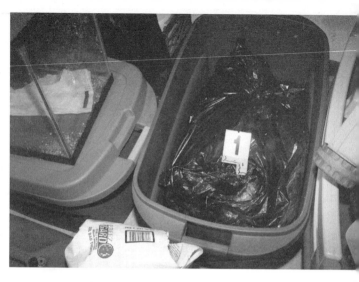

Detective Kozlowski shouted an expletive when he uncovered the bin's grisly contents: Tara's dismembered torso, wrapped in a trash bag.
(Courtesy of the Macomb County Sheriff's Office)

As stunned investigators were finding Tara's torso, Stephen borrowed this bright yellow Dodge Dakota from an unsuspecting friend and fled. Police later were to marvel at his choice of such a conspicuous getaway vehicle.
(Courtesy of the Macomb County Sheriff's Office)

Sheriff's deputies rooted through a Dumpster outside USG Babbitt, the tool-and-die shop owned by Stephen Grant's father, for additional evidence. It later would be learned that the shop was used during the grisly hide-and-seek of Tara's torso. *(Courtesy of The Detroit News)*

Investigators searched Stony Creek Metropark near the Grant home and located a number of Tara's dismembered body parts, including her head. *(Courtesy of The Detroit News)*

Police also found these saw blades in Stony Creek. *(Courtesy of the Macomb County Sheriff's Office)*

Dr. Daniel Spitz, the Macomb County medical examiner, determined in a preliminary autopsy that Tara had been strangled. Spitz is the son of famed pathologist Dr. Werner Spitz, whose expertise has been tapped in famous cases ranging from the John F. Kennedy assassination to the civil suit against O.J. Simpson. *(Courtesy of* The Detroit News)

Remote Wilderness State Park at the top of Michigan's Lower Peninsula was treacherous even to experienced woodsmen. Stephen ditched the Dodge Dakota and plunged into the park with no survival gear as temperatures dipped well below freezing. *(Courtesy of* The Detroit News)

After Stephen was found alive, his attorney David Griem resigned on live television. "I have to look at myself in the mirror in the morning," the veteran lawyer told reporters. *(Courtesy of* The Detroit News)

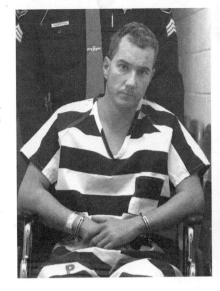

After recovering from hypothermia in a northern Michigan hospital, the captured Stephen Grant was issued prisoner's stripes and wheeled into jail by Macomb deputies. *(Courtesy of* The Detroit News*)*

Members of the media converge on Sheriff Mark Hackel as Stony Creek Park was searched again for body parts on March 3, 2007. *(Courtesy of* The Detroit News*)*

Following the discovery of Tara's remains, friends and family held a memorial vigil on March 8, 2007. More than 200 people gathered with her mother, Mary Destrampe, to honor Tara. *(Courtesy of The Detroit News)*

The detective team on the Grant case included, left to right, Sgt. Pamela McLean, Capt. Anthony Wickersham, Sgt. Brian Kozlowski, Sheriff Mark Hackel, Lt. Elizabeth Darga and Sgt. Larry King. *(Courtesy of The Detroit News)*

Macomb County Prosecutor Eric Smith was known to be one of the region's toughest lawmen. *(Courtesy of The Detroit News)*

Mary Destrampe is consoled at her daughter's funeral in Michigan's Upper Peninsula. The family deliberately chose to hold Tara's final farewell at a church other than the one where she and Stephen were married. *(Courtesy of The Detroit News)*

The case moved Detective Kozlowski to write a heartfelt promise with funeral flowers for the murdered woman. *(Courtesy of The Detroit News)*

The prayer card at Tara's funeral reflected a beautiful, confident woman in the prime of life. *(Courtesy of The Detroit News)*

Stephen Grant is wheeled before Macomb County's Judge Denis LeDuc on March 6, 2007 and charged with first-degree homicide and mutilation of a corpse. *(Courtesy of* The Detroit News*)*

When high-powered defense attorneys Gail Pamukov and Stephen Rabaut were chosen to represent Stephen, the decision generated controversy. *(Courtesy of* The Detroit News*)*

The prosecution team of Therese Tobin, William Cataldo and Prosecutor Eric Smith sought first-degree murder charges against Stephen. *(Courtesy of* The Detroit News*)*

Stephen was not without his supporters, including his sister Kelly Utykanski and her husband Chris. (Courtesy of The Detroit News)

A bailiff escorts Stephen into Macomb County Circuit Court for a pretrial hearing. Generally two or three guards accompanied the prisoner into court. (Courtesy of The Detroit News)

Macomb Circuit Judge Diane Druzinski was known as a soft-spoken judge who handed down harsh sentences. (Courtesy of The Detroit News)

Alicia, shown with husband Erik Standerfer and attorney Patrick Simasko, vowed to seek justice for her slain sister. *(Courtesy of* The Detroit News*)*

The prosecution team addressed the media during the trial.
(Courtesy of The Detroit News*)*

Satellite-equipped trucks from Metro Detroit television stations besieged the Macomb County Courthouse throughout Stephen Grant's murder trial. *(Courtesy of* The Detroit News*)*

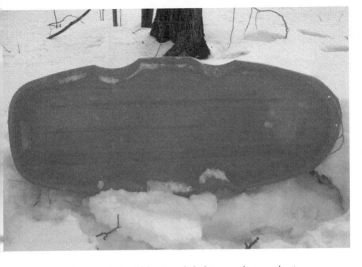

Stephen used his children's red sled to cart their mother's dismembered body parts into Stony Creek park. He confessed that he lost control of the sled, spilling Tara's remains down a snowy hill.
(Courtesy of the Macomb County Sheriff's Office)

Sgt. Larry King testified that his crew found Tara's head wedged underneath this fallen tree. *(Courtesy of the Macomb County Sheriff's Office)*

A tearful Alicia, flanked by Mary and Erik, addresses the media after
Stephen was sentenced to 50 to 80 years in prison.
(Courtesy of The Detroit News)

LOVING MOTHER DAUGHTER SISTER
TARA LYNN GRANT
NÉE DESTRAMPE
JUNE 28, 1972   FEB. 9, 2007

Tara's grave site at the Gardens of Rest cemetery in Michigan's Upper
Peninsula, near the fairgrounds where she competed in 4-H activities.
(Author photo)

58

Sheriff's deputies, prosecutors, media members, and other onlookers squeezed into the small 41-II District courtroom in the rear of the county jail building. Television cameramen and photographers stood with their backs against the south wall, focusing their lenses on visiting judge Denis LeDuc as he ambled into the room.

"All rise."

As was his custom, LeDuc, a gentle, scraggly-bearded man who wears his wire-rimmed glasses on the tip of his nose, thanked everyone for standing. "You may be seated. I thank you kindly for the courtesy," the visiting judge said as he sat down in the high-backed leather chair normally occupied by Judge Paul Cassidy.

The first order of business: Detective Kozlowski had to tell the judge why the arrest warrant was being amended from open murder to first-degree murder. "After Mr. Grant was apprehended, according to the statement he gave to me . . . he, in fact, strangled his wife with his hands, killing her," the detective said.

Once that formality was out of the way, LeDuc called Case #R070196A: *The People of the State of Michigan* v. *Stephen Christopher Grant.*

The camera shutters sounded like machine guns as Stephen was wheeled into the courtroom. The defendant was still wearing Hackel's black-and-white-striped

Halloween costume. The killer's wide eyes scanned the room. As he was wheeled past his sister, who sat next to her husband, Chris, in the front row, they stared at each other for several seconds.

Stephen was not represented by an attorney.

"It's my duty to make sure you know what you're charged with," LeDuc said. The charges: first-degree murder, punishable by life in prison, and disinterment or mutilation, which carried a ten-year penalty.

Stephen leaned forward in his wheelchair and stared intently at the judge as he was advised of his rights.

"The court will indicate that you stand mute to the charges, and a not-guilty plea will be entered on your behalf," LeDuc said. "I'm very concerned that you don't have counsel," the judge told the defendant. "Do you want me to appoint counsel for you?"

"Yes," Stephen answered softly.

Prosecutor Smith then asked LeDuc to hold Stephen without bond. It wasn't a hard argument to win. "Due to the extreme, extreme seriousness of the charges, and the nature of the allegations here, and the nature of the alleged flight, the court agrees with the people. I'm going to order you held without bond," the judge said. "You understand that?"

"Yes," Stephen answered politely.

"I'm going to set the preliminary examination in this matter for Tuesday, March 20, at one-thirty P.M.," LeDuc said. "Do you understand that, sir?"

"Yes, Your Honor."

"Mr. Grant, you are released to the detectives' custody."

"Thank you, Your Honor."

"Thank *you*, Mr. Grant."

With that, the much-ballyhooed proceeding was over. The cameras fired as Stephen was being wheeled away. He briefly scowled over his right shoulder before disappearing through the courtroom doorway.

* * *

Reporters crowded around Kelly Utykanski outside the courtroom. A huge silver crucifix hung from a chain around her neck. She seemed dazed as she tried to answer the rapid-fire questions.

"Do you still support your brother?" someone asked.

"Well, I'm not here to give him a big hug," she said drolly. "I certainly want him to accept his punishment. What he did was horrific."

Kelly said Stephen had called her while he was on the run, but she hadn't spoken to him since. She was asked if she ever imagined Stephen would be capable of killing and mutilating someone.

"No, never in my life," she said. "He's never been a violent person. He's the most docile person in the world. I never would've expected this in a million years."

Were there ever signs of trouble in the marriage? "No, never," Kelly said.

Did she know what pushed Stephen over the edge? "I have no idea."

Eric Smith held a press briefing in a large conference room across the hall from the courtroom; the sheriff's briefing room was too small to accommodate the dozens of people who covered the arraignment.

He announced he would be trying the case—the first case he would try since he'd been elected prosecutor. Critics accused Smith of trying the case for political reasons, although he denied the accusation. "I've always intended to try cases, but I haven't been able to get around to it until now," Smith said when asked why he'd waited until the Grant case to make his courtroom debut.

Smith said he hadn't yet heard Stephen's confession,

although he said police told him some of the gory details. "It's disturbing," he said.

The prosecutor said the Michigan Department of Human Services (DHS) had issued a report recommending Stephen's children be placed with Erik and Alicia. Smith said he supported that recommendation. "They'll be in capable and loving hands," Smith said. He then added that he'd also filed a motion to revoke Stephen's parental rights.

The prosecutor was asked if Stephen was the only suspect. "The sheriff has indicated there are several people he'd still like to take a close look at," Smith said. "But as far as I understand, Stephen Grant acted alone."

Had Smith talked to Verena? "No, we've not heard from the au pair," Smith said. "I would like to talk to her, though, because she could shed light on what happened in the household. Unfortunately, it could take months of dealing with overseas authorities to get her to come back to the States to testify."

Smith concluded his press briefing by mentioning that a trust fund had been set up to help the Grant children. He urged people to contribute. "I realize these are tough times in Macomb County," Smith said. "But no one is facing tougher times than these children, who are now virtual orphans."

At a 3:00 P.M. family court hearing, Referee John J. Kennedy temporarily terminated Stephen's custody of Lindsey and Ian. Stephen was not present. "There will be no contact between the natural father and children in any shape, any form, whatsoever," Kennedy ruled.

With their mother dead and their father in jail, Lindsey and Ian were made wards of the state. A social worker recommended Alicia and Erik keep the children until the next hearing, which was to be held within thirty days. Kennedy agreed, but ordered that the children remain in Michigan. That meant the Standerfers could not take the kids to their Chillicothe, Ohio, home. Alicia would have to stay in Michigan while Erik returned to Ohio to work.

After the hearing, Alicia was asked whether she would seek permanent custody of her niece and nephew. She declined to comment.

Kelly, however, made no bones about it: she planned to fight for custody of Lindsey and Ian. "But I want whatever's best for the kids," she added.

A reporter asked Kelly if there was any animosity between her and Alicia. "We hugged each other last night, and said we love each other," Kelly said. "We don't hate each other. There's no animosity there. We're not going to make this into a horrible battle. I didn't do anything wrong, so I hope they don't hold this against us. Whoever gets custody of the children, the other side wants lots of visitation, and I certainly hope that happens."

Attorney Stephen Donovan, who was appointed by the court on Monday to represent Stephen during the custody hearings, said he visited his client in jail earlier in the day. He said Stephen cried when he heard his parental rights would likely be terminated.

"He was misting up and very emotional about it," Donovan said.

The day after Stephen's arraignment, a source close to the case told the *Detroit News* that prosecutors were looking into a possible affair between Stephen and Verena. Although many people suspected there had been a romantic relationship between the defendant and his teenage former employee, it was the first time anyone connected with the investigation admitted it for the record.

The revelation sparked even more interest in the au pair. Media outlets sent reporters to stake out the girl's home in Germany. *Detroit News* automotive columnist Christine Tierney, who was on her way to Stuttgart, Germany, to cover the possible sale of Chrysler, was told to make a pit stop in Aulhausen. When she got to the au pair's modest home, she found television news crews already on the scene.

Tierney reported that Verena's father, Ludger Dierkes, rushed out of his home to admonish a television reporter who had pulled into his driveway. The man came out of his house several times to shoo away nosy members of the media.

Nobody was able to land an interview with the au pair.

59

On Thursday, March 8, Macomb Circuit chief judge
Antonio Viviano caused a furor when he bypassed a list
of court-appointed attorneys and chose high-powered
lawyer Stephen Rabaut to handle the Grant defense.
The decision was predictably decried by the prosecutor's
office.

"It's still not clear to me why every other murder defendant in this county has to line up to the cafeteria,
while Stephen Grant gets breakfast in bed," said Ben
Liston, Smith's chief of staff. "This is an outrage, and it
reeks of special treatment and cronyism."

Other Macomb County attorneys joined the com-
plaints. Azhar Sheikh, who would have been assigned
the Grant case, if not for Viviano's unusual move, called
Rabaut's appointment "distasteful."

"The whole situation is very suspect," Sheikh said
hours after the judge's decision was announced.

More than one attorney pointed out that Viviano's son
had opposed Smith in the election three years earlier.
Some speculated that Viviano chose the best attorney
available in hopes of handing Smith an embarrassing
defeat in the Grant trial, thus opening the door for his
son to run successfully against Smith for prosecutor
in 2008.

The chief judge insisted the rumors had no merit. He

said he picked the high-profile Rabaut because of the intense media interest in the Grant case—not to help his son win a future election. Still, the judge admitted his decision was unusual. He said it was the first time in his thirty years on the bench that he'd heard of such a move in Macomb County.

"It is rare," Viviano said the day of his announcement. "But this is a unique case with a lot of notoriety, and I wanted an attorney who had the experience to handle the extreme scrutiny this case is under."

Sheikh was not satisfied with the explanation. "That's very unfair to those who are on the list," he said. "If we're not qualified to handle cases, why are we on the public defender's list?"

Rabaut, a well-respected attorney who commanded a handsome fee, had been involved in several recent high-profile cases. In 2003, he represented Youssef Hmimssa, a self-described scam artist who was portrayed as "the Most Wanted Man in the United States" after the September 11, 2001, terrorist attacks because of his alleged connection to a Detroit terrorist cell.

Hmimssa, a citizen of Morocco, testified against four Arab men who were charged with providing support to terrorists in the first federal terrorism trial since the 9/11 attacks. In exchange for his testimony, the government agreed not to charge Hmimssa with having terrorist connections. Hmimssa said he met the alleged terrorists in a Dearborn, Michigan, café, and they frightened him by talking about purchasing weapons to kill infidels.

Two of the men Hmimssa testified against were convicted in June 2004 of conspiring to provide material support or resources to terrorists. A third man was convicted of possessing false documents, and the fourth defendant was acquitted.

U.S. District Court judge Gerald Rosen later threw out the convictions at the request of the U.S. Attorney's Office after it said prosecutors withheld evidence and witnesses crucial to the defense. Rosen also convicted Hmimssa of eleven counts of credit card and document fraud scams in Illinois, Iowa, and Michigan. Hmimssa was sentenced to six and a half years in prison, despite an earlier plea agreement that he be given less time in exchange for his testimony. Rosen ordered a new plea agreement, because he found Hmimssa had committed perjury during his testimony.

Rabaut, a diminutive silver-haired man with a meticulously trimmed mustache, had also defended Warren's 37th District Court judge Susan Chrzanowski, who was involved in a highly publicized love triangle with lawyer Michael Fletcher.

Chrzanowski had just been elected judge in 1998 when she befriended Fletcher, who was still in law school and working as a clerk at the time. Chrzanowski divorced her husband and began an affair with Fletcher, who had a wife and young daughter.

Fletcher's wife was found dead of a gunshot wound in August 1999. She was pregnant with the couple's second child. Fletcher, who had become a lawyer by the time of the killing, was convicted of her murder and sentenced to life in prison.

Chrzanowski was placed on a six-month unpaid suspension for assigning fifty-six public defender cases to Fletcher in 1998 and 1999, approving $17,000 in fees to her lover—more than all other attorneys on the public defender list combined.

Sheriff Hackel was among those who expressed unease about Rabaut's appointment. He was concerned because the attorney was married to Macomb County jail administrator Michelle Sanborn.

The sheriff insisted he trusted Sanborn, his highest-ranking civilian employee, but she often communicated with top police officials about the Grant case, which Hackel said might compromise the trial.

In the end, Rabaut's marriage to Hackel's jail administrator never became an issue.

Stephen had his first visit in the Macomb County Jail the same day Rabaut was appointed to defend him. Inmate #314500 sat behind a bulletproof glass barrier in the jail's visiting room and talked with his sister via telephone for nearly twenty-four minutes. There were signs posted throughout the room warning prisoners and their visitors that their conversations were being recorded.

Prosecutors later released seventy-one audio files of Stephen's visits and phone calls from the time he was arraigned in March until just before his trial in November 2007. The three CDs contained more than fifty hours of the killer's jailhouse conversations.

Thursday, March 8, 2007: Transcript of Macomb County Jail recording of inmate Stephen Grant and visitor Kelly Utykanski

Stephen: So how is everybody?

Kelly: Everybody's pissed off at you. I'm pissed off at you.

Stephen: I know.

Kelly: I love you, but I'm pissed off at what you did. I can't ask you anything about it. I can't ask what happened to make you snap, even though I want to. You can tell me later. . . . That night you went missing . . . I gave the detectives the phone and—

Stephen: You told them where I was.

Kelly: I didn't want you to die.

Stephen: That's OK.

Kelly: Don't be mad at me. I didn't want you to die in a snowbank. I'm sorry.

Stephen: I was close. It was ninety degrees, my body was . . .

Kelly: I saw you helicoptered out. I was pretty stressed out.

Stephen: So how much of it was on the news? . . .

Kelly: When the kids left us, the story was they knew their mother was dead. I used a counselor to tell them. They were too young to understand that you did it. They're not supposed to be told until they're ten and eight. Their understanding was that you were still at the house because the power was out, and that you got very sick from the cold, which was a total lie, and that you were in the hospital for a very long time and they can't see you. Am I allowed to bring you pictures of Lindsey and Ian?

Stephen: (Whispering) Yeah, but I don't want to see them right now.

60

The defense filed motions late Thursday to prevent police and prosecutors from talking about the case, and to preserve Tara's body and the crime scenes.

Rabaut cited "salacious" media speculation as a reason for needing the gag order. *The amount of media exposure in this case has been extraordinary,* he wrote in the motion. *Every day the prosecution and/or the Macomb County Sheriff's Department, or others, leak and discuss various aspects of the ongoing investigation.*

Rabaut also requested that Tara's remains and the crime scenes be preserved so he could gather evidence. A hearing on the motions was scheduled for Monday morning.

More than two hundred people gathered outside the Grant home on Thursday night for a candlelight vigil to honor Tara. Yellow police tape was still draped across the wide front lawn. Mourners left flowers, stuffed animals, and statuettes in the snow just beyond the police tape. A photograph of a young, smiling Tara was dropped off by her former classmates in Perkins. A two-word message—*Miss you*—was written on an accompanying placard.

Mary Destrampe was seen by the public for the first

time since the news broke of Tara's death. She seemed subdued and exhausted. She and Alicia embraced dozens of people, most of them strangers who showed up to express their sympathy.

"The support we're getting from people has just been amazing," Alicia said. "I can't believe the outpouring of love we're seeing."

It was announced that Turning Point, a domestic violence shelter, was organizing a second vigil, to be held Saturday in Stony Creek Metropark.

The Macomb County Bar Association held a press conference Friday afternoon to protest Viviano's decision to bypass the public defender list. "We are severely disappointed that the procedure laid out in the court's own Administrative Order was not followed," said William Staugaard, president-elect of the bar association. "This is the first time anyone in the bar has ever heard of this happening in Macomb County."

Critics of Viviano's decision complained even more when it was announced that a second attorney had been appointed to represent Stephen: Gail Pamukov. Pamukov, a former nurse, spoke softly even when she was grilling someone on the witness stand. One of the highlights of her career was when accused rapist Kenneth Wyniemko walked out of prison in 2003, after serving nearly nine years for a crime he didn't commit.

Pamukov worked on that case for months on a pro bono basis. Working with the Thomas M. Cooley Law School Innocence Project, she was able to prove DNA evidence had been withheld from Wyniemko's trial. Pamukov convinced Macomb County Circuit Court judge Edward Servitto to grant an order allowing for testing of the crime scene evidence. The lab results proved Wyniemko was not the rapist. On June 17, 2003, Wyniemko's conviction was overturned.

* * *

Saturday's Turning Point vigil drew about four hundred people to the park where Tara's remains had been scattered only a few weeks earlier. The 4:00 P.M. event featured songs and speeches. Turning Point director Sue Coats said Tara was a victim of domestic violence, even if Stephen didn't appear to physically abuse her. "This is still about power and control," she told reporters.

A fund in Tara's name was set up to increase domestic violence awareness. Volunteers handed out purple ribbons and a gladiola bulb that would blossom into a light purple flower—purple being the color adopted by domestic violence awareness advocates.

Dozens of people lined up to talk to Alicia after the vigil. Strangers hugged her, and shared their own marital horror stories. Tara's sister had suddenly become a standard-bearer in the battle against domestic violence. As the case moved forward, she rarely made a public statement without raising the issue.

61

Stephen Grant waived his right to attend the hearing on Monday that would address Stephen Rabaut's requests for a gag order and preservation of evidence. LeDuc first granted the defense's request to preserve the crime scene and Tara's remains. Rabaut requested permission to have a second autopsy conducted for the defense. LeDuc agreed, but he stressed it was important to quickly wrap up the examination so Tara's family could hold a funeral.

The judge then denied the gag order. "The court is well aware of the difficulties in balancing the need for a fair trial with First Amendment rights," he said. "That question has kept me busy all weekend." The gag order request had "serious constitutional issues," LeDuc said. After denying the motion, he warned attorneys that while they could talk about the case publicly, they were not to make statements that might taint the proceedings.

After the hearing, Eric Smith hailed LeDuc's decision. "Today was a victory for the First Amendment," he said as reporters crowded around him in the small 42-I District Court hallway. "The public has a right to know what goes on in a courtroom. Justice shines in bright light."

Smith's demeanor changed when he was questioned about the second autopsy granted by the judge. "We bristle at the special treatment this defendant is getting," he said. "I don't know if I've ever heard of a first-degree murder defendant with a public attorney getting his own autopsy."

On the matter of preserving the crime scene, Smith said it was an easy matter to seal off the Grant home, but USG Babbitt presented a dilemma. "The business is difficult, because the defendant doesn't own the business," he said. "We'll try to work it out with the father. This is something that doesn't come up every day, but, luckily, the father is cooperating with us."

Rabaut slipped out of the building without saying much. "We're pleased," he uttered over his shoulder as he bustled through the parking lot.

The next day, Washtenaw County medical examiner Bader Cassin conducted the defense's autopsy. His findings were the same as Spitz's.

Also on Tuesday, Republican state representative Bill Law introduced legislation that would require a life sentence for any homicide resulting from domestic violence, whether premeditation was involved or not.

Law complained that domestic killers were often convicted of second-degree murder because those crimes were usually committed spontaneously. Many of the murderers were paroled after serving the minimum sentence, he said.

Domestic violence advocates hailed the bill, while critics accused Law of trying to exploit outrage over the Grant case for political gain.

Law's bill fizzled.

62

Spitz's office released Tara's remains on Thursday to the Manns-Ferguson Funeral Home in Livonia, which arranged to transfer the body parts to Crawford Funeral Home in Escanaba, near Tara's hometown.

Visitation was planned for Sunday at Crawford, and the funeral would be held the next day in First Lutheran Church in Gladstone, near Perkins. The family had purposely avoided holding the service in the chapel where Tara and Stephen were married.

Tara was to be buried in Gardens of Rest cemetery in Wells, Alicia said.

Wednesday, March 14, 2007: Transcript of Macomb County Jail recording of inmate Stephen Grant and visitor Kelly Utykanski

Kelly: I want to dispose of all your clothes. I don't want them to end up on eBay.

Stephen: You might want to hold on.

Kelly: Well, I'll put them in Rubbermaid containers and put them in my basement then.

Stephen: And there's lots of Rubbermaid containers in the house. (Long pause) Sorry.

Kelly: Have you had a psychiatric evaluation?

Stephen: Yeah. I'm confusing them.

* * *

Stephen Grant made his first public appearance in more than a week, on Friday, when he hobbled into 42-I District Court wearing leg irons and a belly chain. Hackel's Halloween costume was replaced by an inmate's blue jumpsuit.

The defendant waived his right to have a preliminary examination within fourteen days of his arraignment, as required by law. Instead, the examination was scheduled for May 15.

Stephen's attorneys also filed a motion for a protective order to prevent anyone involved in the case from divulging personal information about him. "We have concerns about private confidential information that's out in the media," Pamukov said.

Specifically, the defense team was concerned that stories had been leaked to reporters about a possible affair between their client and his former au pair. The judge said he wanted to weigh the matter before issuing his ruling.

On Tuesday, Juvenile Court referee Deborah Brune lifted the order compelling Lindsey and Ian to stay in Michigan. But Alicia said she would hold off taking the kids home to Ohio until after Tara's funeral. "Our interests at first were in finding Tara," she said. "Now our focus is on what's best for the children."

Kelly said she had talked to Stephen, and that he had no problem with his children living in Ohio while the custody case played out. "My brother wants the kids to go back to school and get into a normal routine as soon as possible," she said.

Stephen Donovan, Stephen Grant's attorney in the custody case, said his client was doing fine. "He was a

little overwhelmed at first, but he's doing a little better,"
Donovan said.

Although Kelly and Alicia were both fighting for custody of the Grant children, Kelly insisted there was no
animosity between the two women. "Alicia and I have
been getting along amicably," Kelly Utykanski said.

*Wednesday, March 21, 2007: Transcript of Macomb County
Jail recording of inmate Stephen Grant and his visitors, father
Al Grant and sister Kelly Utykanski*

Stephen: Dad . . .

Al Grant: I'm so sorry.

Stephen: Hey, that's OK. Shit happens. Kozlowski
apparently came out [and said] that I was
abusing Tara. Is that true?

Kelly: Yeah. Everybody's saying that, by the way.
Turning Point, the abuse place, did the vigil at
Stony Creek, and they all said that you were
an abusive husband for years and years and
years, and it culminated in the murder.

Stephen: Well, you should've told them it was the other
way around. That's what you should've told
them.

Kelly: Well, I can't. I'm trying to get the kids. I can't
bash the dead woman right now. Yeah, she was
the most emotionally abusive bitch I've ever
met—I can't really say that. She was the puppet
master—I can't really say that right now.

Stephen: People want my autograph.

Kelly: Well, you're famous.

Stephen: I had someone offer me a whole box of
donuts for my wristband.

63

Lindsey and Ian were starting to ask questions, Alicia said on Thursday. "They want to know what happened to their mom. They understand that Mom is dead, and they're very, very sad about that. With the funeral approaching, more questions are coming up about what happened. My husband and I are doing everything in our power to help them get through this.

"Every night, we read a book to them about Heaven, to explain their mother's in a better place. I think it's helping. The kids think their father is in the hospital," Alicia said. "We're going to leave it at that until we can sit down with a psychologist to figure out the best way to explain what happened."

At a hearing earlier that day, LeDuc had ruled the Grants' home was no longer an active crime scene, meaning Alicia could retrieve some of the kids' personal items.

"It'll be nice for them to have their own beds, dressers, and things like that," she said. "We'd like them to have their own belongings, to make them feel like they're in a home, instead of being shuffled from one place to another."

Sunday's *Detroit Free Press* carried a front-page tribute to Tara that was written by her sister: *As I write this, I have in mind a photo of Tara and me. Our mother took it years ago when we were kids. In the picture, Tara is clinging to one of our kittens with the biggest smile you would ever imagine.*

Alicia wrote wistfully how Tara's *grin and curly pigtails put a smile on the face of everyone who came in contact with her.* She went on to recount Tara's childhood on the farm, and the joy they shared when Lindsey and Ian were born.

Tara's marriage was never mentioned in the article.

On March 25, about one hundred people crowded into the Crawford Funeral Home—the same funeral parlor where thirteen years before Stephen had charmed Tara by unexpectedly showing up for her grandmother's funeral.

Four fabric-covered boards were propped on easels, each displaying a hodgepodge of photos: Tara holding a basketball; Tara posing with animals; Tara in a cheer-leading outfit. Above her flower-garlanded maple casket was another picture: Tara, Lindsey, and Ian, posing in front of a snow-covered beach.

Journalists covering the visitation tried to be respect-ful, *Detroit Free Press* reporter Amber Hunt said. "Alicia asked that we not interview people at the visitation, and nobody did," Hunt said. "I just tried to stay out of sight. I sat there and focused on Tara's kids, watching them run around."

Lindsey wore a pink flowered dress. Ian was dressed in a blue shirt and blue-and-yellow tie. Their demeanor al-ternated between youthful playfulness and bewildered grief, Hunt said. "One minute, they were just normal kids, running around the funeral home. Then they'd stop and spend a few minutes staring at pictures of their dead mother," she said.

The adults took turns holding Ian, who quipped,

"Thanks for passing me around." It drew a laugh from the group.

Hunt said her parents died when she was young, "so seeing those kids at the visitation really hit home. I could relate to what they were feeling. Lindsey went up to someone and gave him a quarter and said, 'Can you hold this? My mom gave it to me.' I don't know if that was just a quarter she'd found, or if Tara really did give it to her. Either way, it was a touching moment."

Tara's friends and family had managed to keep the mood relatively upbeat during the visitation, considering the circumstances. That changed at the funeral.

Tara's uncle, John Destrampe, tried to read a poem, but he broke down. "Oh, dear God, where do I begin?" he wailed.

Ian sucked his thumb throughout the service, and his sister showed no emotion as the grown-ups around her sobbed.

"Death has done its worst," First Lutheran reverend Jonathan Schmidt said. Then, addressing Tara, he added, "God will not abandon you."

Kelly and her father were there. Al Grant wept.

Lou Troendle described Tara as a woman determined to make her mark in a business world dominated by men. He also said she never forgot her roots. "She was proud of where she came from," he said.

Hackel was at the funeral; he said he felt compelled to pay his respects. And Kozlowski showed a rarely seen sentimentality with a brief note he attached to a bouquet of flowers: *For Tara. I will not stop fighting for you. Detective Kozlowski.*

The seventy-five-minute service was attended by 270 mourners—four times the population of Perkins.

After the funeral, there was a short graveside service. In a gesture encouraged by cemetery staffers, Lindsey touched her mother's maple casket, saying she wanted to leave her fingerprints so she could be with her mom forever. Purple balloons were released after the coffin was lowered into the ground.

"The whole time I covered this case, I tried not to let anything bother me—and there was a lot of gruesome stuff," Hunt said. "But the funeral was really hard to take. It was creepy. I kept staring at her casket, and thinking, 'There's not a whole person in there. It's just body parts.' And all the parts weren't even there—some of them were never recovered. It just bugged the hell out of me."

Wednesday, March 28, 2007: Transcript of Macomb County Jail recording of inmate Stephen Grant and visitor Kelly Utykanski

Stephen: Did anybody mention me at the whole funeral?

    Kelly: No, it was like you did not exist.

Stephen: So it was like I just disappeared.

    Kelly: There were no pictures of you—no wedding pictures; no nothing.

Stephen: That's fucked-up.

    Kelly: Oh, and they released purple balloons, and they all wore purple ribbons at her funeral, because she was a beaten woman.

Stephen: OK, somebody should tell me what the evidence is that I beat my wife. She was never even verbally abused.

    Kelly: I saw her be the puppet master for twelve years, dude.

Stephen: And I kowtowed down.

    Kelly: [A mourner at the funeral] made me gag. He's like, "She's being buried in a maple casket because she liked to make maple syrup." I'm like,

"For the love of Christ, are there barf bags in the pew?" They could not have sapped it up any more. Mom says, why didn't you just put the whole body in the trunk in the airport?

Stephen: (In a jovial tone) Because I didn't do it, Kel, that's why. I had nothing to do with anything.

Kelly: (Talking about a friend's online basketball fantasy league) Somebody named their team Tara's Torso.

Stephen: (Laughs) That's sick. That's twisted.

Kelly: What I want to know is—and this is very disgusting, I realize that for the tape recorder— if they put her back together in the coffin.

Stephen: They probably laid her out that way.

Kelly: Did they dress her, too?

64

The prosecutor's office had been deluged with Freedom of Information Act (FOIA) requests for copies of Stephen's confession, while his attorneys fought to keep it from being released to the media. They said it would negatively influence potential jurors.

On Tuesday, April 3, LeDuc ruled against the defense. "Mr. Grant actively sought out media and gave numerous statements and giving multiple interviews," LeDuc said. "I find great irony that the defendant now raises the issue of pretrial publicity."

Both sides agreed not to release medical records or photos of the crime scene and of Tara's remains. The confession would be released the following week in response to several FOIA requests, the assistant prosecutor Therese Tobin said.

Also on Tuesday, Macomb probate judge Pamela Gilbert O'Sullivan named Alicia conservator of Tara's estate.

The next day, Patrick Simasko, Alicia's attorney, filed a $50 million wrongful-death lawsuit against Stephen in Macomb County Circuit Court. Simasko also filed a petition the same day in the county's probate court to forfeit Stephen's right to be a beneficiary to any of Tara's assets.

The lawsuit stated Lindsey and Ian *have suffered a loss of affection, comfort, companionship, love, society, and financial support, help and service, of which the decedent was accustomed to give and would have given in the future but for her untimely demise.*

The two legal actions were taken to ensure Stephen would not profit from his crime, Simasko said.

65

On Friday, April 6, prosecutors released Stephen's confession to the media, along with dozens of police reports and other documents. Media outlets were quick to post Stephen's chilling confession onto their Web sites.

Finally the public was able to digest Stephen's full confession, just as it had occurred in Northern Michigan Hospital on the night of Sunday, March 4.

Brian Kozlowski and Pam McLean pulled up chairs and settled in near Stephen's hospital bed. Kozlowski set up a tape recorder on a bedside table. At 7:45 P.M., he pushed play.

"How do you feel right now?" Kozlowski asked. "Tired? Exhausted?"

"I'm a little tired," Stephen answered in a subdued voice. "But that's OK."

"Do you think you're of sound mind to talk to us?" Kozlowski asked.

"Yeah." Stephen sighed.

"I'll give you an opportunity to ask us a couple questions first, and then we'll just start," Kozlowski said. "We're in no rush."

McLean added, "We've got all night."

"We're actually staying up here for the night," Kozlowski

said. "No press is going to be coming in here and bugging you. I appreciate you talking to us for a lot of reasons. Obviously, you know, we met under unfortunate circumstances, but I'm not here to judge you. I'm just doing my job."

"I know," Stephen said. His voice was barely above a whisper.

"Okay, so do you have any questions you want to start with?" Kozlowski asked.

"Um, I don't even know where to start with questions," Stephen said. "I just kind of . . . I don't know where to start."

"You do, in fact, know you are . . . under arrest right now?" Kozlowski asked.

"Right," Stephen answered tersely.

"For the murder of your wife, Tara," Kozlowski finished. There was a brief pause. "Yeah."

"OK. Understand that?" Kozlowski asked, making sure there were no misunderstandings that could later be challenged in court.

"I do have a question, and I asked the deputies earlier and they said they couldn't answer," Stephen said, his voice perking up. "What is the difference between levels of murder? First-degree murder—isn't that when you plan it out ahead of time? Is that what it means?"

Kozlowski explained that police had a warrant against him for open murder, and that a determination would later be made as to whether that would become first- or second-degree murder, or manslaughter.

"I know first-degree murder is life without parole, and . . . second-degree is the same, but there is a chance for parole," Stephen said.

"How do you know this?" McLean asked. "How do you know there's a difference?"

"Watching TV," Stephen answered.

* * *

Kozlowski and McLean told Stephen he also was charged with the mutilation of a corpse, a ten-year felony. Then Kozlowski got to the point: "Why don't we go back? Let's start from February ninth."

When Stephen hesitated, Kozlowski tried to reassure the suspect: "I'm quite certain you're familiar with some of our investigative techniques," he said. "I want to tell you from the beginning, I'm not going to overly open up to you and tell you everything that we know, but if you ask me, I will be honest with you and tell you what I know. I'm not here to play tricks on you."

"OK." Stephen sighed.

"I'm not going to be mean, and Pam's not going to be nice or anything like that."

"We're not playing good cop/bad cop," McLean added. "We're just here to talk to you."

Stephen assured the detectives that he understood: "You just gather the information," he said.

"Right," McLean said. "We've been working on this since we talked to you at your house on the fourteenth, so we know a lot. I just want to put that out there, OK?"

"Yes," Stephen said.

"I've seen your kids. I spoke with your sister, and your brother-in-law has been there. We've obviously been to your house. . . . I have obviously spoken to Alicia and Erik . . . and everyone I've talked to, Steve, has said you're a good father," Kozlowski said.

"We haven't heard a negative thing about your being a parent yet," McLean added.

At the mention of his children, Stephen's voice cracked. "OK." He sobbed.

"I know it's going to be difficult for you, but I don't want to make you upset about your kids," Kozlowski said. "I'm glad you are, in fact, alive, because at least your children will be able to see you. You know, anything's possible."

"Well, yesterday, I didn't think that was the case,"

Stephen said. "Yesterday, I obviously thought it would be better the other way. But you're right."

"We know you're a father," McLean said. "That's got to be your primary concern right now."

"That's it," Stephen said. "As of yesterday, I thought it would be better if I just wasn't there, and maybe it is better for . . . the kids to know exactly what happened. I actually started to write things down yesterday."

"Did you?" McLean asked.

"Yeah."

"That's probably a good thing," Kozlowski said.

"It's almost like therapy, writing things down," McLean added.

"I know," Stephen said.

Kozlowski again broached the subject at hand: "OK, go into February ninth, Friday."

"Well, it actually went back to Thursday night," Stephen started. "Tara had called [from Puerto Rico]. I was going to go out to a friend who was playing at Hamlin Pub on Rochester Road in Rochester. At that time, I thought he was playing on Thursday night, so I told Tara that I was going to go to the bar."

Stephen's speech was becoming increasingly animated, prompting McLean to say, "Take your time. There is no hurry."

"Um . . . and Tara had said that she was going to stick around and have dinner. So I said, 'OK, so she had no dinner plans Thursday night.' So once I realized that [my friend] wasn't playing at Hamlin Pub, I called Tara and told her, 'Hey, I'm going to be home.'

"So I called Tara and told her [my friend] wasn't there, while she was at the bar at the hotel. We talked a little bit and that was it. And it surprised me that she was at the bar, because she never goes to the bar. Well, she was talking to an older couple, she had said. So that was pretty much it.

"Then, on Friday morning . . . I talked to her a couple times that day," Stephen said. "I mean, to be completely honest, I really don't remember how many times I talked to her.

"So basically . . . when she got into Newark, she had called me and left a voice mail on my phone. It's still on my phone. It was a saved message. And it's something like, 'I'm at Newark. I'm waiting for a layover. I'm going to be late.' We talked two or three times on the phone."

McLean interjected: "Was it regular conversation, or were you arguing?"

"No, there was no arguing," Stephen said. "I mean . . . there was a little back-and-forth. The weekend before, we had talked about the fact that she travels too much. And she had told me that she was going to try to get things so that they weren't traveling so much.

"And then on Friday night . . . when she got home . . . we started talking. We had been back and forth about the travel schedule. She had unpacked her bag. . . . I was dressed to go to bed.

"I was getting ready to go to bed and Tara came in and we were talking more. And she'd been downstairs, came upstairs, and Tara told me then that she was thinking about leaving on Sunday morning. And I said, 'No, not OK.' And she said, 'Well, I need to go on Sunday,' and she said Lou was going back down there on Sunday. She says, 'I need to go.' I said, 'No, you don't need to go down there with Lou.'

"I said, 'You spend too much time with him already, and you don't spend enough time with us.' I said, 'Why?'

"And she said, 'Fuck off.' She said, 'Too bad.' She said, 'I got to do what I have to do in my job, and it's none of your business.'

"So she started to turn around and I grabbed her wrist," Stephen recalled. "'Stop,' I said. 'Just stop it.

You're not going anywhere. We're going to finish this conversation.' And she slapped me."

"Where was this?" Kozlowski asked. "Up in your bedroom?"

"It was right next to the bathroom," Stephen answered, referring to the bathroom in the master suite.

Stephen continued his story: "So I struck back at Tara," he said. "I don't know. And after that, I don't really remember what happened. I know she—she fell. I know she banged the back of her head on the floor. And then she said something like, 'That's it. I'm going to take the kids. You're going to be fucking homeless. You're a piece of shit.' And I choked her."

"She started to get back up when I put my hand around her neck, because she kept saying that—that it was over, that she was going to take the kids, and because I hit her . . . that was it," Stephen recalled. "And I said, 'No, you hit me first,' and she said, 'It doesn't matter.' She said, 'Cops aren't going to think that. I'm calling the police.' I put my hands on her neck and choked her."

"Was she fighting with you?" McLean asked.

"There wasn't much fighting going on," Stephen said, his voice cracking again. "At one point, she . . ."

"It's OK," McLean said. "Take a break."

Stephen ignored her: "I think at one point she realized I wasn't stopping . . . but it was too late. She scratched my hand. She finally grabbed my hand at one point, but it was too late then, and I couldn't stop then. I knew I was going to prison. I panicked."

The detectives again asked Stephen to clarify exactly where he was when the altercation began, and he reiterated he was near the doorway that separated the master bedroom from the bathroom. Stephen drew a crude map of the layout of the rooms.

"The armoire is here, and . . . there's a window right

here, and a window in the back," Stephen said, referencing the map. "She was standing here, and I was standing here.

"I said something about Lou and her, and she slapped me, and then I hit her back and she fell toward the bedroom," he said, adding details about the beginning of the fight. "I heard something hit. I don't know if she hit her head on the wall, on the floor, but . . . she was knocked for a loop. That's when she started saying shit, right at me. It was venomous—'That's it. I'm done. I can ruin your life now.'

"And she basically [was] lying right there," Stephen said, again referring to his map. "And by then I was here, and that's when I grabbed her as she started to sit back up, and I grabbed her on the back."

"Did you push her back onto the floor?" McLean wondered.

"I don't remember."

"You don't remember," McLean repeated. "OK."

"And I'm sorry," Stephen sniveled. "I—I don't—"

"You don't have to be sorry, Steve," McLean reassured him. "It's OK."

"I just don't remember exactly how it went," Stephen said.

Kozlowski interjected, "I'm not trying to make this graphic, but, unfortunately, some of this—"

"It has to be, I know," Stephen conceded.

"We have to have the details, unfortunately," McLean said.

"I know."

"OK, so just take your time in telling us the answers," McLean repeated.

"Are you on top of her when you're choking her?" Kozlowski asked.

"I think I was kneeling," Stephen said. "I don't think I ever actually got on top of her."

"Were you looking at her face?" McLean asked.

"No, I covered her face up," Stephen recalled. "With a pair of—with gray underwear or a T-shirt."

"So, did you check to see if she stopped breathing?" Kozlowski asked. "How did you know that she had died?"

"She wasn't breathing," Stephen said. "I stood up. I wouldn't call it a rag, because it—I was thinking of it that night as a rag. It was a T-shirt or a pair of boxer-brief gray underwear. I remember gray. It was dark gray. I have lots of T-shirts and underwear like that. I just don't know which it was, and I covered her face up with that.

"And that was it," he continued. "She stopped moving. I went downstairs and I started crying, and I was worried. Really worried. And I sent Verena a text message not to come home."

Kozlowski asked, "Did you send Verena a text message just not to come home?" The detective knew that wasn't true, but he wanted to see what Stephen had to say.

"No, we had been talking," Stephen explained. "Verena and I had been text messaging. . . . We'd been going back and forth for a while, just sending text messages all the time to each other. I knew she was coming home because she sent me a message saying she'd be leaving at a certain time, and I told her Tara was delayed. And I sent her one more. I knew she couldn't come home. I knew if Verena . . . came home, she would see stuff. I knew I had to hide Tara, and I went back up, and she was dead."

"And so Tara is still on the bathroom floor?" Kozlowski asked.

"Yeah."

"As far as you know, she's not breathing?" Kozlowski prodded.

"Right."

Kozlowski's cell phone rang, and at eight minutes and thirteen seconds into the interview, he stopped the tape to take the call.

66

The interview continued a few minutes later.

"We're going back to February ninth," Kozlowski said. "You're upstairs, Tara has come home, you guys have fought—"

"And I choked her," Stephen said. "And then I put something around her neck during this time. I don't remember what. A belt or something. I know at that point if she didn't die, then I would . . . because I'd already put my hand on her neck. I knew I'd hurt her bad. And I wrapped something, a belt or something, around her neck. I think it was my brown leather belt."

"Do you think, Steve, she was breathing at that time?" McLean asked.

"No, I know she wasn't breathing still," Stephen said. "She had stopped, but I didn't know what to do. I had to [find] something to move her with, and I knew I couldn't carry her. She was too big. So I wrapped that around her neck and I used it to pull her downstairs."

"Did you see any other signs . . . that made you think she wasn't breathing?" Kozlowski asked. "Like her skin color, or anything like that?"

"No, she wasn't moving at all," Stephen said.

"OK, did she still have the same clothes on that she had when she got home?" Kozlowski asked.

"She had on black pants and a silver shirt," Stephen

recalled. "She was in the process of basically changing . . . when the whole thing started. She was unpacking her stuff and putting it in the bathroom."

"So what did you do then?" Kozlowski probed.

"Put her in the back of the truck," Stephen said. "I—I don't think I had any clothes on. Like I said, I was . . . when the whole thing started, it was so fast. I was in the bedroom already. I was undressed, and I was ready to go to bed, and it just kept getting worse and worse. And when she smacked me, I—I lost it. For so long, it's been—"

"You guys have had a hard way to go with the traveling and that," Kozlowski added.

"Yeah, yeah, not just the travel, though," Stephen said. "Everything. Tara had—as long as I can remember, she belittled me. And her one way—she knew . . . she knew if she hit me, I'd hit her back."

"Now when you said you didn't have no clothes on, did you at least have a pair of shorts on or anything?" Kozlowski asked.

"I don't think I had any clothes on," Stephen replied.

"OK, like completely naked?" Kozlowski asked.

"Yeah, well, I sleep naked," Stephen said. "I was getting ready for bed."

"OK, so you . . . dragged her body down the stairs?" Kozlowski asked.

"Down the stairs, put her in the back of her truck," Stephen said. "In the cargo area of Tara's white Isuzu Trooper. Um . . . and I dropped her. She was too hard to pick up, and the belt slipped or broke. And she fell, and it was the most disgusting—like, it sounded like dropping a watermelon on the cement. But there was no movement. There was nothing. There wasn't any twinging or anything. I knew then that I had killed her. I didn't know what to do. The only thing I could think to do was to hide her."

"When you said you hid her, how did you hide her?"

Kozlowski asked. "Did you get her back up into the cargo area?"

Stephen explained that he put his wife's body into the back of her truck and covered it with the cargo liner from his Jeep. Then, he said, he heard the garage door open as he was heading into the house. "So I quick jumped in the house, closed the door, and ran upstairs and put pajama pants on," he said.

"What did you do then?" Kozlowski asked.

"I walked back downstairs and I heard Verena walk in and I said, 'Go, just go!' And Verena thought I was talking to Tara. She said, 'Well, what do you mean?' I said, 'Nothing. I thought you were Tara. Come back.' And she said, 'OK,' and she said, 'Where did she go?' And I said she was back down to the airport, and I was thinking as fast as I could.

"My brain was going a mile a minute. And I kept thinking, 'We've got a body in this garage. What the hell do I do with the body?' And I'm thinking, 'I killed my wife.' I'm thinking my life was over."

Stephen told Kozlowski and McLean that he talked with Verena for several minutes that night.

"What did you tell Verena?" Kozlowski asked.

"That Tara had left," Stephen said. "I mean, pretty much the same thing that I had told you guys initially— that Tara had turned around and left. She came home and left."

Stephen said Verena noticed the scratch on his nose.

"What was that scratch from?" Kozlowski asked.

"Tara hitting me," Stephen said. "And I told Verena that. I told her Tara slapped me, and—"

At that point, eight minutes and twenty-three seconds into the interview, the tape ended. Kozlowski stopped Stephen, switched tapes, and continued the questioning.

"You were talking about the scratch on your nose," the detective started. "Tara hit you."

"Oh, and I told Verena that Tara had slapped me," Stephen continued. "And then she said, 'OK.' And I think I told her that I called Tara a whore or something. I made something up for a reason that Tara would hit me and Tara left. And she believed that."

"So what did you do all night?" Kozlowski asked. "Did you just stay awake? Did you stay in your room?"

"I can't remember," Stephen said. "I talked to Verena some more, and basically tried to convince her that Tara had left."

"Do you think that Verena believed you?" Kozlowski asked.

"I think she did," Stephen replied. "I'm pretty sure she did. I don't think she would not believe me. I was worried about that. I had to convince her that Tara had left. Because I knew it was going to be her backing up what I had said. And—"

"[Did] Verena go to sleep?" Kozlowski asked. "[Did] she go to sleep in her room?"

"I don't remember," Stephen replied. "The next day, though, she slept in my room. Saturday morning, I went out and I—I really did it. I went to the bank and the post office and I, uh, something else . . . just errands. And then I came home and I had driven around some, too. Just thinking, trying to think."

"And were you driving Tara's Trooper or were you driving the Commander?" Kozlowski asked.

"I was driving my Jeep."

"OK, so Tara's body's still in the back of her car?" Kozlowski asked.

"Yep. In the garage." Stephen added that he had locked the doors to Tara's Trooper. "I didn't know what to do. I thought about it all day on Saturday—about what I could do. I planned to get up Saturday night and hide Tara somewhere. But I didn't know. It was too cold.

And I knew I wouldn't be able to hide. So on Sunday morning, I took her to the shop.

"I told Verena I had to go into the shop to do something. And I took the truck in, and I called my dad to make sure he wasn't going to be coming in on Sunday. And he said no, he was somewhere. And I said, 'OK.' And I called him back, just to make sure, because I didn't want him walking in on me.

"There was a plastic tarp that was at the house, and I had taken that with me," Stephen said. "And I had taken my bow saw, like a tree-cutting saw. And thinking that would do it. The problem was, it wasn't like she was lying flat, or curled up in a ball. You know? One of her legs was, like, kind of out to the side, and her arm was out to the side, and she was much bigger then."

"So she was hard to move, right?" Kozlowski asked.

"Yeah, very hard to move. And, uh, I—"

Kozlowski interrupted: "So you took her into the shop. How did you get the vehicle into the shop?"

"I backed it in."

"You backed it into the bay door?" Kozlowski asked.

"Yep. And closed the door and there wasn't enough room. So I had to move everything that was in the shop. And I put the piece of plastic down and I put her on the piece of plastic, and then I pulled the truck out so it wouldn't be sitting in there while I was doing what I was doing. And I weighted the four corners of the plastic sheet down with pieces of steel from the shop, and I tried to cut something. Her hand."

Stephen explained that the bow saw didn't work. "I started panicking. I washed my hands off. And I went out to the truck and I had brought something with me. A blanket, or something we had—a pint—we had at the house. And a couple big gulps off of that and then I shredded everything that was in her briefcase. And by the time I was done shredding, I decided, 'OK, now I can do this.' And I went back over. And I couldn't do it.

"So I took her laptop computer and put it on the band saw and cut it into pieces, but the disc drive shattered and there's glass everywhere, and I had to clean that up. And then I had to move all of the steel out of the way again, because there's little pieces from the box of the hard drive everywhere. And I got a piece in my finger. I had to get a tweezer and pull it out. And I'm like, 'Oh, my God, there's blood here now.' And I panicked. I just didn't know what to do."

Stephen said he put the shredded laptop pieces into a box. "And I put her computer bag, I put her purse . . . I put everything in a paper bag. All the stuff I had to make disappear. Because Tara's not going to travel without her computer. She's not going to travel without her phone. She's not going to travel without her computer bag.

"And I emptied her suitcase . . . her travel suitcase. And that's why I came up with the whole [story that] she had a second suitcase. So I'm formulating things as I'm going along, trying to think of the stuff, and I can't. I'm thinking, 'I killed my wife. I killed my wife. I killed my wife. What the hell do I do?' And I was panicked, absolutely panicked."

"OK, so you shred the computer," Kozlowski said. "You put everything else in a box."

"No, I shredded the documents," Stephen corrected. "Like the papers and stuff that were there, business cards, I ran through the shredder at the shop. I tried to run some stuff through the shredder, it wouldn't go. So I had all the stuff that I cut up—the computer and stuff like that—I thought pieces, any of it, that they would be able to identify, I'd put all of that in a box. A cardboard box. And then I put the other stuff in a paper bag, or . . . a computer bag. Her purse, stuff that I just couldn't shred or cut up. And then I threw that stuff away."

Stephen said he later discarded the items in a Dump-

ster in Sterling Heights, near the home where he grew
up. Then he went back to telling the detectives how he
dismembered his wife's body.

"I had tried to cut something—her hand or something—to make her smaller," he said. "And I had taken
a bucket with me—one of the storage buckets at the
house—and we had, like, four or five empty ones."

"Like a Rubbermaid container?" Kozlowski asked.

"Yep. Yep. And I had a blue one. Um, it was a blue one
and some garbage bags, and I brought that sheet of plastic. I had one at the house. I kept thinking I can't go buy
any more plastic because it's going to look funny—'He's
at Home Depot buying plastic.'"

Stephen and the detectives chuckled, then the murderer continued. "So I looked around the shop. I was
looking for something. I was looking for a hacksaw or
something, and we have a big band saw. I thought, 'I'll
use the band saw.' And I'm like, 'No, you can't use the
band saw. It's going to be too much of a mess.'

"So I remembered that my dad had . . . needed a hacksaw for something, when he had one of the band saw
blades break. They stay very straight, perfectly straight.
They're, like, an inch wide, and they're ten teeth per
inch, and they're high carbon steel. So I took one of the
old ones and I broke it and snapped another piece off, and
I wrapped a washcloth or a blue towel around it and
I started cutting with that. And it worked, but then it got
dull fast. It was used blades. So I thought, if I got a new
blade and do the same thing . . .

"So I got a new blade and broke it into pieces. I cut
Tara's hands off. And I cut her next joint, and the next
joint, and at some point I threw up. And I threw up
again. And I drank some more whiskey. And then I just
told myself, 'Look, if you don't do this, you're going to
prison for the rest of your life.' And I kept cutting her."

"When you cut the pieces off, like her hands, what did
you do with them?" Kozlowski asked.

"Left 'em sitting there on the tarp."

"OK, no blood at this point or anything?" Kozlowski asked.

"Very little, like very little," Stephen recalled. "And it surprised me, to be honest. It . . . really surprised me. There was that little blood. Um, I couldn't get her pants off. So I just ripped the pant legs up to the waistband. And I cut as high as those, but the blade kept catching in the cloth. It would do everything, but it wouldn't go through the cloth.

"And when I was done, we had some plastic bags there at the shop. We had a roll of them. Another roll that had come from the house also—that was the garbage bags I had brought. But they were real thin. So I wrapped the pieces that were in there and I put 'em all in the bucket."

"The Tupperware thing?" McLean asked.

"Yeah, the Rubbermaid bin, in the bucket. I'm sorry. And then I put that over to the side. And I had taken everything and put 'em in these plastic bags, and that was still on the big piece of plastic, and then all that was left was Tara's torso. And I wrapped it in plastic. I think I put newspaper in there, too. At one point, there was some blood. It was real thicklike, like syrup. And so I put some newspapers down just to make sure it stayed put, and I rolled it all up and . . . that fit right on top of the bucket, just on top of the Rubbermaid bin. It fit just inside the rest of the parts that I had cut up."

"So you had Tara's entire body in one—" Kozlowski began.

"—in one Rubbermaid container," Stephen finished the sentence. "And I put all the dirty rags and the blades and the band saw blades in there also. Even the ones that hadn't been used. I put 'em all in there. And then I went and cleaned up the floor. Blood hadn't really gotten through, but there was some body matter that had gotten through. So I cleaned the floor the best I could and I kept throwing out the dirty rags in the . . . Rubbermaid container with the rest of Tara's remains."

Stephen said he backed Tara's Trooper into the shop. "I put the big . . . Rubbermaid container in the back with the . . . garbage bag . . . that had the laptop computer bag and her purse and all that in it. I put all that in the back of the truck. And I put the box that had the actual chopped-up computer and her phone and all that up in the front seat with me, because I said I was going to throw that out.

"I kept worrying someone was going to see me littering, and then I was going to get pulled over or something. So that's why I waited until Monday. Sunday afternoon, I went home and I stayed home as much as possible."

67

"On Sunday, I tried to make things as normal as possible for everybody," Stephen said. "And I continuously flirted with Verena, because I thought that was the only way I was going to be able to get through this was if she . . . She was a nice girl. She still is a nice girl."

"Yeah, she is," Kozlowski agreed.

"She's a very nice girl," McLean added.

"I kept thinking, 'What am I dragging her into?'" Stephen recalled. "And then I would think, 'Well, I'm going to get killed in prison. I don't want that.' And I'd do what I had to do. If I was fifteen years younger . . . because I had fallen in love with Verena anyhow, easily. Because she was a sweet girl, and she was nice and she was kind. And this whole time, she's thinking that Tara's left me, so she's trying to be comforting."

"We're on Monday now?" Kozlowski asked.

"Yes," Stephen replied. "Sunday night, Tara's body's in the back of her Trooper. We had a red sled in the back of the garage. I put the red sled in the back of Tara's Trooper. The blue bucket's in there and I drove around, trying to find somewhere to hide it. And I didn't know where I could go. I just didn't know. I kept thinking, 'You've got to think of something.' I was going to put the whole blue bucket in a Dumpster. But I'm like, 'No, the garbage man is going to dump it out. They're going to see pieces falling out and somebody's going to notice something.' So I'm like, 'Let's bury it, hide it.'"

"All the pieces that are in the Rubbermaid container, they're not wrapped? They're in one big piece of plastic?" Kozlowski asked.

"No, some were two pieces in one plastic bag," Stephen said. "They're these clear plastic bags, real paper-thin, like the kind they use for bottles and cans at Meijer. Real thin, clear forty-gallon bags. So I had wrapped them up, rolled them up."

"So this is Monday morning?" Kozlowski asked. "You're driving around with the sled?"

"At, like, three in the morning," Stephen said. "I left really early."

"Verena's home, your kids are at home?" Kozlowski asked.

"She's sleeping, the kids are sleeping," Stephen said. "And it wasn't that odd for me to go into work. Three o'clock early? No, but four, I've gone at four. So I go and I find somewhere that I thought would be good. There's an electrical power . . . line. Have you guys found this yet, or no?"

"Yes," Kozlowski said.

"OK, did you guys find all the parts?" Stephen wanted to know.

"Not all of them," Kozlowski said. "But I'm familiar with the power lines."

"We know what you're talking about," McLean added.

"OK. I had offered the guys earlier today to . . . if they . . . if you needed me to draw a map. I didn't know if you knew where any of it was."

"Did you drive up to the power lines?" Kozlowski asked.

"No, I didn't drive up," Stephen said. "Not in Tara's truck. I parked Tara's truck on the road because . . . I thought I was going to get stuck [in the snow]."

Stephen said he parked his wife's truck near an open

field. "So I put the sled . . . on the ground," he said. "And I put the blue bucket on the sled and balanced it. So I slid it back down the road, and I walked it up—pulled it up—that hill, and once I got up there . . . I could kind of see. I had no light, though. That was the problem."

Kozlowski asked how much snow was on the ground.

"It was before the big snow fell, [but] it was enough to move the sled pretty easily. I could pull it up there."

Stephen said he began pulling the sled up a snowy hill. "I got about a third of the way in before the hill starts dropping down," he said. "And . . . soon as I started going down, it was like Keystone Cops. The sled took off and now I'm chasing after the sled with Tara's remains and cut-up body in it down a hill.

"It had gone down maybe a hundred yards. I'm not sure exactly. I finally got it stopped when it fell over and it spilt. So now all these pieces are now fallen all over the place. So I took Tara's torso and I buried it in the snow. And then the pieces I put on the sled and I buried that in the snow. Just in the woods there."

"Were they all together on the sled?" McLean asked.

"They were all together on the sled," Stephen said. "And the torso was by itself. And then I dispersed all of the saw blades, and I had a pair of black shoes that I had been wearing, and, um—"

"By 'dispersed,' what do you mean?" Kozlowski asked.

"Threw away," Stephen said. "All away, all around there. I was standing where the sled was and I would throw a shoe, and I would throw a thing just to make everything kind of disappear into the forest. Again, at the time, I'm not thinking straight. I'm like, 'I've got to get rid of this. As far away from each other as possible.' Shoes, saw blades, the bow of the bow saw that I tried to use initially. Everything. Some rags.

"I did a very bad job of hiding anything," Stephen said. "It's right there in the open. So Tuesday, I went back. Tuesday afternoon, I was on the way home and called Verena and told her I was going to go running. Which isn't out of the ordinary at all. It's pretty normal. I'm trying to think what the closest way to get out there would be."

Stephen said he parked his Jeep and ran through a nature trail in Stony Creek Park. "A bunch of people saw me," he said. "I kind of freaked out by it. I'm like, 'Okay, no one's going to recognize me.' I had a hat on, gloves on. It was cold. It snowed a little more that Monday night, I think. So I ran north . . . back down where the power lines were, and I . . . ran in."

Stephen then backtracked to Monday morning: "After I had hidden everything, I had left that big blue bucket there still. And I knew I had to get that out of there. So later Monday morning . . . I'm sorry, I got confused."

"That's OK," McLean said.

"OK, so Monday morning . . . I'd taken the blue bucket up the hill, on the sled, and it dumped. I panicked and ran away. Then I went back in my truck later. I'd gone home, saw the kids, pretended nothing had happened, left, and Verena said something to me. She said, 'You've been up since early.' I said, 'What do you mean?' She's like, 'I heard you rustling around.' I'm like, 'No, I've been here all the time.' I figured she heard the car leave."

At that point, the tape ended. McLean slid another minicassette into the slot and pressed record.

68

"I was explaining how I had gone back into the house after dumping the bucket and running away in an absolute panic," Stephen began.

"Now the bucket's still got the body parts in it, right?" Kozlowski asked.

"And it's fallen over and it's broken," Stephen replied. "The blue bucket has a chunk fallen out of the corner, where it hit the log sliding down the hill. So I go back to the house, put Tara's truck away, walked in and went downstairs, and sat on the couch and turned the news on, and just hung out basically until Verena and the kids woke up. So I then went out and said good-bye to the kids, good-bye to Verena, and left in my truck."

Once again, Stephen headed back to Stony Creek Park. "I drove my truck this time, parked at the top, pulled in as far as I could, walked back to see if you could see my truck, and I didn't think you could," he said. "I'd driven my truck up the hill because I knew my Jeep could make it up, no problem. So I went down to where the bucket was dumped and I had put a pair of—Tara bought a box of, um, vinyl gloves for dyeing her hair. They were too small but I got 'em on my hands anyway.

"I went down and moved everything around. That's when I made the pile on the sled of the parts, and then her torso was buried separately. And then I took the blue bucket and put it in the back of my truck. And I think in the blue bucket there were some gloves and some of the plastic, like extra plastic. And I put that in the blue bucket so that it wouldn't be sitting there.

"And then I put the blue bucket in the back of my truck," Stephen recalled. He said he again drove to the Sterling Heights neighborhood where he grew up to dispose of the bag containing Tara's laptop computer, her purse, and other items. He said he threw the incriminating evidence into a Dumpster.

"So at this point, Tara's torso is buried in the snow, and the sled is buried in the snow with all the parts in the sled?" Kozlowski asked.

"This is on Monday?" McLean added.

"This is still on Monday, yes," Stephen said. "I'm sorry. I had gotten confused. But I had forgotten—what had reminded me was, I knew I had taken my truck in there. So then on Tuesday after work, I told Verena I was going to run. So I parked it [near the power lines] and ran north across and down, and some guy . . . There's a shooting range right there. And his dog chased me out in the road, and he said it was a nice dog, don't worry about it. And I kept thinking, 'Oh, my God, that guy saw me.' And I'm going to hide the body, you know?

"Nothing I can do about it," Stephen said. "So I went out, found the sled. Couldn't find the torso at first. Panicked a bit. Found it also. Took the sled down—there's a trail . . . that goes around through in there. So I took it down, across the woods.

"Once you get on the trail, it's easier to follow the trail, because there's skier tracks and stuff on it, or snow tracks. So I figured that would be an easy way to follow that. Went about maybe a quarter mile, half mile down, it felt like farther, but I could see a tree or a house up ahead of me that was lit up. So I didn't want to go too close that way."

Stephen said he walked back through the woods toward the power lines. "It seemed like it was real low ground there, and there was a lot of fallen trees. So I proceeded to take all of the parts off of the sled, and I [took the items] out of the bags and hid them. At first, I was going to do the same thing with the metal stuff and just disperse them, and I thought that would be a bad idea. And then, I don't know how I got the bright idea of hiding things up in the trees. That's pretty much what I did with everything. Under all the fallen trees. The hands, feet, Tara's head—everything."

Stephen said he put the too-small rubber gloves and all the excess plastic into a gallon Ziploc bag he'd brought from home. He then said something that contradicted a statement he'd made only minutes before: He said he'd purchased the rubber gloves, along with razor blades to cut open the plastic bags, at a local store. He said he bought coffee filters as well.

"And if you're thinking, 'Why did I buy coffee filters?' Because I told the lady I was making a project making flowers, and we were going to dye them, and that's why I needed the rubber gloves. But then I thought about it and went, 'Oh great, now I look like a crystal meth manufacturer.'" Stephen shared a laugh with the detectives.

"Well, that's what they always say on the news!" Stephen said in a jocular tone. "They're always buying coffee filters and rubber gloves. I'm thinking, 'Oh great, now they're calling the police, telling 'em that I'm manufacturing—'"

Kozlowski, always the cop, interrupted. "You didn't manufacture any crystal meth, did you?"

"I didn't make any crystal meth, I promise," Stephen replied.

Stephen's recollection of purchasing rubber gloves contradicted his earlier statement that he'd used rubber gloves Tara had purchased to dye her hair.

Stephen said he threw his hat and his knit winter gloves into the Clinton River. He said he hid the plastic

Ziploc bag in a tree—a move that would ultimately be his undoing when Sheila Werner found it a few weeks later.

He then said he removed the black fleece undergarments he'd worn that day and his running shoes, and put them all into a paper bag. Then, Wednesday morning, when he drove from his home to police headquarters to make the initial missing persons report, he again ventured into his old Sterling Heights neighborhood and threw the paper bag into a Dumpster, not far from where he'd disposed of Tara's laptop and other personal effects.

"So I made the report, paid that ticket. Oh! The other thing I did Tuesday was pay the other tickets," Stephen said. "Because I didn't want anything to pop up."

"Nine hundred dollars' worth of tickets," McLean said.

"In Clinton Township," Stephen said. "Yep. Because I had a lot of parking tickets, and one, two, I don't know—two tickets, plus the speeding tickets. And I had forgotten about the ones in Rochester, or I would have paid those on Tuesday also. But then . . . I told Deputy Hughes that I had an outstanding ticket and he's like, 'In Rochester.' So the light went off in my head, and I went, 'Crap. That ticket.'

"So I went and paid that one, and there's one in Troy also. I paid those two and then I was in the parking lot in Rochester when my brother-in-law Erik called me. And he said to me . . . he asked me something, and that's when I called and I ended up talking to you. They put me through to you. I thought I was so smart. And nothing."

"No problem," Kozlowski said, recalling the phone call he'd gotten from Stephen the afternoon of February 14, just a few hours after Stephen reported Tara missing. "So we came out to your house. You talked to us. You know what happened there. You had nothing in the house, right?"

"No, there was nothing at that point," Stephen said.

"At what point did you feel the need to contact an attorney?" McLean asked.

"That night," Stephen said. "After you guys left, I

called [a friend], but he's not that kind of attorney." He said he called another friend, who recommended David Griem. "And Thursday, David Griem told me to come straight to his office. Do not come in to you guys. Go see him first. He said he'd just finished a trial, and I was lucky, he said."

"Did you think you were going to tell Pam and myself [about the murder] when we were at your house the other night?" Kozlowski asked.

"No," Stephen replied.

"Did you have any intentions of telling us what happened at that point?" Kozlowski asked again.

"I thought about a lot of stuff," Stephen said.

"How do you think we treated you, Pam and I, Wednesday night?" Kozlowski asked.

"Cool," Stephen said. "You scared me at the end. And that was all it was. And whoever listens to this, I want them to understand—you guys were very nice. Right up until the end."

"So Thursday morning you . . . retained David Griem," Kozlowski said.

"Yep. And then he called you guys," Stephen said, "and told you I wasn't coming in. And then I left his office."

Stephen then complained about being pulled over by police on February 15. He said earlier that day, officers stopped Verena near his home. "She said there was two cars parked at the end of my road, where the new bus stop is. [An officer] got out of their car and told her to stop. And she was like, 'What is it all about?'

"They said they were looking for me," Stephen said. "They asked her if I was at home. And she said no. And they said, 'OK, we'll wait here for him.' That's what they told her. Because when I called, she was crying in the garage, and I was like, 'What are you crying for?' And she explained."

69

"OK, let's get that over," Kozlowski said. "You got stopped, you got arrested. Your attorney said I interrogated you in the jail. Which—"

"Oh, no, no," Stephen interjected. "All I told him was that everybody who I had run into—every policeman that was there—kept asking questions. And they did. They were like, 'What happened? What are you in here for?'"

"That's normal, just doing the booking process and they always do that, just getting you in and out," McLean said.

"So what happened?" Kozlowski prodded. "You got out of jail Thursday night?"

"Thursday night," Stephen confirmed.

"And then what?" Kozlowski asked.

"Nothing," Stephen replied. "A week and a half, nothing. And then, the following Wednesday . . . the sheriff announced he was going to search the park. And I thought, 'I'm screwed. They're going to find that torso that at this point was still buried in the snow.' So I tried to get up . . . Thursday night to do it, and I couldn't wake up. I set my alarm, and my alarm didn't go off or something. So then Saturday morning, at like three-thirty in the morning, I woke up and I waited around, so it wouldn't seem weird."

"This is after you dropped off the laptops when I saw you on Friday?" Kozlowski asked.

"Yep. Yep. Yep. It was that night, into Saturday morning," Stephen said. "And I ran from the house because I didn't want my mom (who was visiting from Arizona) to hear the car driving away, wondering why I'm driving at five in the morning."

Stephen said he jogged from his house to Stony Creek Metropark. "I located the torso," he said. "And I was worried because I kept thinking someone might see my footprints. Because the snow was crunchy by then, I was thinking they would see the footprints when they're searching. So I found the torso, where it was, and literally carried it. And it was so heavy, and my legs were hurting so bad."

"Was it in the bags, in the garbage?" McLean asked. "What was it in?"

"It was still wrapped in that plastic," Stephen said.

"How did you carry it?" McLean asked.

"I put it over my shoulder and carried it," Stephen said. "I mean, it was frozen. *She* was frozen." Stephen said he tucked the torso behind a tree in the park, then ran home. "And then I told [my mother] I was going to get her a cup of coffee. And then I took two black garbage bags with me."

"You drove back there in the Commander?" Kozlowski asked.

"Nope, in Tara's truck," Stephen said.

"OK, so you went back and got the torso," Kozlowski prompted.

"Yep. And put it in the back of the truck."

"Put it in the back of the truck," Kozlowski repeated. "In the bags, or . . . ?"

"In the bags. Yep. [The torso] in one bag, and put the bag in another bag," Stephen recalled. "Stuck that in the back of the truck, thinking that there was no bleeding or anything. So then I got home and I went to get coffee, and the coffee place was busy . . . so I went to Speedway (a local gas station) instead, got a newspaper and a . . . a—"

"Coffee," Kozlowski finished.

"And . . . went home and told my mom the coffee place was too busy. I couldn't get coffee. Left it at that. Went back to the truck. It was Saturday."

"So that was the search that day," Kozlowski said.

"It was the search that day," Stephen agreed. "At about twelve, I . . . drove to the shop. And drove with the torso in the back of the truck. Tara's truck. Drove to the shop and hid the torso in the shop, up on top of the roof in the shop. I had put it in three or four black plastic bags at this point. It was frozen. Now I was concerned that it was going to thaw out in the shop. So I left it there until the night you guys searched."

"So you left it there until Thursday," McLean probed.

"Until Thursday."

"On top of the roof of the shop?" McLean asked.

"On top of the roof of the office," Stephen corrected.

"Yeah, I know what you mean," Kozlowski said. "You've got a built-in room. OK. You've got it up there in the blue container."

"Nope. Nope. No, no, no."

McLean corrected her partner: "In the plastic garbage bags."

"Yes," Stephen said. Then he explained the layout of his father's shop: "It's a big shop, and there there's like . . . offices. With a roof."

McLean was confused: "Is it on the outside where you put her, or—"

"Built-in room," Kozlowski said. "I saw it. A room that's up in top of the shop."

"The office has ceilings," Stephen explained. "And then there's a ceiling of the building. And . . . the shop building is about twice as tall as the office . . . and there's a wood floor up there (on the office roof), and some metal and stuff. And I kind of hid [the torso] behind something up there. And then I was worried. I'm like, 'What am I going to do with her?' And I don't know why I . . . When did you do your search? Friday?"

"Friday night," McLean said.

"OK, so Friday morning I went and got the green bucket . . . no, Thursday?"

"Can we back up a little bit?" McLean asked. "The day of the search, the day they searched Stony Creek, they didn't find anything. Were you surprised?"

"Oh yeah," Stephen said. "And by then, I thought I got away with it."

"I couldn't believe that that morning I was able to run out there, dig up that torso, and hide it in the back of the car," Stephen recalled. "You have to understand that I was shocked—I mean, absolutely shocked that I didn't get found."

"OK, so it's, like, Thursday night," Kozlowski said.

"No, I think it was Thursday during the day . . . that I put the torso back in the bucket. So now . . . from Saturday it's in there—Sunday, Monday, Tuesday, Wednesday. Must be Thursday morning and nobody has searched anything. I kept thinking, 'Wow, I got away with it. I can't believe I got away with it.' I'm thinking, 'Now what do I do? The torso is in the shop. It's got to get disposed of.' So I figured the parts were hidden. If you didn't find them, then they're hidden real well."

Stephen said he took his wife's torso from the office roof and put it into her Trooper. "Friday morning, I got up, took the green bucket up, back out of the back of . . . Tara's Trooper, put it on the ground, slid it behind my truck and just . . . hid it over there. And then . . . I had cleared a little spot out and put the green bucket where it was out of the way. And I really don't know what I was going to do with it."

"So Thursday during the day, somehow you bring

up a green Tupperware container from home . . . Rubbermaid . . . ," Kozlowski said.

"Rubbermaid," Stephen confirmed. "A different one. The blue one I had already thrown away. I didn't want it kind of sticking out, so I moved some of the kids' stuff over to make the space wide enough to put it," Stephen said. "And I put it in."

Then, Stephen said, he went to work because a storm had knocked the power out to his home. A few hours later, "when I was driving home, Deputy [Anthony] Szalkowski pulled me over, that I knew from previous dealings with kids in the neighborhood," he said. After Szalkowski made the stop, Captain Wickersham, who had been waiting in a separate police cruiser, informed Stephen he had a warrant to search his home.

"OK," Kozlowski said. "So you go up, you get back up to the house, get your keys, and talk to the people there at the house."

"Yep."

"And then you leave."

"Yep," Stephen said. "I was in an utter panic. I kept thinking, 'They're out in the garage searching. They're going to, like, get me. Right now.' I'm thinking, 'Why should I sit in the car with Deputy Szalkowski?' I figured you found something already. And then I went home and you were just searching the house. And I'm like, 'I've got to run.'"

"OK, so you get out of the house, take the dog," Kozlowski probed.

"And [Mike Zanlungo] came along, picked me up, they told me to call somebody. So Mike took me to his house. I was in a big hurry to get out of there. I kept thinking the first place you're going to start is the garage. Or, I mean, I didn't know where you guys started, but I knew that bucket was going to get found eventually. So I turned my phone off, again, because I thought you tracked me last time using my phone, so I turned it off. And Mike lent me a car. He lent me the yellow truck."

"And what did you do?" Kozlowski asked.

"I drove to my sister's, and I kept thinking you'd be sitting on the house, like staking it out or whatever," Stephen replied. "And so I called my sister from a pay phone, using a phone card. And I talked to her, and she said they were at church still. So I went to say good-bye to the kids and asked Kelly if I could borrow her key to put the dog away and get something to drink. Um, what I really wanted was a .38. I was going to kill myself. That was the plan."

70

Stephen said he couldn't find the gun in his sister's house. "Looked everywhere," he said.

"Good thing, eh?" Kozlowski asked.

"It would have been real fast," Stephen answered.

"OK, so you go to her house," Kozlowski said.

"Go to the house. Leave the dog there. Searched. Quickly as I could. Couldn't find anything, so I took . . . Chris had some Vicodin, so I took those."

The tape again ran out, so McLean turned the tape over to side B and the interview resumed. "So you were searching for pills," Kozlowski began.

"Looking for something I can take because I can't find the .38," Stephen said. "I figure I've got to do it with something, and there was a bottle of Ambien. It was empty. And she had these little tiny pills. She gets migraines. So I figure it has to be some pretty heavy narcotics to make a migraine go away, so I figure it would be something pretty good to take. I took some of those and I took something called Toprodeck. And then I left.

"Got in the truck and then I drove around," Stephen continued. "Oh, and I borrowed my sister's phone. She had given me her phone, or Chris's phone, actually. And she kept mine. And I kept telling her, 'I'm going to get arrested,' and she's like, 'For what?' I'm surprised I didn't tell her at the time. So I told her, [a friend] told me if they find one drop of blood, I'm going to prison. So I said I'm going to drive around for a while, and Kelly said, 'OK.' I don't think she . . . I don't think . . . don't know—she might have put two and two together, but I don't think she really thought about it that way. I called her a couple times. I called my voice mail a couple times from different places."

"What different places did you use a pay phone?" Kozlowski asked.

"Pay phone and that cell phone," Stephen said. "I knew they might be able to look at the cell phone, so I kept turning it off. And then I'd turn it on and call, and turn it off. Man, I drove everywhere. I mean, I drove all over the place. I'm trying to think of somewhere to go. So I remembered the first trip Tara and I took was to the Wilderness State Park. We stayed in a cabin."

"I saw pictures of it on the Internet. It looked pretty nice," Kozlowski said.

"Did Kelly tell you?" Stephen asked.

"Tell us what?" Kozlowski wondered.

"That I went there."

"No," McLean said.

"Oh. I called her," Stephen said. "Again, I think I was reaching out."

(In fact, Kelly had told police Stephen was in Wilderness State Park, but the detectives weren't going to tell that to the suspect.)

"So how did you get up here?" Kozlowski asked. "What was your route?"

Stephen described a chaotic search for the correct expressway, one that took him through various suburbs, including Warren, where he stopped at a gas station across from General Motors' fabled Tech Center, to Big Beaver Road in tony Troy, where he buzzed right past a police station. "I don't remember how I got to Lansing," Stephen said. "Maybe the Vicodin . . . the painkillers had calmed my nerves down, too."

"So you're in Lansing," Kozlowski said.

"I'm in Lansing. And I was going to call [a friend]. The lawyer. And have him turn me in. But I couldn't do it. I couldn't bring myself to make the phone call."

"Why would you call [your friend] and have him turn you in, and not your attorney?" McLean wondered.

"Because [Griem's] a dick," Stephen said. "Don't tell David, but he's a dick."

"Can I tell him?" Kozlowski asked.

"That I said he's a dick? No," Stephen said amid laughter.

Kozlowski then asked, "Can I tell him that I think he's a dick?"

"Sure," Stephen answered.

"We have no problem with that," McLean joked.

"Because he is," Stephen continued. "I don't know . . . He's mean. There were some things that I thought he would be good to do, like talk to you guys. He said, 'No, only faxes back and forth.'"

"If we sat down and talked to you, would you have told us what happened?" McLean wondered.

"Maybe," Stephen answered. "You don't understand. In this three-week ordeal, I wanted to tell somebody."

"I believe it," Kozlowski said.

"We believe you," McLean chimed in.

71

"What counts is, you're telling now," Kozlowski reiterated a little later.

"That's what matters," McLean added.

"You know what people remember?" Kozlowski asked. "They'll always remember what your last good act was. OK? So . . . you get up near the Lansing area."

"Yeah, I don't know how I got there," Stephen said.

"Did you ever buy a phone?" Kozlowski asked.

"I bought a phone at Rite Aid at five minutes to ten, because they were closing at ten, and I wanted in. I had to pee so bad. And I'm standing there, kind of dancing on two feet, and the ladies are [asking], 'What are you looking for?' And I said, 'I need a phone.' And they're like, 'They don't come precharged.' So I bought an Energizer phone charger. And it didn't fit. So I'm like, 'Damn it.' So I had to use a plug somewhere.

"So I stopped at a rest area somewhere," Stephen continued. "And I used a plug and I left it plugged in for just . . . No, I didn't. I didn't end up doing that because I was going to do it, and I turned the phone on. It worked. It had, like, one and a half batteries. I'm like, 'OK, I'll warm it up.' So I put it in my pocket and heated the battery up. It generates more power. It's rechargeable. And it got enough power to work. And I kept it in my pocket the whole time. Off. Turned off. Because I didn't know if they could ping that, too."

Stephen said he continued driving north, into Michigan's "thumb" area. "I stopped at a couple different places, and I was by Flint, and then I went across and I came back down to [Highway] 69. And I took 69 into Lansing. That's how I got there."

"Somewhere I bought a box of razor blades and sleeping pills," Stephen said. "And I was blown away. I was thinking of them, saying, 'Oh, I can't sell you that.' Let's see—self checkout." Stephen shared a laugh with the detectives. "Well, if you saw someone buying razor blades and sleeping pills, wouldn't you have said something?" Stephen asked.

"You would think a lot," McLean agreed.

"Hey, I guess when you think about it, I guess I'd think the same thing, too," Kozlowski said. "But you know, them scanner people, they just scan it."

"No, she wasn't there," Stephen said. "No, I went to self–scan. But, still, people saw me buying stuff. And I'm thinking to myself, 'How is somebody not going, "Hey, you have razor blades and sleeping pills?" No! No! No! No! "Did you need to talk to a crisis person or something?"'"

"So you buy it at Meijer self-check, get out of there," Kozlowski said.

"Yeah," Stephen said. "I bought something else. And I tried to stay at a hotel, too."

"What happened?" Kozlowski asked. "You didn't have a credit card?"

"No, I had cash," Stephen said. "Five hundred dollars."

"Where'd you get it?" Kozlowski asked.

"At a gas station," Stephen answered. "But they had LaSalle banks. I don't get charged with a service fee. I know it doesn't make any sense." There was more laughter.

"OK, so . . . you're running," Kozlowski said. "You got five hundred dollars out. But you find a LaSalle Bank so you don't get charged a service charge."

McLean, still laughing, commented, "But you're intending on committing suicide."

"Yep."

"You're all right in my book, Steve," Kozlowski joked.

"Keep going," McLean added. "This is getting good."

"OK, wait," Stephen said. "Let's go back. I'm driving north on some road and that's where I stop a couple times. I've got to eat. Oh, it was on Lapeer Road. I go north on Lapeer Road from the Palace (of Auburn Hills, home of the Detroit Pistons basketball team). And I listen to the message from Captain Wickersham . . . at the house, saying he wanted to know where the key was to the wine cellar. I wasn't going to call him so he could ping me. I'm telling you that's what I thought at that point. I thought, 'No way. I can't call. And then they'll know right where I am.'

"So I drove north on Lapeer Road," Stephen continued. "And at some time, I called my sister and I called my dad. And that's when your two deputies were at my sister's house. I was on the phone with her. That was about the same time I was on the little cut across the road by the Palace. A policeman's on the corner—there's something going on at the Palace. It was the first time I thought, 'OK, he's going to pull the gun and point it at me, and I'm going to die.'

"So he didn't. He just waved me through," Stephen said. "I keep driving north, driving north, and driving north. And then I stopped a couple places. At some point, I bought the first pint of Jack Daniel's. And then a fifth of Baileys at some little liquor store in Lapeer. And I saw a sheriff's deputy then, too. Drive right past him. He didn't come up behind me and flip his lights on—

which I figured by this time . . . if there's a found corpse at the house, I figured I'm a wanted man.

"Then I figured they don't know what car I'm driving, but they had to have written down Mike's license plate number when he picked me up. And then I thought, 'Well, it's a company car. He works for Chrysler. It was a company car. Maybe they won't know who it is.' So I cut across all the little back roads to the Rite Aid, where I bought the phone, the pay-to-go phone. And I stopped at a couple of them gas stations and nobody had one. So one guy had one, but it was a piece of junk. But I found one at the Rite Aid and it worked."

72

Stephen told the detectives he stopped at a rest area and called the 800 number in order to activate his new cell phone. "And that tells me it could take twenty-four to forty-eight hours to make it work. And I'm like, 'God-damn it!' I wasted all that time to find a phone and it's still going to take a day, so I'm not going to be able to say good-bye to anybody.

"So I drove into Lansing, and that's when I bought the sleeping pills. I stopped three times. I bought sleeping pills and razor blades, a toy gun, a Sharpie to make the red end of the toy gun black, because I figure if it came down to it, I'd point the toy gun at the policeman and he'd shoot me. And he would have done that—if you point a gun at a cop, you're going to get shot. That's what I figured."

"You bought the gun at Meijer's?" Kozlowski asked.

"Yeah, at Meijer's," Stephen confirmed. "Then I went on [Highway] 127 to 27 to Clare. I stopped in Mount Pleasant and actually went into the Soaring Eagle Casino and tried, figuring they'd have a room. They didn't have a room. So I went to another hotel and they didn't have any rooms, and I said, 'Forget it!' So I drove to Clare."

Kozlowski stopped the recorder at that point to take a break.

* * *

At 9:46 P.M., the tape again started rolling. "So where was I?" Stephen asked. "I couldn't get a hotel. The casino didn't have any rooms available. There was some conference, or country concert going on, so they . . . hooked me up with a place up in . . . must have been Clare. I think at some point into Mount Pleasant and Clare is when I decided I was going to drive up here. So I turned and got on 75 somewhere. I kept thinking I could go north on 127, but for some reason I kept thinking I was going to get pulled over because they were going to be looking for the car again. I kept thinking, 'I've got to get rid of this car. A bright yellow four-door pickup truck—how many of those are there?'

"And then I started seeing some bright yellow four-door pickup trucks. I'm like, 'There's a lot of them.' I was still worried. I didn't want to get pulled over. So I . . . I drove the weirdest way up here. I drove 75, then I'm like, 'I can't get into Grayling,' so I . . . cut across West Branch somehow. And in West Branch I was going to get a hotel room, then I started getting paranoid. They had to be looking for me, I'm thinking.

"So I bought the *News* and the *Free Press*. And there's [the headline] 'Cops Search the Grant Home,' and there's nothing (about police searching for Stephen). And I listened to the radio. They don't have (the AM news station WWJ) 950 up there. Because on 950 back home, they would pipe in every two minutes: 'We're looking for Stephen Grant.'"

A new tape was put in, and Stephen continued recounting his journey across Michigan: "I got off at Seven Mile Road in Grayling, just south of Grayling."

"Four Mile," Kozlowski corrected him.

"Four Mile. I got off there and drove across. And there, I got on some dirt road that I thought would take me back to 27. And it was an oil field. And I got completely lost in this oil field. Like, totally. I thought, 'I'm going to be stuck out here.' I'm thinking, 'This is not where I want to die!' I kept thinking, 'No, this is not going to end this way.' So I put the truck in four-wheel drive. And I knew I was just south of Camp Grayling (a Michigan National Guard training center), and there's oil fields just south of that. There's military roads running north and south, and there's oil fields off of there. But it didn't go anywhere. I got on this road and every time I got to a corner of the thing, it dead-ended," Stephen recalled. He said he approached a sign: *Do not go any farther; unexploded ordinance.*

"I'm thinking, 'OK, so now an MP is going to come out here and he's going to get me,'" he said. Finally, Stephen said, he approached Wilderness State Park. "Tara and I had gone there," he said. "And that was the first place we'd ever went, our first trip ever. It's a good place to end it."

73

Stephen careened around the sparsely driven country roads, finally ending up at the corner of Lakeshore and Lakeview Roads, right next to Sturgeon Bay.

"So I sat there for a while at the south entrance to the park, and I tried to write a note to the kids. I hadn't taken any sleeping pills yet. But I'd taken enough Vicodin that I was really loopy by that point. I mean, I could barely see to drive. I actually went back in to buy more whiskey because I figured I'd drink whiskey with sleeping pills—that's how they do it on TV, kill themselves. That's how the rock stars go. Go off to sleep and freeze to death.

"It was weird," Stephen said. "I was hallucinating. I was seeing stuff. I don't know if it was lack of sleep, plus the booze, plus the Vicodin, but I wasn't seeing straight. So I tried to write out a couple times to the kids, just explaining. But I couldn't do it. Some guy on skis—when I got back from buying the alcohol, the guy on skis . . . saw me, waved at me. And I waved. And I started walking.

"I put the notepad in a bag . . . and an extra pen in my pocket and the booze in there, and the sleeping pills I put in there and by now empty Vicodin bottle. Put that in my pocket. Before I left, I called my sister. And she told me that she wanted to know. Basically, I'm fucked-up. I said 'Tomorrow morning call the DNR and tell them where they can find my body. Basically, [that's] what I wanted them to do, so I wouldn't just rot out here in the woods."

Law enforcement officials would later comment on the irony of Stephen worrying about rotting in the woods, after the way he left his wife's body parts in Stony Creek Metropark.

"There's a cabin out there," Stephen said. "There's a cabin on the north end, and there's one you can only access in the summer. But I figured with snow, I could make it there, and I didn't have any match with me, so I knew I wouldn't be able to make any heat. So I figured I'd just freeze to death out in the cabin. And so I figured that way I could just sit and write. And I told Kelly that I'd already taken all the sleeping pills, and she asked, 'What?' And I asked her what the little pills were, and she didn't know what they were. She couldn't recognize what they were. I'm sure I was slurring my speech.

"I told Kelly about Waugoshance. 'That way you'll know what park it is.' I said, 'Really, you aren't going to find out until . . .' I didn't give her the spelling. 'Call and find out where there's a cabin called Waugoshance,' I said. 'I'm there,' I said. 'My body will be in the southern cabin. At the south end of the thing.' And I walked out. I started to go through the woods, and it was too hard going. So I went down to the lake, and I walked up the ice. I kept seeing somebody behind me and somebody in front of me. I kept thinking I was being followed."

"Were they real people or were you just hallucinating?" McLean asked.

"I think I was just trying to find somebody, or find a reference point to see if the person was moving," Stephen said. "I'm like, 'If they're by a tree, they're not going to move.' And . . . they're looking for somebody—that's what I was thinking. By the time I got to the sign—there's a sign ahead of me—I thought the sign said, 'Waugoshance

Cabin in here,' uh, but it didn't. 'Wilderness area'—no. 'Bird nesting area, keep off the grass.' And I walked up over the sand dunes and got in the woods, and I realized why they call it Wilderness State Park. It's a wilderness. I mean, it hasn't been developed. No trees have been cut out of there. I was literally walking through fallen trees and trees," Stephen said, "then I got in that valley, and I couldn't find my way out. It's way down."

"You were nowhere near the cabins," Kozlowski observed. "You were far from the cabins."

"No, the cabins on the north," Stephen said. "I know where the four are. But there's one south one. And I thought, 'I can make it.' In the middle of the night out to that cabin. I talked to people to stay awake."

"Who'd you talk to?" McLean asked.

"The trees."

"OK," she said.

"I told you, there were people out there," Stephen stressed. "There were a lot of people out there. There's nobody. But in my mind . . . Alicia and Erik were out there, and they were sitting there, like in judgment of me. And everyone I talked to wouldn't talk back, I thought, because they hate me."

"So at any point did you run from people?" McLean asked. "Did you run from officers that were trying to apprehend you?"

"You're down in the valley," Kozlowski said. "You're stuck down there, right? You don't have any way to get out of there, right?"

"I laid down," Stephen said. "I'd been [running] for so long, and I kept falling. And I kept [running]. I put my hands on the branch and I kept falling off."

McLean said, "Well, I'm not a doctor or anything like that, but I would guess with the alcohol, the pills, the stress, the hypothermia . . ."

"Oh yeah," Stephen agreed. "I'm thinking the same

thing. Yeah, I'm not a doctor, either, but I figure that's exactly—"

"What's the next thing you remember?" Kozlowski interrupted.

"Someone telling me, 'Get down, motherfucker!'" Stephen said. "And I'm like, 'I think they have a machine gun.' Like an MP-5 or something."

74

Kozlowski tried to get Stephen to describe the moments before his capture. "It looked like they were tracking you, and it looked like you were probably stopping in spots," the burly detective said. "Did you take anything with you when you were out there? Did you drop stuff along the way?"

"Yeah, I had that bag," Stephen said. "I had that bag that had the . . . booze and the—what'd I have?—the pen."

"What ever happened to the pistol?" Kozlowski asked.

"Oh, that was in the bag, too," Stephen recalled. "The plastic bag. I must have dropped that at some point, too."

"I guess, according to the sheriff, it appeared, you know, that you were stopping at spots and laying in the snow," Kozlowski told Stephen. "And that might have been when you were trying to get out of there, and you were sitting down and resting and moving."

The second tape ran out, and McLean put a third cassette into the machine at 10:03 P.M.

"I know that [I] walked in the woods, and it was just too hard going," Stephen said. "I know I'm getting far enough away from the car to die. 'Would someone find me?' was my concern. And I wasn't running from anybody. I was just trying to get far enough that by the time they tracked me down, I'd be frozen stiff. That's really it. I might have stopped. I have no idea. I don't really remember stopping and going."

"What do you remember?" Kozlowski asked. "Do you

remember the helicopters? Do you remember the guy coming up to you and saying—"

"Oh yeah," Stephen said. "I do remember now. OK, and then they carried me out, and two really big men picked me up and told me that I had to walk back. I couldn't walk. And I remember them putting me in a basket, like an Easter basket, and we were in that helicopter, and it was . . . uh, it was the Coast Guard or something, was it?"

"Yes," Kozlowski confirmed.

"The only reason—they make a certain noise, and we have them fly over the shop all the time, and they give a different noise than a regular helicopter," Stephen said. "They have that turbine in the back through a regular propeller, so it doesn't make the same noise, and I knew that's what it was, but it didn't land. It actually, like, just came in and hovered."

"Right," Kozlowski said. "I understand they pulled you up in the basket."

"Yep, and then that last thing, and then this morning waking up," Stephen said. "I remember somebody coming in there to cut my feet off, or saying something. They were going to take my feet off, and I . . . remember saying no, and I don't think she was listening to me, and I remember her saying they were going to amputate my feet off. I remember saying no, or that was on my mind."

"OK, that puts us to right now then," Kozlowski said.

"Yep," Grant said.

Kozlowski wanted to go over a few things that Stephen had told him. "It's a whole lot of information, and it's a whole lot of time."

"I hear ya," Stephen said.

Kozlowski started to ask a question, but Stephen interrupted him. "Can I ask what they found? Like what pieces they're still looking for?" Stephen asked. "Maybe I could help."

"Sure," Kozlowski said. "They obviously found her torso, found Tara's head. We found both her hands, one of her arms—basically what we're missing is from the knee down and one of the arms."

"It's all under the trees," Stephen said in an easy tone. "Like, if they look in the same area—I didn't walk but twenty-five yards in any direction to find a tree."

"OK," Kozlowski mused.

"Did they find the sled?"

"No," both detectives answered.

"Oh, that's right there somewhere," Stephen said. "It's, like, right by the edge of the woods, where the power lines start. Because I put it there, and that same morning, I was going to take the torso and bring it down to the same area, but it was getting late, and—"

"Was the sled buried or anything?" Kozlowski asked.

"I kind of tossed some snow over it, but it was a bright red sled," Stephen said. "I didn't want it to be visible that you would see it, but I didn't never take it out of there. Someone may have taken it that walked that trail, you know? 'Hey, I found a free sled.'"

McLean deadpanned, "Uh-huh."

"Right," Stephen answered. "It's got blood all over it."

"It does?" McLean perked up.

"Yeah, yeah," Stephen said. "I mean, I would assume it does. It had bloody stuff on it—the bags, and stuff in the bags tore when I was taking them out of it, and then I used the razor blades that I bought with the coffee filters and stuff to open the bag."

"So when you went back to move her torso, you did not remove some or any other parts?" McLean asked.

"I didn't know where they were," Stephen said. "It was that morning of the search, and I figured I was going to get in there, because I figured that stuff was hidden well enough because I had put it up under trees and stuff.

"I figured unless they bring dogs in there that know how to smell for that kind of stuff, then there's no way,"

Stephen said. "But did I figure you guys would find it? Yeah, I figured for sure you guys would find that stuff."

"Now, when it wasn't found that day, and we still weren't coming to your house, you were thinking you got away with it, correct?" McLean asked.

"Yeah, that's exactly what I thought," Stephen said. "And I kept asking David, 'Why don't they search the house? Why don't they search the house?' But there was nothing at the house—I mean, was there stuff at the house?"

"There was stuff, but nothing other or larger than the torso," McLean said. "There were other things we needed."

"Oh," Stephen said.

Kozlowski added, "But for the most part, everything you used to cut Tara up was all those blades from the band saw."

"That's all it was," Stephen said.

"And you cut her up at the shop?" McLean probed.

"At the shop, on a piece of Visqueen, or plasticlike—it was drop cloth, that's right, it was too thin. If it was thicker, it wouldn't have ripped. That's why I cleaned the floors," Stephen said. "And I actually cleaned the floor at the house on Sunday, but that's normal. We always clean the floor at the house."

"OK," the detectives said simultaneously.

"It's a wood floor," Stephen explained. "So I cleaned the floor on Sunday just because you could see a—I think I could see a line, like when I dragged Tara . . . in the wood. And I kept thinking I can see something."

"The kids?" McLean asked.

"Excuse me?" Stephen wanted clarification.

"When you were dragging her downstairs, or anything—do they usually sleep that soundly?" McLean asked.

"That concerned me," Stephen said. "But right after I got her down, I checked on the kids."

At that point, the tape was stopped so the three could take a break.

75

"We're just going to ask you a few more questions, Steve, all right?" McLean started.

"No, we're fine," Stephen said.

"Thanks. Let's clarify some things. We're going to go back to February ninth," McLean said.

"OK."

"OK, February ninth, when Tara comes home—can you just tell us again what transpired that day?" McLean asked. "I just wanted to go over it one more time to make sure we got it straight."

"Tara brought her bags in. She was listening to her headphones when she came in . . . because I yelled down to her and she didn't answer. And I walked down and she had her headphones—her iPod in her ear—and I got kind of disgusted.

"Then she came upstairs and went downstairs and upstairs a couple more times, and she was in the bathroom putting her stuff away, and she came out and she had told me that she was going to try to travel back on Sunday. It was more important. And I told her, 'No, I want you home,' and I said something about Lou—that 'you're only going down there because Lou's down there,' and she said no. She said, 'Why do you always think Lou?'

"'I don't know,'" Steve recalled the conversation with his wife that night. "'It's just weird how you get to travel that much together.' And she said, 'Well, what the hell do you think I'm doing?' and somehow that elevated to the point where I called her something—'Are you fucking him?'—and she slapped me, and I hit her back."

"Did you punch her back, or open hand? Closed hand?" McLean asked.

"Open. Prior to that, I grabbed her wrist. And she spun. She started to turn and told me, 'I'm not talking to you any more,' and I grabbed her wrist and I said something, and that's when she slapped me, and I don't even know how I hit her."

"OK," McLean said.

"I think I just . . . I went to hit her and I think I hit her on the side of the neck," Stephen continued. "And I kind of . . . I don't know, like knocked the wind out of her, but she fell backwards, then she thumped. But she was fine.

"And she started telling me that we're over, and that she's going to take the kids, and I hit her, and if a man hits a woman, he goes to jail and she gets the kids and the house and everything. And she said, 'Screw you, you'll never see your kids again.'"

"And that pissed you off," McLean ventured.

"I grabbed her neck," Stephen said. "And at first I was only grabbing her neck to make her stop talking—to make her shut up."

"What were you thinking?" McLean wanted to know.

"Shut up, stop it, don't say that," Stephen said. "And then—"

"She grabbed your hand," McLean finished the sentence.

"It wasn't then. It wasn't that fast," Stephen said. "She didn't really try to fight me then."

"OK," McLean said. "Was she still talking, with your hand on her neck?"

"No, she wouldn't fight right away, and I just squeezed, and she . . . um, that's when I realized that I was going to go to prison for hurting her," Stephen said. "She was going to tell somebody. I've got to make her not tell."

McLean would later divulge how disgusted she was that Stephen was able to discuss the murder and dismemberment of his wife so casually, as if he were discussing the latest hockey scores. But she continued questioning the subject without a hint of her true feelings.

"OK, so she was getting up, you put your hand on her neck," she said. "You squeezed her neck. How did you—"

"Well, she . . . she hadn't really gotten up, that was the thing," Stephen said. "She'd fallen backwards, and she was still kind of halfway sitting up. Her mouth was going a mile a minute, saying, 'You're done, you're done, you're done.'"

"OK, at what point in time did you think that . . . what did she do that made you let go of her?" McLean asked. "Did she go limp? Did she shut her eyes?"

"She quit moving."

"Just quit moving?" McLean asked.

"Yeah, I just kept squeezing. Just kept squeezing, squeezing, squeezing, and wouldn't let go. And that's when I covered up her face."

"And then what did you do?" McLean asked.

"Then I held it over her face and I kept squeezing her neck. I was only covering her face . . . so I wouldn't have to look at her. Couldn't look at her."

"So something was right by you that you could grab while you were still holding on to her neck?" McLean asked.

"Yeah, it was just to my left," Stephen recalled. "I remember grabbing it in my left hand, and . . . there's laundry there. I mean, it was right there, where the laundry basket is."

"And you grabbed it, put it over her face."

"Yep."

"Still held on to her neck."

"Yep."

"And then she went limp? Quit moving?"

"She was dead."

"So you let go of her?"

"Yep."

"What did you do then?" McLean asked.

"That's when I decided I had to put her somewhere," Stephen said.

"How did you know she was dead, and wasn't unconscious?"

"It was too long."

"Too long?"

"Oh yeah, yeah, too long," Stephen said. "Too much time had gone by. I knew she was dead. She wasn't moving at all. I didn't feel a pulse. I didn't feel anything. I'd been squeezing as hard as I could. I wanted her to shut up."

Kozlowski, silent for several minutes, asked Stephen when he put the belt around his wife's neck.

"That's where I'm going," Stephen replied.

"Were you still upstairs?" McLean asked. "You stayed upstairs with her?"

"And the belt was right there by the thing," Stephen said referring to Tara's body. "I knew I had to take her downstairs and get her out of there, and I was going to take her and put her in the truck and make the truck go away before Verena got home. Because when I had gotten her out in the garage, and the belt broke, and Tara . . . her head fell back on the cement and made that noise."

"Was she bleeding some?" McLean asked.

"There was no blood."

"There's no blood?" she asked again.

"There was no blood," Stephen repeated.

"Did the back of her head hit the cement, or the front of her head?" Kozlowski asked.

"The back of her head," Stephen said. "When she fell backwards . . . because it—the belt that I'd been dragging her with was old."

"How were you dragging her?" McLean asked. "Was she facedown? On her back?"

"On her back."

"But at no point did your kids hear anything, or get up to say anything to you?" McLean asked.

"No, like I said, she went totally quiet. She went totally silent. So when I grabbed her around the neck, she was quiet. I had to make her stop."

"So you took her downstairs," McLean said. "You drug her downstairs?"

"Yep."

"Put her in the back of the truck—"

"Yep. But . . . that's why the belt broke, because the only thing dragging was her feet. I was holding her up . . . when she was dragging, like, her butt was hitting the stairs."

"Right. Only her feet were hitting the stairs," McLean said.

"Yeah, because I was pulling so hard to keep her up, because I didn't want her to wake the kids. And then the belt broke. Literally. I had just gotten to the truck and just opened the back of the truck and there wasn't very much space in between the truck and the door. The whole back end of that Trooper opens up.

"It was a big door, and I lifted her up," Stephen said. "I think I just yanked one time to put her up, and she got maybe waist-high. She fell backwards and banged her head."

"You kept her in the back of the Trooper all day Saturday, right?" Kozlowski asked.

"Uh-huh. I didn't know what to do."

76

The subject turned to Stephen's e-mails to his ex-girlfriend Deena Hardy, and their reference to Tara's boss, Lou, as "the Old Geezer."

"I called Lou and apologized to him," Stephen said. "I told him he wasn't 'the Old Geezer.' It wasn't me saying that. It was something [Deena] had said from a conversation we've had a long time before that. I had never even used the phrase 'Old Geezer.' They would text message back and forth like fourteen-year-old girls. Literally. They would send these text messages that didn't make any sense.

"So that, I think, is what Deena was talking about. Cheating Wife and the Old Geezer. It wasn't Cheating Wife. To be honest, I don't think Tara was."

"That's what my next question was," McLean said. "Do you think she was having an affair?"

"No. I mean, from the bottom of my heart, no."

The next several minutes of conversation were redacted in both the print and audio portion of Stephen's confession. Law enforcement officials said they omitted that part because Stephen was discussing a possible affair by Tara with an ex-boyfriend, whose identity they wanted to protect.

* * *

McLean changed the subject: "So Friday, you dropped the computers off," she said. "If we would have said, 'Steve, do you want to talk to us?' you probably would have talked to us."

"That's why I apologized," Stephen said.

"We know," McLean answered.

"I could tell you wanted to talk," Kozlowski said, "and I actually wanted to talk to you." Kozlowski then asked Stephen why he didn't join in the first search of Stony Creek, when Hackel alerted the press about the search.

"I wanted to be out there," Stephen said. "I thought you would have found something."

"Why didn't you decide to go out there?" Kozlowski asked.

"Because David wouldn't—he told me he'd fire me," Stephen said. "'If you go, I'll fire you.' And I was like, 'What do you mean?' 'You can't go, you can't go.' He refused to let me go. Something . . . that the sheriff had a small quote in the paper."

"So he created that whole thing that you weren't going to help in the search because of something the sheriff said?" Kozlowski asked.

"David came up with that," Stephen said. "Because I was ready to go. I was all ready to go."

Kozlowski then asked: "What was your relationship with Verena?"

"We were friends," Stephen said. "We became close friends. We kissed one night."

"Did you do anything more?" McLean asked.

"Before February ninth? No."

"What happened after February ninth?" McLean prodded.

"She thought that Tara had left. She thought we could do whatever we wanted. A lot of nights I slept in her room. I needed someone to hang onto."

"It's understandable," Kozlowski said.

"No, it's not," Stephen said. Then he added, "It is."

"She's a young girl," Kozlowski said. "She's good-looking. You know, she didn't know what was going on. She's acting a certain way. . . . Verena . : . didn't know that you killed Tara?"

"She had no clue."

"OK," Kozlowski said. "And then you guys are sleeping together days after, when your relationship . . . your relationship was sexual at this point."

"We never actually had sex, but, yeah, I know what you mean," Stephen said. "We never had intercourse."

"Did you exchange oral sex with her?" Kozlowski asked.

"I did," Stephen said. "She slept in my room."

"Did she have plans of staying?" Kozlowski asked. "I know from talking to her that she wanted to stay here, obviously, and that . . . I don't think she wanted to go back to Germany."

"She didn't," Stephen agreed. "She didn't want to go back to Germany. She didn't want her family to know. The kids loved Verena."

"How are the kids doing?" McLean asked.

"I don't know."

"The last time you talked to them, they were OK?" McLean asked.

"They're fine."

77

"All I want to do, Steve, is . . . I want to have a basic timeline," McLean said. "I'm going to say it to you. You can agree with me or disagree with me, so I have it correctly. Tara comes home on the ninth. She gets home about ten-thirty?"

"I think it was after the phone call ended," Stephen recalled. "It was maybe five to ten minutes. Or she might have been talking to me still when she pulled in the garage. Yeah, I think she was on the phone when she pulled into the subdivision."

"And then you go through, and then you kill her," Kozlowski said.

"We had gone back and forth, arguing about stupid stuff, and, yeah, I said something wrong, she turned away and I grabbed her hand and I grabbed her wrist," Stephen said. "She was spewing venom and she slapped me."

"I know you made a call at ten-thirty that night," Kozlowski said. "And it was to Verena. Was that before or after you killed [Tara]?"

"I really . . . Again, I'm sorry," Stephen stammered.

"That's fine, that's fine," Kozlowski said. "So you take Tara—"

"I know I sent [Verena] a text message after," Stephen said.

The first side of the third tape ended. McLean turned the cassette to side B and continued recording.

Stephen and the detectives continued discussing the events of February 9, after Tara was dead.

"[Verena] answered her phone. It was ten thirty-two," Kozlowski stated.

"And I talked to her?" Stephen asked.

"Yes. It wasn't a long conversation. It was something quick. When I asked Verena, Verena told me that she basically said in that conversation, 'You have to quit texting me, or my girlfriends are going to know what's going on.' I'm basically trying to . . . narrow it down to when you killed her, Steve," Kozlowski explained.

"Tara's probably home for thirty minutes," Stephen said.

"You initially told me you called Verena and told her not to come home," Kozlowski said.

"No, I texted her and said don't come home," Stephen corrected. "I don't think I remember what I said—Oh, you mean the text message I sent? That was, like, at eleven, I think. What I had sent her was basically saying that she didn't have to come home because Tara was delayed again. Basically, I was trying to get her not to come home.

"At some point, [we were] sending messages back and forth, and I told her she owed me a kiss, and I actually wrote it on a note on her bed that night, that she owed me a kiss, that the shit hit the fan with Tara."

"Do you think Tara knew about you and Verena?" Kozlowski asked.

"No way," Stephen said. "Tara wouldn't have had a clue. What had happened prior to then was . . . I said some off-color joke to Verena—it's a guy joke (about Verena having a threesome with a female friend of the Grants'). I said, 'God, I'd love to see that,' just a joke, and as soon as the words came out of my mouth, I was embarrassed. I thought, 'Oh, God, Verena's going to kill me.' And she laughed. She thought it was funny.

"Tara was in London. That was the week I was e-mailing Deena," Stephen said. "We talked for a couple of days, and I was going to go meet her. And the last e-mail I sent to Deena was 'Look, I can't do it. I can't ruin my kids' lives over a stupid relationship,' and she said she understood, and she was pissed, but she understood. It was the second time I had done it. A couple years before I had stood her up."

Tara's January trip to London—and the e-mails Stephen allegedly found in which Tara had written to her ex-boyfriend—apparently had driven Stephen to solace from any woman he could get near.

"When Tara was in London was when I told Verena that I wanted to kiss her, and it was nothing. It was just . . . we were talking about something, and I'm thinking another bad thought basically, and I said, 'This time, I'll keep it to myself,' and she insisted, 'No, no, no, tell me. Tell me what you're thinking.' I was like, 'No, I can't say it because it will get me in trouble.'

"And she said, 'No, just tell me,' and I told her that I wanted to kiss her. Verena said something . . . and that was it. She was, 'Oh, I can't believe you said that,' and we talked maybe twenty minutes after that, just kind of standing in the hallway.

"And then Tara was home that weekend, and it was a good weekend at home. We talked about a lot of stuff; about the future, and I thought things were getting better. But a lot of times, over the years, I thought things were getting better, and, um, they don't. They didn't."

"Just let me ask you," McLean said, "You had told us earlier that you would text message her, or call Verena and say, 'you don't have to come home because Tara's not home yet.'"

"Right, meaning that she didn't have to hurry up to come home," Stephen said. "Well, I had text messaged her something, or I . . . went on the phone with her that she still owed me a kiss—same thing that I had put on the note. Then the last text message I sent said something to the extent of, 'You don't have to come home yet.' Basically, I was trying to stall her, giving myself more time."

After going through the timeline a final time, Kozlowski said, "OK, Steve, it's getting kind of late." Then he asked the suspect to provide a written statement about the events of February 9. Stephen agreed.

"OK, we'll let you rest up here," Kozlowski said. "When you get back to the jail, we may want to talk to you again. Do you think at that time you'll want to talk to us again?"

"Yes."

Kozlowski then read aloud the time: 10:56 P.M.—more than three hours after the interview had started. "Anything else you want to say before I turn the tape off?" Kozlowski asked.

"No."

"Anything you want to tell us that we didn't ask?" McLean asked.

"No, I can't think of anything I didn't tell you," Stephen replied. "I think I've told you everything. I mean, as much as I can remember exactly. It might be out of order."

"Thanks, Steve," Kozlowski said.

"Thanks, Steve," his partner repeated.

"No problem."

PART IV

78

By mid-April, the Grant case, awaiting trial, was being bumped off the front pages by news of radio shock jock Don Imus's reference to the Rutgers women's basketball team as "nappy-headed hos," and stories about German automaker Daimler's impending sale of its Chrysler unit.

Still, a constant stream of new developments kept the Grant story from falling too far from the radar. Prosecutors on April 27 released documents from evidence technicians, the Emmet County Sheriff's Office, and Michigan State Police that offered new details about the case, including the disturbing fact that the Rubbermaid bin that held Tara's torso had once been used to store Ian's clothes.

Smith's office also released a video of the Grant home that was shot by evidence technicians during the execution of the search warrant. The footage offered followers of the case a glimpse inside the Westridge home: Lindsey's pink bedroom, Ian's green-and-white room, which was cluttered with toys, the master bedroom and bathroom, where the killing took place, and the beige-carpeted stairs Stephen said he dragged Tara's body down after killing her. Footage of the garage search was not released.

* * *

On Tuesday, May 1, Alicia filed a petition to terminate Stephen's parental rights permanently. The same day, Kelly filed a petition to adopt Lindsey and Ian.

Kelly, who earlier had promised she wouldn't fight for custody of the children, now said she wanted to adopt them because the kids were more comfortable with her side of the family. She made it clear she didn't want Alicia to get Lindsey and Ian.

It was the first public indication of the bitter tug-of-war between the two women over custody of the children.

Also Tuesday, the winter Arbitron radio ratings were released. In the Metro Detroit market, news-talk WJR-AM (760) and all-news WWJ-AM (950) both did well: WJR topped the overall ratings for listeners twelve and older, and WWJ came in second. Radio executives credited the Grant case for the high ratings.

"We had breaking news just about every day," WWJ vice president and general manager Rich Homberg told *Detroit News* feature reporter Susan Whitall.

Sheila Werner, whose discovery of the bloody Ziploc bag in Stony Creek Metropark led to the break in the Grant case, revealed her identity to the public on May 15 at Hackel's annual Sheriff Recognition Awards ceremony, held in the Macomb Intermediate School District Building.

There was a larger media turnout than usual. Hackel handed out fifty-six awards. Dispatcher Tom Stawski received a Lifesaving Award for his work on February 11, 2007, when, during an emergency telephone call, he provided a distraught mother with directions for performing CPR on her seventeen-month-old baby. Stawski said he knew his efforts were successful when he heard the baby crying in the background.

A Professional Excellence Award was given to Lieutenant Darga and Sergeants King, Kozlowski, and McLean for their work on the Grant investigation.

But Werner was the award recipient the media was waiting for. Reporters crowded around the attractive brunette after Captain Wickersham presented her with a Civilian Award for helping to crack the Grant case.

"It was divine intervention. How else do you explain it?" she said of finding the crucial bloody bag. "People think it was some kind of voodoo that led me to that part of the park. In all the years I lived there, I never went to that area. But I went there that day.

"It was the first warm day we'd had for a while, and I decided to take a walk through the woods. I knew the police had been searching the woods (for evidence in the Grant case), and I wanted to see if I could find anything. I saw the bag near a tree. I had no idea what it was, but the Tara Grant case did run through my mind. I took the bag home and called the police. I made sure I didn't touch anything inside the bag."

Werner said she wasn't worried about testifying in the same courtroom as Stephen in the upcoming murder trial. "I'm not afraid of him," she said. "He looks to me like a cowardly person."

The following day, two court decisions prevented Stephen from profiting from Tara's death. Macomb probate judge Pamela Gilbert O'Sullivan revoked Stephen's right to control Tara's assets; and Macomb County Circuit Court judge Matthew Switalski awarded Tara's estate $50 million in the wrongful-death lawsuit filed by Alicia.

In the wrongful-death hearing, Alicia was called to the witness stand on that afternoon to explain how Tara's murder affected her family. "Tara was a fantastic mom," Alicia said. "Even though her job took her from home, the children were never far from her thoughts. She called them every night to tell them she loved them.

Lindsey and Ian are very confused. They don't know why their dad did this to their mom. They're also very angry about it. Emotionally they'll be scarred for the rest of their lives."

The $50 million figure was arrived at in part by calculating $750 per day in damages for Lindsey and Ian over their expected life span. "That's just a figure we came up with," Patrick Simasko, Alicia's attorney, said. "It's actually low. How much is it worth to lose your mother? But you have to come up with some figure, and that's the one we arrived at."

The lawsuit also sought $17,000 in funeral expenses, and Tara's salary of $168,000, compounded over thirty years. "We don't expect to see any of that money," Simasko said. "But what this will do is prevent [Stephen] from profiting from a book deal in the future, or selling any pictures on the Internet. We stopped that."

In the probate hearing, O'Sullivan ruled Stephen could not collect from Tara's two life insurance policies, her 401(k) plan, or her half of their home. O'Sullivan took less than five minutes to decide for Alicia. "I have no hesitation in granting this request," she said.

79

As expected, Stephen's attorneys mounted a vigorous defense. They filed another change of venue motion. They filed a motion demanding Judge LeDuc remove himself from the case. Stephen Rabaut and Gail Pamukov wrote that the judge showed a *complete and unequivocal violation of the due process rights of Stephen Grant* because he'd disclosed a request by the defense to allow a psychologist to examine Stephen.

When LeDuc refused to step down from the case, Stephen's attorneys appealed to chief district court judge Paul Cassidy. On May 31, Cassidy ruled against the defense.

On Tuesday, June 5, LeDuc bound the case over for trial after a two-day preliminary examination, in which Kozlowski was the chief witness.

"I'm satisfied that Stephen Grant did, with premeditation, murder Tara Grant," LeDuc said. "Mr. Grant said he did not like looking at the victim's face as he was strangling her, so he put a pair of boxers or a T-shirt over her face. Also, within minutes after he strangled her, he told police he took a belt and used that to transport her in an effort to conceal the body, thus beginning an elaborate concealing of the crime that lasted over a period of several days."

* * *

On June 6, circuit court judge Diane Druzinski was chosen by random draw to preside over the Grant case. Druzinski, a mother of three, had a reputation on the bench of being fair but harsh. Her courtroom manner was understated but effective, and although she worked hard to ensure defendants got fair trials, she also was known for handing down harsh sentences.

"She'll smile at you while giving you the toughest sentence possible" is how one attorney described her.

Druzinski was elected judge in 2002. Prior to her election, she was a civil litigation attorney.

Prosecutors were happy Druzinski was chosen for the Grant case. "She's a very fair judge," Eric Smith said when asked about the choice. "We're confident she will handle this case properly."

The trial was scheduled to begin September 19.

A second high-profile missing person case that turned into a murder investigation surfaced in normally tranquil Washington Township during the summer of 2007: the fatal stabbing of Marilou Johnson on June 14—four months to the day after Tara was reported missing, and less than two miles away from the Grant home.

Johnson, fifty, was the live-in girlfriend of millionaire Roger Blanchard, owner of a nearby auto parts factory. Blanchard, seventy-two, reported Johnson missing to police on June 15.

Reporters thought they had another domestic homicide drama on their hands after the *Detroit News* on June 21 printed a story revealing that Blanchard had filed a personal protection order against Johnson the previous year, and hired off-duty police officers to guard him because he said he felt "threatened and harassed" by Johnson and her sons.

Blanchard alleged in the petition that Johnson kept *calling my home and cell phones, harassing myself and my family, and I fear for my safety and that of my family.* But those titillating details had nothing to do with the murder. It turned out that David Wright, a plumber who was working at Blanchard's mansion, stabbed Johnson during a robbery in which he stole her $250,000 diamond necklace.

Police found out that Wright had been working at the home during the time Johnson came up missing, and they tailed him. They saw him dump evidence into a trash can outside a fast-food restaurant, and when they searched his car, they found the diamonds from the stolen necklace.

Wright confessed that he'd killed Johnson and then dumped her body in Cass Lake in nearby Oakland County. Wright said he hadn't meant to kill her—he was trying to force her into his truck at knifepoint when he slipped, inadvertently stabbing her.

Prosecutors scoffed at the claim, pointing out that Johnson had been stabbed six times, and that her throat was slit twice.

Wright was convicted of first-degree murder.

Friday, June 22, 2007: Transcript of a collect call from the Macomb County Jail

(Kelly tells her brother she's in the car, driving Lindsey and Ian to her condo to go swimming.)

Kelly:	Say hi to Stephen.
Lindsey and Ian:	*(in unison)* Hiiiii.
Stephen:	*(Laughs nervously)* Hi.
Lindsey:	*(In a formal, polite tone)* How are you?
Stephen:	Good.

(A few seconds of awkward silence ensues.)

Kelly: Okay, they wanted to say hi to you. They asked how you are over there.

Stephen: Thank you.

Kelly: *(Suddenly breaking into an excited voice)* Wave, because we're passing.

Stephen: What?

Kelly: We're passing you right now.

Stephen: *(Sarcastically)* Oh, thanks.

Kelly: *(Jauntily)* You're welcome. *(Lowers her voice)* They know that you're in there. It's OK.

Stephen: *(In a testy tone)* Nice.

Lindsey: Can he see me?

Kelly: No, he can't see you.

Stephen: Have fun with the kids.

Kelly: They worry about you a lot. They say they understand you must have been really mad to do what you did, because you're a really nice guy.

Curiosity seekers and bargain hunters swarmed the Grant home at a July 14 estate sale. Alicia said the proceeds from the sale would go to Lindsey and Ian. Most of the furniture was sold. By the end of the day, only the blond wood bed, dresser, and armoire remained in the master bedroom, while two beige suede love seats were left in the den.

Lindsey and Ian's toys, the plates, the spoons, and the forks the family used to eat with, all were scooped up by the dozens of people who flocked to the house. So were the Grant family Christmas ornaments. Some of those who showed up admitted they weren't planning to buy anything. They just wanted to tour the infamous Grant home.

Although interest in the Grants' personal belongings

was high, there were no takers when the Macomb County Sheriff's Office put the house up for auction a few weeks later. Even though the sale price of $221,468.73 was significantly lower than the state equalized value of $267,000, it still wasn't a good bargain, real estate foreclosure experts said.

"It would probably have to be listed for one hundred fifty thousand or so for it to be a good deal," said Bob Mackenzie, of Real Estate One in St. Clair Shores, who showed up to the sheriff's auction. "Anything more than that isn't worth bidding on."

Sarah Reis, a foreclosure specialist at R.A. Williams, a Warren-based real estate investment firm, said many of the one hundred homes that were auctioned that day were mortgaged for more than they were worth—and the Grant home, she said, had an added issue. "That place is tainted," Reis said. "I know I wouldn't buy a house where there's been a murder—especially one as infamous as this one."

Family court judge John Foster had harsh words for Alicia and Kelly at a July 16, 2007, custody hearing.

Assistant Macomb County prosecutor Jodi Debbrecht, who represented the Michigan Department of Human Services in the custody case, said officials in Ohio had recommended Kelly not be allowed to see the children.

"DHS in Ohio stopped visitation with the paternal relatives," Debbrecht said. "The two [children] are having behavioral issues at this time—"

Foster interrupted her before she could finish her sentence: "Well, maybe part of it is, they aren't seeing the family members they like, as well as the other family members," he said. "I'm not going make a decision based on some caseworker in Ohio sending you a letter saying that they shouldn't see these children.

"The children have seen [the Utykanskis] their whole

lives, and now they aren't good enough to see them? Why are the Standerfers good enough to see them? Am I going to have to order these children to come back to Michigan?" Foster asked as he ordered both sides to work out a visitation agreement.

"Whatever you do should be done in the best interests of the children."

The fight between Alicia and Kelly was getting ugly. Each side dropped snide, off-the-record comments about the other, and their public statements often dripped with thinly veiled contempt.

Kelly told the *Detroit News* that Stephen wanted her to have custody of the kids. "He would not sign his parental rights over to Alicia, because he doesn't want the kids to go to her," she said. "The kids know us better, and both Stephen and I feel they would be better off living with us."

Kelly said Stephen was upset with Alicia for telling his children the details of how their mother was killed. "They're still too young," Kelly said. "If it were up to us, we would have told them later. Stephen is afraid they're going to be raised in a negative environment. Even if they never want to forgive him for what he did, it's the responsibility of whoever raises the kids to get them through this ordeal as best as possible, and to raise them with as positive an outlook as possible. You shouldn't raise them as if they're going to be scarred for life. Kids can overcome tragedy."

Kelly, who was unable to have children of her own because of an undisclosed medical condition, said if she was granted custody of Lindsey and Ian, she would let them visit their mother's side of the family. "But Alicia isn't giving us the same courtesy," she said. "We haven't seen those kids since Easter. That's ridiculous. If she's trying to punish me because she can't punish Stephen, she needs to know she's only punishing the kids."

Alicia wouldn't comment for the record about Kelly's statements.

On July 31, Druzinski ruled against several motions that had been filed by the defense. She denied their motion for a change of venue. She denied a motion to quash the evidence in the case. And she declined to throw out Stephen's confession.

The judge did, however, grant Rabaut and Pamukov's request for a gag order. To the chagrin of reporters and others hungry for more information about the case, Druzinski's ruling meant there would be no more leaks. There would be no more evidence released.

Those who wanted their questions answered would have to wait for the trial. And it was announced in mid-August that the wait would be even longer—the trial was postponed until November 27 to allow Eric Smith to recover from an August 17 throat surgery.

80

Rabaut and Pamukov filed a motion on Thursday, October 18, asking to be removed from the case. They said they couldn't properly prepare for the upcoming trial because they said Smith had withheld evidence until "the eleventh hour."

The defense claimed Smith had waited until Monday to provide them with more than thirty hours of audiotapes of Stephen talking on the telephone and in the Macomb County Jail visiting room.

In the motion, Rabaut and Pamukov asked to be removed from the case because they claimed they would not have time to review the new material. Druzinski denied the request.

Rabaut raised the ire of the judge the following month, when, less than two weeks before the trial was to begin, he gave an interview to Channel 7 reporter Ray Sayah. The television station touted the interview all day November 16, promising that Rabaut would reveal salacious new details about the case.

"Only on 7, Stephen Grant's lawyer tells all," trumpeted promos for the 11:00 P.M. spot.

It turned out to be November sweeps-week hyperbole. Rabaut didn't specifically talk about the Grant case, although he did say he thought Stephen was a likeable person. "I think there are good human qualities in all individuals," Rabaut told Sayah. (Sayah, who resumed the use of the first name Reza, now works as an international correspondent for CNN.)

Smith immediately filed a motion to have Rabaut found in contempt of court for violating Druzinski's gag order. *Given Mr. Rabaut's defiant and wholly inexplicable behavior, this court should hold him in criminal contempt of court,* the filing read. *Mr. Rabaut cannot believe this court is naive enough to entertain the excuse that he cannot control the marketing and production of this interview that he voluntarily and contemptuously submitted to with the television station."*

An emergency hearing was held on Tuesday, November 20. Reporters were surprised to discover that Rabaut was being defended by Geoffrey Fieger, the bombastic attorney who had defended assisted-suicide doctor Jack Kevorkian. Fieger had handled other high-profile cases, including his defense of Jonathan Schmitz, who murdered his friend Scott Amedure after Amedure revealed on Jenny Jones's television talk show that he had a gay crush on Schmitz.

Fieger further surprised reporters by explaining that he was handling Rabaut's case for free. "I do a lot of things for free," Fieger said after the hearing. "Although I didn't consider this as doing something for free—I considered it an honor to represent Mr. Rabaut, because I think he's an American hero for representing someone who everyone views as a pariah. Sometimes you just have to do what you think is right."

Druzinski denied Smith's motion to hold Rabaut in contempt of court. But she made her displeasure with Rabaut known. "The court is not pleased to be dealing with these issues right now," she said. But she added that Rabaut hadn't specifically discussed the case, even though the Channel 7 promotional commercials promised he had.

"Mr. Rabaut had no control over the editorializing of the media prior to this interview," Druzinski said.

Rabaut would not be kicked off the case. The trial would proceed as planned.

Wednesday, November 21, 2007: Transcript of Macomb County Jail recording of inmate Stephen Grant and visitor Kelly Utykanski

(Stephen and Kelly discuss the fact that their jailhouse conversations have been turned over to prosecutors.)

Stephen: Steve (Rabaut) says that some of them sound bad. He said it sounds like I'm not respectful enough about the whole situation. But what are you gonna do?

Kelly: I'm trying to keep your spirits up.

Stephen: I told him we're just talking how we'd talk anyway. But he said they're going to make it look—

Kelly: —like you're taking it lightly. Which you're not. It was a very serious thing. It was a horrible, horrible thing. Nobody takes it lightly.

81

Media interest in the case reignited as the trial date approached. *Dateline NBC, 20/20, 48 Hours,* and Court TV all applied to cover the proceedings. Interest was predictably high among the local outlets, with Channel 2, Channel 4, and Channel 7 all on hand, as were radio stations WWJ and WJR. Print media was represented by the *Detroit News,* the *Detroit Free Press,* the *Macomb Daily,* and the *Source.* Stringers for *People* magazine were also in town to cover the trial.

The intense scrutiny prompted Judge Druzinski to deviate from her normal procedure. She wanted five hundred potential jurors summoned, three times more than usual, to ensure enough people could be found whose opinions about Stephen hadn't already been swayed by media accounts of the case. Druzinski also decided to seat sixteen jurors instead of the usual fourteen, allowing for four alternate jurors rather than the customary two. The judge also allowed defense attorneys and prosecutors the opportunity to each dismiss up to eighteen potential jurors without cause, rather than the twelve preemptory exemptions typically allowed each side.

In another unusual move, attorneys on both sides agreed to forgo the routine practice of questioning the potential jurors in groups. Instead, each candidate would fill out a twenty-three-page questionnaire. It took eleven cases of copier paper to print sufficient forms. The questionnaire was adapted from the Scott Peterson case, said William Cataldo, the prosecution's chief of homicide, referring to the wife killer now serving time in California's infamous San Quentin prison.

Some of the questions were predictable, such as whether prospective jurors had formed opinions about Stephen based on the media's portrayal of him. But the surveys also delved into more personal details, asking: *Do you have a bumper sticker on your car? Do you currently or have you in the past owned any pets? Do you have any opinions about people involved in extramarital affairs?*

The prosecution and defense each had a hand in choosing the questions, which were designed to reveal candidates' personality traits, Cataldo said. "Picking a jury is dealing in stereotypes," he said. "In each trial, you have to figure out—Do you want a factory worker? Do you want an engineer? Jury selection is a crapshoot, and there's not much time to really get to know the people in the jury pool. So you go with basic stereotypes."

The questionnaire allowed both the defense and prosecutors to get an idea quickly about which stereotypes the jury candidates represented, Cataldo said. "In this case, we were looking for a professional, college-educated woman in her mid-thirties," he said. "We wanted a woman with children who was in a stable relationship."

The prosecution didn't want female jurors who had been abused by their husbands, because instead of empathizing with Tara, they likely would blame her, Cataldo said.

"Many times, women who are in abusive situations blame themselves for the abuse," he said. "So, instead of blaming Stephen, they might blame Tara, and say, 'I brought the abuse on myself, so Tara must have brought the abuse on herself.'

"That's not what we wanted. We wanted someone

who was an advocate for female organizations that say domestic violence will not be tolerated."

Attached to the survey was a list of potential witnesses, with instructions for jury candidates to circle the names of anyone they knew personally. Of the eighty-two names on the witness list, which included police officers and Tara and Stephen's relatives, one immediately jumped out to the press: Verena Dierkes.

Was the young au pair going to take the stand? Prosecutor Eric Smith had said several times before the gag order was implemented that he wanted to question Verena. He said that would be difficult without her cooperation, however, since the teen was a German citizen, who hadn't been accused of committing a crime. Reporters still phoned her home in Germany periodically, but she still wasn't talking.

Verena's appearance on the witnesses list provided hope for answers to several lingering questions. Followers of the case wondered: What did the au pair know about the events of February 9? After all, police said Stephen had called her several times that night. What was the extent of her affair with Stephen, to which he briefly alluded during his confession? And what was life like behind the Grants' closed doors?

If prosecutors had the answers, they weren't talking. Because of the gag order, reporters were unable to verify whether Smith had been able to interview Verena or convince her to jet back to Michigan and testify against her former employer. Witness lists often bear the names of people who are never called to testify, so there was no guarantee the nanny ever would be heard from in a court of law.

The unanswered questions only titillated the media corps, and as journalists prepared to scrutinize the trial from every possible angle, court officials made it clear they would be keeping a close eye on them. Strict rules were laid down. Reporters were told a Macomb County sheriffs deputy would be stationed outside the courtroom door each day, issuing passes on a first-come, first-served basis. All cell phones were to be turned in to the deputy before a spectator entered, and anyone who left the courtroom during the trial for any reason whatsoever would be locked out until after the next break.

To further cut down on any chaos in the courtroom, Druzinski issued an order on Friday, November 9, allowing only one pool photographer and one video camera into the proceedings. But much to the woe of journalists and the general public, the judge banned live broadcasts. Television stations and Web sites would not be allowed to air footage of the proceedings until after the court had finished its business for the day. Attorneys for Channel 4 and Channel 7 later filed motions with Druzinski, challenging the ruling.

The stringent rules were put in place to ensure Stephen got a fair trial in the face of all the media scrutiny, court spokesman Phil Frame said when reporters called him to complain. He said the judge held several meetings with bailiffs and other court employees before the trial to go over the logistics of handling the expected media crush. The media's motions would be addressed by the judge the following month. Meanwhile, preparations for the trial of Stephen Grant continued.

82

Despite all the planning, the first day of jury selection, November 27, was chaotic. Macomb County's sprawling 1960s-era courthouse was packed with hundreds of potential jurors, who overflowed the fifth-floor jury room and milled around the corridors for hours.

It was a long morning: Tuesday's proceedings were scheduled to start at ten-thirty, but there was a three-hour delay because the jury candidates hadn't yet filled out their questionnaires. The holding room, which was about the size of a typical high-school classroom, was crammed with dozens of Stephen Grant's prospective jurors. They were seated at small school-style desks, jotting down answers to the 130 questions on the surveys.

While they waited to be called to court, potential jurors viewed a patriotic video stressing the importance of jury duty. To the amusement of some, they also were shown a twenty-minute tourism film touting the dining and nightlife establishments in downtown Mount Clemens.

Afterward, administrators allowed the pool to watch television to while away the wait—but then the TV was mistakenly tuned to a local news broadcast, which aired a story about the Grant case. The next day, court officials yanked the TV set from the jury room, and banned wireless Internet use in the courthouse.

· * * *

Finally, at 1:30 P.M., the "court in session" light above Druzinski's second-floor courtroom was turned on, and a buzzer sounded, alerting everyone in the corridor that the proceedings were about to get under way.

Lieutenant "Wild Bill" Donovan, the officer in charge of security for the Grant trial, passed out laminated red media badges to the seven reporters covering the jury selection. Only one green public pass was given out, to a white-haired, bearded gent who declined to give his name, identifying himself only as a "court watcher." The man attended the entire trial. The nonstop jury selection coverage was not reflected by the sparse turnout, although that would drastically change once the actual trial began.

But court officials had planned for a packed courtroom, and for the time being, they stuck to their plan. Six deputies stood guard inside the near-empty room. Sheets of copier paper bearing FAMILY, PUBLIC and MEDIA were taped on the end of each row, directing the eight spectators where to sit.

Members of the media were assigned the last row, to a bench about a third smaller than the other rows in the courtroom. Because there wasn't enough room there for seven people to sit comfortably—and because the rest of the benches in the courtroom were empty, except for the white-haired onlooker—permission was eventually granted for reporters to take seats elsewhere. The seating designation signs were removed a few days later, and despite public interest in the case, there never were more than ten people present at any time during jury selection.

Stephen was escorted into the courtroom. He sported a new look for his first public appearance in street clothes since his arrest. The defendant now had a close-cropped haircut and wore a black business suit. His ankles were shackled, but his hands were free. Sitting at the defense table with his leg irons obscured, he looked like he could have been any young attorney awaiting trial, rather than an accused murderer.

In addition to his new clothes and hairstyle, Stephen's green eyes didn't seem as "bugged-out" as usual. He later revealed that Pamukov had instructed him to practice softening his expression for the trial. Stephen said his fellow inmates in the Macomb County Jail often teased him about his wide-eyed expression, urging him "do the Stephen Grant eyes." A recurring theme in discussions about the Grant case was how spooky his saucerlike eyes looked during his television interviews, and Pamukov knew that wouldn't play well with a jury. So, Stephen said, he worked on relaxing his eyelids.

Stephen had been shuttled into the courthouse via an underground tunnel that runs beneath Cass Avenue, connecting the Macomb County Administration Building to the court building. The two-hundred-yard-long tunnel is part of a system of underground passages that dates back to the late 1800s, the heyday of Mount Clemens's fame as "Bath City." The tunnels accommodated the dozens of bathhouses that were built in the city after subterranean mineral-water wells were discovered there in 1862. The underground passages allowed access to the wells.

When the county's administration building was built in 1997, another tunnel was constructed connecting the new structure to the courthouse, to allow employees a sheltered path between buildings. The tunnel also provided an opportunity for famous witnesses and defendants to circumvent the media while entering and leaving the courthouse. Stephen was afforded the same secret route as famous rapper and Macomb County resident Marshall Mathers, more commonly known as Eminem, who'd sneaked in and out of the building through the tunnel during a highly publicized 2006 divorce hearing.

The first prospective juror in the Grant trial, a well-dressed Asian woman, walked through a door on the left side of the courtroom and took a seat in the jury box. Juror Number 1 said she hadn't formed any opinions on the case, and was certain she could render a fair verdict. When neither prosecutors nor defense attorneys raised any objections, she was asked to return for the next round of questioning.

In all, twenty-one prospective jurors were interviewed the first day, of whom ten were disqualified because they said they were biased in some way about the case. Peggy Przybylski, of Shelby Township, gave a typical response: "My personal opinion is, there should be an eye for an eye," she said after it was revealed she'd stated in her questionnaire that Stephen should suffer the same fate as his wife. She was excused.

Przybylski was one of the few rejected jurors who agreed to be interviewed by the reporters who descended on each of them as they left court. Most newspapers and television stations supplemented the one journalist each outlet was allowed inside the courtroom with other reporters, cameramen, and photographers stationed in the hall outside.

After Druzinski called an end to the day's proceedings at 5:30 P.M., attorneys and reporters grumbled about the prospect of having to wade through hundreds more identical interviews.

"Long day?" Eric Smith was asked.

He smiled tightly. "Back at it tomorrow," he said.

83

On Wednesday, the same cast assembled for another long day of jury selection. The turnout was again sparse. Kelly was one of the few spectators to file into the courtroom. A few minutes after she took her seat in one of the pews denoted FAMILY, a bailiff approached and whispered something to her. She tensely gathered her coat and walked out of the courtroom. It was later explained that Kelly was not allowed to attend the proceedings because her name was on the witness list.

Another forty jury candidates were interviewed on Wednesday, including a teacher of autistic children who told the court she could not render a fair verdict because she was "heartbroken" about the plight of the Grants' offspring. The woman said many of the kids she taught came from violent homes, and that the murder of Tara Grant had struck a nerve with her. When the woman mentioned Stephen's children, the defendant bowed his head and closed his eyes for a brief moment.

Another man was excused after he told Pamukov that Stephen had discussed the murder with his friend who had served time with the accused murderer in the county jail. "I know he's guilty because he told my friend in jail he was," the man said. When asked by Pamukov to clarify his testimony, the man said, "I wouldn't lie to you, sweetheart—"

Druzinski cut the man off: "She's not a sweetheart. Treat her with the proper respect."

Stephen broke into tears when a woman identified as Juror Number 448 testified that she was the mother of someone on the witness list. It was later revealed, in a strange coincidence, that the potential juror was Deena Hardy's mother. Stephen's first public display of emotion since his arrest didn't last long, though. He quickly wiped the tears away with his sleeve, and his face again became an impassive mask.

By the end of the second day of jury selection, the judge, prosecutors, and defense all agreed that the process was taking longer than anticipated. There were hundreds more juror candidates still to be interviewed.

It was an exhausting ordeal for everyone. Druzinski tried to move things along as quickly as possible. She adhered to a stringent schedule: an 8:30 A.M. start, lunch from noon to 1:30 P.M. and ten-minute breaks midmorning and midafternoon. She usually ended the day between 5:30 and 6:00 P.M.

The media intensity died down as the days wore on, and court employees and officers relaxed. A routine was established, and faces grew familiar: the baseball-loving deputy who manned the front-door metal detector; the swarthy cook/cashier in the basement cafeteria who proudly displayed near the cash register photos of his brown-eyed daughter, a lieutenant, who in his younger days had served as a diver for the sheriff's office, who was nearing retirement and looking forward to moving to a house in the country with his wife, and the reporters, prosecutors, and defense attorneys who sat together in the same room for hours on end.

At the center of it all was Stephen, who hobbled into court each day wearing the same dark suit and a vacant expression. Every now and then as he was being led into or out of the courtroom, he would glance at onlookers before quickly averting his eyes.

* * *

On December 6, the eighth day of jury selection, Druzinski started the morning by addressing two motions. First she postponed ruling on the defense's request for a change of venue. She didn't give a reason.

Next the judge ruled on a motion filed earlier in the week by two television stations requesting to be able to broadcast the trial live. In a move that surprised and dismayed many, Druzinski decided not only to uphold her decision about live broadcasts, but to take it one step further and ban still and video cameras from the courtroom altogether. Only reporters and sketch artists would be allowed to cover the case.

In her ten-page ruling, Druzinski said the media frenzy prompted her decision. *During the November "sweeps" month, competing television stations apparently engaged in a game of ratings one-upmanship in an effort to manufacture an audience,* Druzinski wrote.

She also cited concern for the Grant children: *If the Court were to allow the trial to be filmed and televised, and thus preserved in perpetuity, the details of their parents' relationship and the accusations against their father would be permanently preserved in a visual record that this Court believes will scar them emotionally for the rest of their lives.*

84

Jury selection wrapped up with surprising abruptness at 9:30 A.M., Friday, when Rabaut unexpectedly announced he was satisfied with the jury as seated, even though the defense had used less than half of its allotted eighteen preemptory exemptions.

The arduous nine-day process was over. The jury was seated: ten women and six men. Among them were two registered nurses, an ambulance driver, and a man who said he enjoyed reading murder mysteries.

After months of anticipation, the Stephen Grant murder trial was about to be under way.

At 10:15 A.M., the courtroom light was turned on and a line formed outside the heavy wood double doors. Word had quickly spread that the trial was about to begin, and although the number of reporters who'd been covering the jury selection remained the same, deputies issued about a dozen passes to the public. Among those who were issued green public passes were several attorneys who'd already been in the courthouse and decided to pop in.

After everyone was seated, Stephen was escorted into the courtroom. Before Druzinski could ask the bailiff to bring the jurors into the room, Stephen Rabaut announced his client wanted to plead guilty—to the charge of mutilating a dead body.

Stephen was called to stand before the judge to enter his plea. "I mutilated a dead body," he said in a subdued voice. The plea was expected and elicited little court-room response. Legal experts had predicted that Rabaut and Pamukov would instruct Stephen to plead guilty to the mutilation charge, a ten-year felony, in an effort to keep discussion of the dismemberment out of the trial.

The speculation proved correct. After Stephen's guilty plea, Rabaut petitioned the judge to ban testimony about the mutilation of Tara's body. "The court should inform the jury that the case has changed, and that they shouldn't even think about the dismemberment," he said.

Therese Tobin, the assistant prosecutor, accused Rabaut of trying to sanitize the case. "There's no way to talk about the murder without also discussing the muti-lation," she said. Druzinski sided with the prosecution, ruling that evidence of the dismemberment was relevant because it may have been done to conceal the murder.

Then, the defense asked for a ruling on its motion for a change of venue. Gail Pamukov pointed out that nearly all the potential jurors had testified they'd seen media accounts of the case, and she insisted Stephen couldn't get a fair trial in Macomb County.

Tobin pointed out that a change of venue had been rejected in another high-profile Michigan murder trial, in which a man named Lawrence DeLisle was convicted of first-degree murder in 1990. He killed his four chil-dren by deliberately driving his car into the Detroit River.

As expected, Druzinski denied the request to move the case to another county.

The judge called the jurors into the courtroom. They solemnly filed into the jury box and took their seats.

Druzinski didn't tell them that Stephen had just pleaded guilty to chopping up his wife's body, but she did inform them that Stephen was charged only with first-degree murder.

At 10:40 A.M., Eric Smith began his opening statement with a thunderbolt: "Have you ever wondered what goes through the mind of a man who just murdered his wife?" he asked jurors pointedly.

Smith paused a few seconds for dramatic effect before answering his own question: "Sex."

Moments after the murder, Smith revealed, Stephen sent a text message to his off-duty au pair. *You owe me a kiss,* the "Mr. Mom" typed into his cell phone.

Then, Smith said, Stephen penned a similar message and left the note on Verena's pillow. "To do so, he has to walk by the still-warm and lifeless body of his wife, while his children slept nearby," Smith said grimly.

Smith revealed that Stephen had set up a sexual rendezvous with Deena Hardy after sending the e-mails—"but he canceled because of Verena," Smith said. "During the week of February ninth, their relationship turned physical, and the defendant had fallen in love with Verena," Smith said. "When he slept with the au pair, it marked the end of Tara's life."

As jurors and spectators listened avidly, Smith described the night of the murder: how an enraged, naked Stephen had strangled Tara, and then hid her body in the cargo area of her garaged Isuzu Trooper.

"He then calmly spent the day Saturday watching television with his children, all while his wife's dead body is in the back of her car in the garage," he said.

"Then, on Sunday, he takes the crime to a new level," Smith said, recounting how Stephen transported Tara's body to his father's shop and hacked his wife, the mother of his children, into fourteen pieces by hand with sections of saw blades. "He tells us something only a butcher would know: how the saw blade dulls as it cuts through bone and flesh," Smith said.

Smith disclosed that Stephen had left several messages on his wife's cell phone in the days after the murder in an attempt to cover up his crime. He told the jury they would get a chance to hear Stephen's phone calls to the woman he'd just murdered—including an angry call he made minutes after dismembering Tara, saying she owed it to her children to call them.

Smith concluded his thirty-five-minute opening statement by asking the jury to "hold the defendant responsible for his horrific actions."

Several spectators stood up to stretch when Smith finished his statement. It was 11:15 A.M.—not yet lunchtime—and there would be no break.

Within seconds of Eric Smith taking a seat, Gail Pamukov rose and headed for the podium. "This is a terrible, tragic story," she began. "There are no winners, and at the end of this trial, there will still be no winners."

Pamukov stipulated that Stephen killed his wife. "He did it. Your job is to determine what happened that night. Mr. Grant was a good parent," she said. "Tara's frequent absences were a source of friction. The events of February ninth were the result of a pot that had simmered for a long time and finally boiled out of control."

Pamukov described the argument the night of the murder: "Tara made demeaning statements to Mr. Grant, and he lost control," she said. "The evidence will show that, at best, his thinking was chaotic. His actions were impulsive. Fueled by anger. Fueled by jealousy."

She said that when Stephen dismembered Tara's body, "his actions were those of a scared and desperate man trying to cover up the killing of his wife. But he reacted to what he did—he didn't plan it beforehand."

Pamukov's twenty-minute opening statement ended with a plea to the jurors to keep an open mind, and to only consider the evidence that was presented during the trial.

As soon as Pamukov finished her statement, Druzinski told the prosecution to call its first witness.

Macomb sheriff's deputy William Hughes took the stand. He was the officer who took Stephen's initial missing persons report on February 14 at the sheriff's headquarters.

Hughes said he talked with Stephen for more than an hour in the police station lobby. Stephen had told the deputy he hadn't seen his wife for five days, when she left their house following an argument about her travel schedule.

"I noticed a scratch on his nose, and I asked him if the argument was physical," Hughes said. "He denied there was a fight."

Hughes also testified that Stephen said of his wife, "I don't think I want her to come back. In fact, I don't care if she ever comes back."

After Hughes's testimony, which ended about noon, Druzinski broke for the day. She informed the attorneys she would be taking Mondays off to attend to other docket matters, and ordered the trial to resume at 8:30 A.M., Tuesday.

Druzinski reminded the jury to refrain from talking about the case. Then reporters rushed into the hallway, dialing their cell phones as they went.

85

Alicia and Erik Standerfer were met by a media feeding frenzy as they exited the courthouse elevator on the second floor at about eight-fifteen, Tuesday morning. The corridor was filled with the sound of shutters clicking, and the blinding glare of lights shining from a battery of television cameras.

The Standerfers appeared steeled for the barrage. They calmly walked past the assembled media and sat on a bench outside Druzinski's courtroom. As they waited for the trial to start, they appeared to ignore the camera operators and photographers who continued snapping pictures from every conceivable angle.

Alicia, wearing a brown sweater over a white blouse, was the day's first witness. She told Eric Smith about her childhood with Tara in Michigan's rural Upper Peninsula. She said the sisters had always been close, and that they remained that way through adulthood. "We were best friends," she said. "We talked every couple weeks."

When Smith asked Alicia whether Tara had any children, Stephen bowed his head and closed his eyes. Alicia answered that her older sister had two children, and that Tara spent as much time with Lindsey and Ian as her hectic schedule allowed. Alicia said her sister called home every day from Puerto Rico, and that when Alicia sorted Tara's belongings after her death, she found dozens of cards that her sibling had sent home to her children. "She was a fantastic mom," the murdered woman's sister said.

Smith showed Alicia a photograph and asked her to identify it. "That was my sister, Tara, and her beautiful smile," she said wistfully. She said she spoke with her sister twice the day she was killed, and that they discussed the Grants' upcoming vacation to Arizona, where the family planned to stay at Stephen's mother's house. During their final telephone conversation, Alicia said, they also discussed the upcoming annual trip in March to their hometown, to make maple syrup at Dusty's Sugar Shack, the rustic hut named for Tara and Alicia's father.

Alicia also testified that Tara had told her she planned to return to Puerto Rico on Monday, not a day early as Stephen claimed. She said she found out her sister was missing after receiving a telephone call from her mother on Tuesday, February 13. She said her mother explained that Stephen had just called her to say Tara hadn't been heard from since the previous Friday night.

Alicia testified that she immediately called her sister's cell phone and e-mailed her, to no avail. Then, she said, she called Troendle, who told her he hadn't heard from Tara, either. She said Stephen left a message on her phone later that day, asking, "Can you call me when you get a minute? It's no big deal." Stephen didn't mention on the message that Tara was missing, Alicia said. When she called him back, she said her brother-in-law told his story about Tara leaving in a black sedan following an argument. Alicia said that Stephen sounded oddly casual, considering the circumstances.

Alicia recounted for the court how she and Erik drove to Michigan immediately and distributed pictures of Tara throughout Macomb County and in Metro Airport. She said Stephen didn't offer to help. She described having dinner at a Chili's restaurant with Stephen and his children one night during the search for Tara.

"Stephen drove Tara's Isuzu Trooper," she said. "He insisted we all ride together in the Trooper." Alicia had no clue at the time that her sister's body had been in the back of the vehicle only a few days earlier.

She said the last time she and Stephen spoke was on March 2, about an hour before police began searching his house. He'd told her that he'd released a family videotape to several media outlets, and that a reporter from one local television station would be upset because Stephen earlier had promised to release the footage exclusively to him. "He asked me to lie and say I released the tape," Alicia said. "I said, 'I'm not going to lie for you.'"

Prosecutor Smith announced he had no further questions and defense attorney Pamukov approached the podium. Alicia tightened her lips.

"How long does it take to drive from your home in Ohio to Washington Township?" Gail Pamukov asked. Alicia said it took five hours.

"I'm assuming you didn't physically visit much?" Pamukov asked. "When was the last time you saw your sister?"

Alicia said the last time she'd seen Tara was on Thanksgiving 2006, when the Grants traveled to her Ohio home for dinner.

"And your ability to see Tara with the children was limited to those visits?" Pamukov asked.

"Yes."

"I assume you and Tara argued."

"All siblings do," Alicia answered.

Pamukov asked whether she'd argued with Tara that Thanksgiving, and Alicia acknowledged that she had. "Was it always lovey-dovey? No—we were sisters," she said. "We argued sometimes."

Pamukov then raised the issue of Tara's business travel. "You knew your sister had a heavy travel schedule?"

"Right."

"She was gone all week usually, right?"

"Yes."

"It's my impression she did whatever was demanded for her job," Pamukov said; to which, Alicia retorted, "But she never put her job before her children."

Pamukov next brought up the fact that the Grants had gone through several au pairs. Alicia testified there had been four au pairs who stayed in the home for more than a few days, "and numerous others who came and went." She said her sister had decided to hire an au pair the year Ian was born, in 2002.

When asked what kind of father Stephen was, Alicia acknowledged that he seemed to be attentive, and that he took care of Lindsey and Ian's day-to-day needs.

Pamukov then produced an article from the February 20 edition of the *Detroit Free Press,* in which Alicia was quoted as saying Tara planned to go back to work a day early the weekend of the murder, as Stephen had claimed. "Your statement to the newspaper is different from your testimony today," Pamukov said.

Alicia said the quote in the newspaper was due to a misstatement on her part. She explained that she hadn't been sleeping much when she gave the interview, because she was worried about her sister. "Stephen said she was leaving a day early, so I might have just told that story to the media," she said. "But I can tell you, Tara said she was going back on Monday."

"But isn't it possible that Tara may have told you she planned to cut the weekend short?" Pamukov asked.

"It's possible," Alicia said, "but that's not what I remember."

Pamukov then asked Alicia whether Stephen ever called her at home over the years. She said he did. "Early on in Tara's traveling, he'd call when she was out of town," Alicia replied. "He said he was lonely and needed someone to talk to."

Pamukov asked Alicia if she knew anything about Tara's goals and dreams. "My sister was a private person," Alicia said. "Our conversations were usually about our children," she said.

Pamukov then asked, "Did Tara ever say she wanted to stop being so controlling and domineering in the marriage?"

Alicia was quick to defend her sister: "She wasn't the domineering personality in that marriage," she said. "She was the breadwinner, but she wasn't the dominant one."

Pamukov asked Alicia to recount what Stephen had first told her about his argument with Tara on February 9. "He indicated to me that he told her it would be less disruptive to the family if she just stayed in Puerto Rico instead of coming home," Alicia said.

Pamukov barely had time to leave the podium when Smith began his redirect, with questions obviously designed to portray Tara as a loving mother, despite her dedication to her job.

"Did Tara ever indicate that her travel was a source of discontent?"

"No."

"And in relation to her children, which came first— her job or her children?"

"Her children," Alicia said. "As a mom, you can sense where the priorities lie, and it was with the children."

Smith indicated he had no further questions, and Alicia stiffly stepped down from the witness stand. She appeared to be exhausted.

86

Lou Troendle was the next witness. Although he had been a key figure in the case since the beginning, little was known about Tara's well-dressed, silver-haired, fifty-year-old boss.

Perhaps Troendle's appearance on the witness stand would reveal if there was any substance to Stephen's suspicions about Tara having an affair with the man he'd referred to as an old geezer.

Troendle testified that he'd known Tara since 1994, when she started working at Washington Group International. Troendle was a project director at the firm, where he was in charge of a team that oversaw construction projects around the world. Washington Group had been acquired by URS Corporation of San Francisco in November 2007 for $3.1 billion. "I was the one who interviewed her," he said, adding that he quickly identified her as management material.

He said he and his wife, Leslie, were friends with the Grants outside of work, and that they often got together for parties and other functions. He said the last time he'd seen Stephen was when the Grants spent a weekend together in Puerto Rico in mid-January.

When Smith asked Troendle if Tara had ever mentioned her travel schedule being a problem in her marriage, he said she hadn't. "Tara kept family issues to herself," he said. "She usually confined her conversations to talking about her children."

Troendle said Stephen called him the morning of Monday, February 12, asking if he'd seen Tara. "Of course, I hadn't," the executive said. He added that Tara was due back to work on Monday, and that he hadn't asked her to report a day early, as Stephen had claimed.

Stephen called him again later that night, and Troendle asked whether he'd called the police. "The answer was that he had not," Torendle said. "It was a strange discussion. He kept asking things like, 'When is someone legally considered missing? Is it forty-eight hours?'"

Troendle said he couldn't understand why Stephen hadn't called authorities. "My exact words were 'Do you want me to come up there and go with you?' I kept telling him, 'You need to do this.'" Throughout the conversation, Troendle recalled, Stephen's manner was "reasonably calm."

Troendle told the court the last time he talked to Stephen was on March 2, when Stephen called him to find out if Tara's health insurance was still valid, because he said one of the kids was sick.

Then it was Gail Pamukov's turn to cross-examine Troendle.

"You and Tara worked together for thirteen years," Pamukov said. "It sounds to me that Tara was an apt and capable student who was on the leadership track." Troendle agreed.

The defense attorney continued. "And I'm assuming as operations manager of the Puerto Rico office, she was instrumental in deciding who would stay, and who would go?" Again, Troendle agreed.

"So this was no shrinking violet?" Pamukov asked.

"I don't know what you mean by that terminology," Troendle replied, "but she was a good leader."

"You spent a good deal of time together in the Puerto Rico office," Pamukov said. "Were there times when Tara's phone would ring, and you'd know it was Stephen Grant?"

"Yes."

"Did she take those calls?"

"Most of the time," Troendle said.

Pamukov asked about the difficulty the Grants had in keeping au pairs. Troendle responded that Tara had told him she was very particular about the people she allowed to watch her children. "She had to go through a lot to find an au pair who fit the family," he said.

Troendle was then excused. Stephen's suspicion that his wife was sleeping with her boss was not addressed by either the defense or the prosecution.

87

Pam McLean was called next to the witness stand. Struggling to speak through a nasty cold, she recounted how she and Kozlowski visited the Grant home the evening of February 14, hours after the missing persons report was filed. McLean said Stephen was home with his nanny and children that night. She said she spoke with Verena briefly, but the au pair seemed to be in a hurry to leave the house.

She recounted for the jury that Stephen told her the same story he'd told Deputy Hughes earlier that day about his wife angrily leaving in a black sedan after calling someone and saying, "I'll be right out."

"He was convinced Tara's boss, mother, and sister knew where she was, but he said they were keeping it from him," McLean said.

McLean said Stephen allowed the detectives to look through the house. "The home was very tidy," she said. "I noticed that Tara's closet was full. There were no spaces to indicate any clothes had been removed." The detective sergeants also spied three pairs of eyeglasses on the bedroom nightstand. "These were things I thought she would need if she was leaving," she said.

The detectives were at the Grant home for about an hour, McLean said. "In my opinion, he appeared nervous," she said. "He kept going off on tangents."

McLean said Stephen's demeanor changed as the interview wound down. "He became sad toward the end, and started crying," she said. "He only started crying when we suggested he come in the next day for further questioning."

McLean said she verified the next day that Tara had a flight scheduled to return to Puerto Rico on Monday, which she said called into question Stephen's story about Tara leaving early. McLean said she contacted the U.S. Border Patrol and the Immigration and Naturalization Service (INS) to see if Tara had used a passport since her trip to London in January. She hadn't. Her trips to Puerto Rico, a U.S. territory, hadn't required one.

Checks through the credit-reporting agency TRW, the airlines, and San Juan hotels all turned up nothing, McLean said. The last credit card activity police could verify was when Tara used her American Express card at 9:32 P.M. on February 9 to pay for parking at Metro Airport.

Detectives obtained search warrants for the records of the Grants' home phone, Stephen and Tara's cell phones, and Verena Dierkes's cell phone. McLean said the phone records revealed some interesting facts:

- Stephen and Tara exchanged eleven phone calls on February 9.
- Stephen also called his au pair five times that night, including three short calls that were made around the time Stephen claimed he'd been arguing with Tara.
- In the days following Tara's disappearance, Stephen also placed ten calls to his wife's cell phone.

But tellingly, not a single call had been placed from either Tara's cell phone or the home phone around the time on February 9 that Stephen claimed she'd called someone and left in a black vehicle.

McLean said detectives hung a placard in police headquarters, chronicling all the calls that had been made. She said the decision was also made to put Stephen under surveillance.

On February 26, McLean said, an undercover officer saw Stephen stop his car and place a call from a pay phone. He waited for Stephen to drive away, and then the officer dialed his own home number from the pay phone, she said. The sergeant explained that the officer called home so that police could later pinpoint the call Stephen had made—on the log sheet, it would be the call placed just before the officer's home number was dialed.

When police obtained the pay phone's records, it was determined that Stephen had dialed an international number. "I recognized it as the home number of Verena Dierkes," McLean said.

Under cross-examination, Stephen Rabaut asked about other calls Tara had made the day of the murder. "Did you ever investigate those other calls from Tara's cell phone?" Rabaut asked.

McLean said that police did investigate the calls, but that the calls weren't pertinent to the investigation.

Rabaut then asked McLean if the Grants' au pair had ever indicated there were problems in the marriage. "I was informed of Verena's opinion that there were problems," McLean said.

Deputy Adnan Durrani, a Macomb County evidence technician, was the prosecution's next witness. He was sent to the Grant home after the interview by McLean and Kozlowski, the night of February 14, to take pictures of Stephen's injuries. Durrani said Stephen appeared nervous and apologetic.

Durrani said he photographed the scratch on the left side of Stephen's nose, a small bruise on his left leg, and a scratch on his right hand. He said Stephen claimed to have cut his nose on a metal shaving at his father's shop, and that he'd cut his hand while trying to start his snowblower. He did not have an explanation for the bruise, Durrani said.

After Durrani's testimony, the prosecution called Deena Hardy, the ex-girlfriend to whom Stephen had written the racy e-mails two weeks before the murder.

Pamukov was ready with her objection: She asked the judge to disallow the e-mails from being entered as evidence. Pamukov characterized the messages as hearsay, and said they served no other purpose "than to make the jury hate Stephen Grant."

Smith argued that Hardy's statements about the e-mails would be relevant. In his opening, he had claimed Stephen killed Tara to facilitate his affair with his au pair. "Evidence of marital discord is relevant," Smith said.

Pamukov started to cite a 1974 case, when the judge cut her off: "I don't think they had e-mails in 1974," she said. Druzinski promised to rule on the matter after the midday break.

88

To court watchers, although the morning's testimony had so far revealed some interesting information, it had largely been an uneventful day.

That would change.

After lunch, Druzinski ruled that the e-mails were admissible. She said they were not hearsay, as the defense claimed, because they showed the defendant's state of mind in the weeks leading up to the murder. But the judge ruled that while prosecutors could talk about the spicy messages, they could not provide transcripts to the jurors.

Hardy, wearing a tan suit, took the stand. Upon questioning from Eric Smith, she told the jury she'd known Stephen since childhood. The attractive redhead testified that she also had dated Stephen in 1992 and 1993, when they both were in their twenties.

"After we broke up, he'd call me about once a year to see how things were going," she said. Although most of their conversations were matter-of-fact, she said that changed in early 2007. "At the end of January, he called me," she said. "It was more flirtatious this time."

Hardy said they exchanged e-mail addresses and Stephen continued flirting with her online. On January 25, she said, Stephen sent her a series of sexually explicit e-mail messages. They also talked on the phone about ten times that day. "It sounded like he wanted to hook up," she said, adding that they agreed to meet for dinner on either January 30 or 31, which were weekdays when Tara would be out of town.

During one of their conversations, Hardy said, she asked Stephen if he was still working for his dad. "He said no. He said he had a different job that required him to travel a lot," Hardy recalled.

Then Smith read aloud to the courtroom the sexually charged e-mails Stephen and Hardy had exchanged on January 25. The entire time, Stephen stared intently at Hardy. She, however, didn't return the gaze, although she appeared embarrassed as the prosecutor recounted their racy correspondence.

"Did you ever discuss these e-mails with Mr. Grant?" Smith asked.

Hardy testified that she'd talked to Stephen after the *Detroit News* published the e-mails on February 21. "He was a little upset about the e-mails being published," she said.

But, Hardy added, Stephen seemed to enjoy the media attention the case was getting. "He bragged that a reporter from *Dateline NBC* kept calling him," she said.

Gail Pamukov cross-examined Hardy. "You said you agreed to meet with Stephen Grant," the attorney said. "Did you have sex with Mr. Grant in January 2007?"

"No."

"So, even though there was some sexual content in those e-mails, you didn't act on that?" Pamukov asked. Hardy answered that Stephen called her and canceled the scheduled meeting.

Hardy was excused from the stand. She appeared relieved as she walked out of the courtroom, doing her best to avoid eye contact with her ex-boyfriend.

89

As spectators were still digesting the appearance of Stephen's ex-girlfriend, they got another adrenaline surge when the prosecution called its next witness: Verena Dierkes.

Earlier that day, scuttlebutt among reporters held that Verena might testify. There were unconfirmed reports that she'd flown in from Germany the previous evening. During the lunch break, the rumor was verified when someone opened the witness room door briefly and a Channel 4 cameraman captured a few seconds of footage of the Grants' au pair. The pale young woman wore a gray suit, and her hair, which had been blond when she lived with the Grants, was now dark brown.

Prosecutors had shuttled Dierkes into the courthouse through the same underground tunnel Stephen was using. She was then whisked into the witness room, where she waited until the bailiff summoned her to testify.

"Are you nervous?" the assistant prosecutor Therese Tobin asked.

"Yes," Verena answered, smiling self-consciously.

As artists sketched pastel portraits of the "other woman" in the Grant household, Tobin warmed up by asking Verena a few personal questions: How old was she? Verena said she was twenty years old. What was she currently doing in Germany? She said she was studying English and theology, with hopes of becoming a teacher.

Verena said she joined Au Pair in America in August 2006 after graduating from high school in Germany that June. She said she lived with her first American family for a few weeks before joining the Grants on August 21.

Speaking in a soft German accent, Verena told of living with the Grant family. She said she enjoyed her time there. She said she worked forty-five hours a week taking care of Lindsey and Ian, and had weekends off. On Wednesdays and on weekends, she said she would get together with other au pairs.

Verena testified that Tara's travel schedule wasn't too hectic when she first moved in with the family. But she said Tara's assignment changed in October, and she began spending all week in Puerto Rico.

"Was there a time when your relationship with Stephen Grant changed?" Tobin asked.

Verena softly answered, "Yes." She said she'd been taking classes at Macomb Community College, when one day toward the end of January, she came home and Stephen asked her to read some e-mails.

"I thought it was something in German he needed translated," she said. Instead, Verena said, the e-mails had been written by Tara. They were messages to an ex-boyfriend, she said. "The e-mails made it obvious the relationship was intimate," Verena said.

Verena said Stephen told her he felt trapped. "He said he didn't want a divorce, because his parents had a divorce and he had been through hell," she said. "He kept saying, over and over, 'I don't know what to do.' Then he apologized and said I shouldn't tell anyone about these e-mails."

The nanny's mild-mannered boss proved increasingly manipulative behind the scenes. During a telephone conversation the next day, Verena said, Stephen told her not to act any different around Tara. "He said, 'Don't say anything to her about the e-mails, even though she deserves a kick in the ass,'" Verena said.

Later that night, as she was getting ready for bed, Verena said, Stephen told her, "You're beautiful. I want to sleep with you."

"I started laughing," the nanny recalled. "I didn't know how to react." She said they talked for four hours that night, finally going to their separate bedrooms at about 2:00 A.M.

Verena went to her computer and typed up an e-mail to her brother, wishing him luck on an upcoming test. As she sat at the desk, she got the feeling someone was watching her. She turned around. Stephen was standing in her bedroom doorway. "He said he was going to take a shower, and he asked if I wanted to join him," she said. "I said no."

The next day, Verena said, Stephen called her cell phone from his father's shop. "He said he was glad I was still talking to him," she said. "He said he was afraid I'd pack my suitcases and leave."

Despite his apparent contrition, however, Stephen continued his lecherous advances toward the teenager. That night, as Verena was preparing to go out with friends, she said, Stephen poked his head into the bathroom and told her she looked good. He also told her Tara was en route home.

The Grants' final weekend together was uneventful, Verena recalled. On Saturday, she said the couple went grocery shopping. The next day—Super Bowl Sunday—Verena said the family ate dinner and watched the Indianapolis Colts defeat the Chicago Bears. "They hugged each other a very long time, and I thought they had talked about the e-mails, and everything was all right again," she said.

But later that night, Verena said, Stephen sent her another flirtatious e-mail: *For what I'm thinking I know I'm going to hell,* wrote the "Mr. Mom" from his bedroom computer, just across the hall from where his two children slept.

Verena said Stephen sent her another e-mail Monday morning, telling her he'd been looking at her breasts. He said he hoped she was "itchy," and he went on to explain that "scratching the itch" was one of his euphemisms for having sex.

On Tuesday, Verena said, Tara left for Puerto Rico. She said Stephen had activated text messaging on her cell phone that day, and when she was in class later that evening, she received a text from Stephen: *Do you want me to do your laundry to see if you are itching?*

When she got home that night and logged on to the Internet, she said there was an e-mail from Stephen waiting for her. It said: *If you come downstairs, I've got you. If you stay in your room, I'll understand that you hate me.*

She said she went downstairs and told him, "I don't hate you, but you don't 'got me,' either." She said he gave her a hug. Then they sat down on the couch to watch television together, she said.

Verena said Stephen touched her feet, prompting her to demur, explaining that she didn't like her feet touched. That, Stephen insisted, was all in her head, and he said he wanted to help her get over her "problem."

"He said he was giving me therapy," she said. She endured it and tried to focus on the television while Stephen played with her feet.

Even after she'd retired to her bedroom later that night, Verena said, Stephen kept texting. In one message, he asked her to come out of her room to see him one last time for the night. When she opened her bedroom door, she said, he was standing there, waiting for her. "He told me he wanted to have sex with me, but I said no," the nanny testified.

But, Verena admitted, she did allow him into her bed. They slept for about an hour, she said, before he woke up and went to his own room. The next morning, Verena recalled, Stephen asked her to come to his room. "He pulled down his pajama pants and said we could now have sex, because I now knew what he looked like naked."

On Thursday—the day before the murder—Verena said, she was resting in bed when Stephen called and asked her to meet him for lunch. She said she thought that was odd, since Stephen had always disliked going to restaurants with his wife. "He was always embarrassed to have lunch with Tara," Verena explained. "He said she was always dressed nice, and he was dirty from working in the shop."

Verena said she declined the invitation. "I was about to go pick up Ian from school, when Stephen came home," she said. "He said I made him smile. He said I made him happy."

Later that night, after dinner, Stephen drank a beer. "He said it made him dizzy," Verena recalled. Stephen went to his room eventually, and she turned in a short time later. As she was getting ready for bed, she said, Stephen came into her bedroom and said, "Good night. I love you."

"We sat down on my bed and talked," she said. "He said, 'I won't repeat those three little words again, but I am falling in love with you.'" Verena said they cuddled on her bed for a short time. "But he kept asking if we could spend the night in his room," she said. "He pulled me out of my room, and I followed him."

In a quiet voice, she added: "We had oral sex. He did me."

Verena said she was startled when her alarm sounded at seven o'clock the morning of February 9. She hurried to her room to shut off the clock; then she retreated down the hall and climbed back into bed with Stephen.

In her haste, she forgot to close the door to the master bedroom. "Lindsey came walking into the room," she testified. "I was hiding under the blanket."

As the seconds ticked away on Tara Grant's last day on earth, her husband's pursuit of their young nanny grew increasingly frantic. Throughout the day, Verena said, Stephen kept asking her how she felt about him. "I said, 'I don't know,'" she recalled.

Later that evening, as she hung out at the bar with friends, her phone kept coming alive with calls and text messages from Stephen. "I felt annoyed," she said.

Verena said she found a private spot in the restaurant and called Stephen to ask him to stop pestering her. "The girls were wondering what was going on," she said. The text messages stopped for a while. Then, at about 10:30 P.M., another message from Stephen appeared on her cell phone: *Tara is going to be home in a few minutes. You owe me a kiss. Make a noise when you get home so I can get my kiss.*

Verena said when she arrived home about an hour later, Tara's Trooper was in the garage. As she walked into the house, Stephen came running down the stairs, screaming, "What the fuck are you still doing here?"

Recognizing the au pair, he apologized and said he'd thought she was Tara. Verena noticed a new scratch on his nose. Then, she said, Stephen went into the dining room, sat in a chair, and started to cry. There had been an argument, he said. Tara had left him. "He said he could have walked away, but he wanted to fight," Verena recalled. "He said they were arguing about traveling.

"He said he expected to get divorce papers on Monday," she said. "He said it was going to be hard, and he would understand if I wanted to leave. But he said he needed me."

Verena needed to keep quiet about their budding

relationship, Stephen added. "He said he would lose the kids if anyone found out about the affair," she said. "Then he took a flashlight and went into the garage."

Later he asked her to delete the text messages he'd sent her earlier that night. "I started to delete one of them and he took my cell phone from me and deleted all of them," she said.

Meanwhile, Stephen asked her to help him wash the sheets from the master bedroom. After that, she said, they went to their separate rooms.

Verena said Stephen asked her the next morning to watch the kids while he went to the post office and the bank. When he returned a few hours later, she said, she went out to meet some friends.

"I came back around midnight," she said. "We talked a little. He said he left messages with Tara, but she didn't call him back. We slept together again, kissing and cuddling. On Sunday, he said I needed to watch the kids for two hours because he needed to do some work at the shop. He didn't come back for four hours."

That evening, Verena said, Stephen told her he'd left "mean" messages on Tara's cell phone. "He said he left Tara a message saying he wouldn't be home Monday," she said. "He said . . . she was a bitch and she should call her kids."

Verena said she left the house for a few hours. "He sent me a text that said the kids know I liked strawberries, so they bought strawberries for me," she said. When she got home that night, she said, Stephen ran down the stairs to greet her. He kissed her and asked, "Did you miss me?"

On Monday, however, Stephen offered some strange advice. "He said he doesn't know what's going on with Tara," she said. "He told me there was a gun in his room, and he said if she goes in there, I should take the kids and leave."

Verena said they again slept together in her room that night, but did not have sex. "On Tuesday, he told me he called Tara's mom and boss, but they didn't know where she was," Verena said. "He said he was going to report her missing Wednesday morning.

"He kept wanting to know my feelings," she said. "He said he was in love with me. He said, 'Are you falling in love with me?'

"I said, 'Yeah, maybe.'"

90

Verena said, on Wednesday, as planned, Stephen reported Tara missing. She said she briefly spoke with Detectives Kozlowski and McLean that night before leaving to meet friends.

Three days later, she said, she spoke with a private detective, who was a friend of Stephen's. She said she told the private eye about the e-mails Tara had written to another man. "He told me I can't tell anyone about those e-mails because the police might think [Stephen] was jealous and did something to Tara," she said.

When Kozlowski interviewed Verena a few days later, she said, she didn't tell him about Tara's e-mails. "I didn't tell him about our relationship. I wanted to protect [Stephen]." Verena began openly weeping on the stand. "I believed everything he said. I believed the story he told me about Tara leaving."

Verena glared at Stephen for a brief moment. He showed no emotion.

On February 16, Verena said, her community counselor at Au Pair in America told her she would have to leave the Grant home immediately because of the pending missing person case. "I packed my stuff," she said. "I was upset. I didn't want to leave."

Stephen came to her room. "He called my counselor and asked if I could spend one more night," she said. "I slept with him in my room, kissing and cuddling." Verena said she flew back to Germany on February 21, but she continued to call or e-mail Stephen at least once a day. "We made up new e-mail addresses," she said. "Steve said the police knew the regular e-mail addresses, and he said we couldn't talk the way we wanted."

The nanny's testimony climaxed with a description of calls from the fugitive Stephen Grant. She had stopped crying by now, and she answered the lawyer's questions in a low, measured voice. Stephen phoned her on March 2 as he fled from police. "He said, 'The police are searching the house.' He explained if police found one drop of blood, he was screwed," she said.

The next day, she got another call from Stephen. "He said, 'I'm just calling to say good-bye.' He told me he's going to prison the rest of his life, but he said it was an accident. He said, 'Tara smacked me, so *boom*—done,'" Verena recounted. "He said I should call the kids and tell them he was sorry, and tell them that he loved them. Then he wanted me to say I loved him."

Tobin asked Verena, "Did you love him?"

The witness paused for a second. "I think so, yes."

Verena said she called Kozlowski later that night, and that he told her Stephen had confessed to murdering his wife. "I was crying because I realized that Tara is dead," she said, again breaking into tears on the stand. "Steve told me not to tell the police about our affair, and he kept saying he was innocent. He said a lot of people in jail are innocent, and he didn't want to be one of them.

"I wanted to protect him," she said, but she finally told Kozlowski the truth after reading Stephen's confession. Then she wrote a forty-page document, telling all she knew.

Verena had taken the stand at 2:10 P.M. After an hour

and ten minutes of spellbinding testimony, Tobin announced that she had no further questions.

Pamukov stepped up to begin cross-examination. "Based on what you said, you had one contact with oral sex," Pamukov said. "You and Mr. Grant slept together several times, but you never had intercourse, correct?" Verena concurred.

Pamukov then asked Verena about the text message Stephen sent her the night of the murder, and asked her to clarify whether he'd told her to make a noise when she came home. "This whole thing about making a noise was to avoid detection because Tara was supposed to be home, right?" Pamukov asked. Verena agreed.

Pamukov then asked what kind of father Stephen was, and Verena replied that he was a good, attentive father. Verena also testified that Tara didn't reveal much about her relationship with her husband, although she said she saw them argue from time to time.

Usually, though, Verena said, the Grant home was quiet. She said Stephen stayed home with the children most nights, and that he did various chores, such as cooking and laundry.

"In terms of the flirtation, did you enjoy the attention?" Pamukov asked.

"Yes," the nanny replied.

Pamukov announced she had no further questions.

Verena appeared drained as she left the stand. She and Stephen exchanged a brief glance as she walked past him and out of the courtroom.

Druzinski then called for a fifteen-minute break.

91

As the afternoon wore on, jurors and courtroom observers were jolted from the salacious drama of the lovestruck nanny and the lecherous employer, nearly twice her age, to the harsh reality of the murdered woman's fate.

Sheila Werner, who had stumbled upon the bloody debris that broke the Grant case open, took the stand after the afternoon break. Dressed in a red silk shirt, the attractive brunette explained to jurors that she lived near Stony Creek Metropark and that she often walked there with her small children.

She briefly recapped how, on February 28, she took advantage of the 40-degree weather and went for a hike in the park about 12:30 P.M. She said she'd been walking along Mount Vernon Road for about ten minutes when she decided to cut through the woods. Passing through the wooded area, she saw something unusual sticking out of a snow-covered tree stump: a large plastic Ziploc bag, which prompted her to call the police.

Deputy John Warn, who responded to the call, replaced Werner on the witness stand. During his brief testimony, he verified that he'd met with Werner and that she turned the bag over to him. He said Werner took him to the spot where she'd found the bag. Then, he said, he turned the evidence over to Kozlowski.

* * *

When Warn stepped down from the witness stand, Druzinski called a halt to the day's testimony. After the jury was escorted out of the room, the defense and prosecution discussed which pictures would be shown in court.

Prosecutors said they wanted to introduce as evidence three autopsy photos, along with a video taken of the Grants' home. Therese Tobin argued that the video showed nothing objectionable. She said the video merely depicted someone taking the top off a plastic container, revealing only a bit of skin. "I know it's gruesome," she said, "but to just say there was a torso found in the home doesn't give this jury what they need to see."

Tobin said every effort had been made to ensure nothing too gory would be shown to jurors. She said there had been several pictures taken of Tara's decapitated head, but the photos the jury would see only showed a portion of her hair, not her face. Tobin said showing the pictures would illustrate to the jury how Stephen tried to cover up his crime. She added that juries regularly are forced to deal with gruesome evidence during murder trials. Tobin assured the judge that prosecutors had cropped the three autopsy pictures so they would be less shocking.

Stephen Rabaut argued that the pictures would prejudice the jury. "There's no way the defense can get a fair trial when the jurors see body parts in the snow," he said.

Druzinski announced she would rule the next morning whether to admit the photos into evidence. Then Stephen Grant was escorted out of the courtroom.

It had been an emotional, exhausting day.

92

Testimony was delayed for about an hour on Wednesday while Judge Druzinski conferred with attorneys in her chambers about which photos to admit into evidence. As the clock neared 10:00 A.M., Druzinski made her ruling: most of the photos prosecutors wanted to show the jury would be admissible.

Druzinski did say, however, that the pictures that showed Tara's body parts would not be allowed, because she said they would only prejudice the jury while adding nothing to the case. The judge also ruled the video of the Grant home could be shown to the jury. She asked that the portion of the video showing Tara's torso in the garage be shortened to ten or fifteen seconds. Bill Cataldo agreed to stop the video when the judge directed him to, and fast-forward through the part she didn't want the jurors to see.

Sergeant Mark Grammatico, a sixteen-year veteran of the sheriff's office, was the day's first witness. He said everyone in the detective bureau had worked on the Grant case at one time or another. "That's very unusual," he said. Grammatico told Eric Smith that the sheriff's office received hundreds of tips in the days after Tara Grant was

first reported missing. "I took each one individually to see
if they were credible," he said.

Smith's questioning then moved to the events of
March 2. Grammatico was among the officers executing
the search warrant on the Grant home that day. About
fifteen officers, including evidence technicians, swarmed
the residence. In order to stay out of the way of the evidence techs, Grammatico said, he and a group of officers decided to stay in the garage. "We were just standing
around discussing the case," he said. "Then I heard Sergeant Kozlowski say, 'What the fuck!'"

He said Kozlowski had been looking in a large green
plastic container. Officers gathered closer and saw black
plastic bags covering an unknown object. He said Kozlowski cut open the bag to reveal a human torso. "Koz
told everyone to back off so we wouldn't taint the evidence," Grammatico said. "Several of us left to look for
our prime suspect, Mr. Grant."

Eric Smith then announced that he was going to play
the video of the Grant home, which had been filmed by
an evidence technician the night Tara's torso was discovered. As the video played, Grammatico narrated what
was happening on the screen.

The shaky video appeared at first to be a tour of a
normal upper-middle-class home. In an upstairs bedroom, there was an unmade bed; while in the bathroom
next door, a towel was shown draped over a shower cur-
tain rod. In the basement, the camera scanned past a
child's basketball hoop, workout equipment, and a wine
cellar.

But then the video moved into the garage.

Tara's mother, Mary, shifted slightly in her seat as the
camera zoomed in on a green plastic container. On the
screen, a gloved hand was shown moving aside a black

plastic bag to reveal flesh. Then the video was stopped, and Smith announced he had no further questions.

During cross-examination, Stephen Rabaut asked Grammatico whether he'd found any evidence that Stephen had planned the murder. Grammatico admitted he'd never found any plane tickets, maps of where to hide the body parts, or any other indications that the crime or cover-up was premeditated.

Detective Sergeant David Kennedy took the stand after Grammatico. Kennedy was among the officers who searched USG Babbitt, Stephen's father's shop, where the dismemberment had occurred. Kennedy described the small shop as "disheveled, and cluttered, with metal shavings everywhere." He said detectives confiscated a computer and a handheld global tracking system unit.

Police also took into evidence some saw blades, and Kennedy said he saw a loft area where a rectangular imprint was left in the dust. The imprint was about the size of the Rubbermaid container used to store Tara's body parts, Kennedy said.

Next to testify was Captain Anthony Wickersham, chief of staff at the MCSO. At the time of the murder investigation, Wickersham had been in charge of the detective bureau. He said he was the first officer on the scene on March 2, and that he had formally informed Stephen about the search warrant.

As Wickersham spoke, another video, which had been recorded by a Channel 4 cameraman, was shown. It depicted Stephen walking his golden retriever, Bentley, in the driveway of his home, while huge snowflakes swirled around him.

Wickersham said he told Stephen he was free to leave, and Stephen was cordial as he let the officers in. "He asked us if we were going to tear up his house searching for evidence," Wickersham said. Then Stephen took his dog for a walk. By the time police discovered Tara's torso, the bereaved husband was gone.

As was now well-known, the man who was now a murder suspect had already borrowed a truck and was headed north. The neighbor who loaned the truck, Michael Zanlungo, was the prosecution's next witness.

Smith asked Zanlungo about his relationship with Stephen. They had been friends for a few years, Zanlungo said, noting that Stephen had coached his daughter's soccer team the previous season, while Zanlungo served as assistant coach.

At soccer games, "Tara was a fixture," Zanlungo said. He recalled her always smiling and cheering the girls on. "She cheered for all the girls, not just her own daughter."

As Zanlungo began to recount all the parties he and his wife had attended with the Grants, Rabaut objected, arguing that the discussion wasn't relevant.

Smith replied it was important to show what kind of parent Tara was. "Clearly, this has been made an issue in this case."

Druzinski overruled the objection, and allowed Smith to continue the questioning.

"Did you ever get the impression that the Grants' relationship was troubled?" Smith asked.

"No," Zanlungo said. "In fact, my wife and I envied their relationship. They seemed to have the perfect life together."

"Did you ever hear Tara belittle Stephen?" Smith asked.

"No, they seemed happy together," the witness replied. "She was proud of him being a soccer coach." Zanlungo said the only time he'd ever seen the Grants argue was over a trivial matter at a soccer game: they'd left Lindsey's cleats at home and "argued back and forth about who was going to go back to get the shoes."

Smith then asked Zanlungo about the days following February 9. Zanlungo said Stephen had called him that week and asked if he'd seen Tara. "He said she was missing," the witness said. "He said he hadn't gone to the police yet because she'd taken off like this before. He said, 'She wasn't Mother of the Year.'"

Stephen seemed to grow increasingly bitter as the search for his wife continued, Zanlungo said. "He was telling people that Tara had been having an affair. He alluded to people he thought she was having an affair with. He was upset that his wife had left him and was out with another man, supposedly. He was very angry."

Zanlungo said Stephen disparaged the police who were looking for Tara. "He said he was upset with the police, and said that they were badgering him. He'd make fun of them."

Zanlungo said Stephen called him one day and asked him if he'd be willing to be interviewed by a Channel 7 reporter to vouch for his character. Zanlungo said he told the reporter that Stephen was a "good guy."

"Did you ever get the impression that the notoriety he was getting was bothering him?" Smith asked.

"No," Zanlungo said. "I think he was glad to have it."

Then Smith led Zanlungo through a recap of the events of March 2, when he unwittingly loaned his yellow Dodge pickup to a then-fugitive Stephen Grant. When the news broke a few hours later that a torso had been found in the Grant home, Zanlungo said, he called Stephen's cell phone, which was answered by Stephen's sister, Kelly.

"I asked if there was a police officer in front of [Kelly's] house, and she said there was. I said, 'Put him on the phone.' When the officer came to the phone, I told him what kind of truck Stephen was driving," Zanlungo said.

Under cross-examination, Pamukov asked Zanlungo why he didn't tell police what he'd just told the jury when officers questioned him while Stephen was on the run. "All this content you just gave to the jury, you sat on it for months," she said. "You never volunteered this to law enforcement?"

"We know what happened when I volunteered something," he answered, referring to when he offered Stephen use of his truck. "I felt if they wanted to talk to me, they'd call me."

In an apparent attempt to show that Zanlungo didn't know what went on behind the Grants' closed doors, Pamukov asked how close he was to his neighbors. Zanlungo said he mostly saw the Grant family during the weekends.

"So these interactions between you, your wife, and children were in public?" she asked.

"Yes."

"And you weren't a confidant of Tara's?"

"No."

"So what went on in the privacy of their home, you can't speak about?"

"That's a fair statement," Zanlungo said.

Pamukov changed the subject: "Is it true that you offered Mr. Grant use of your vehicle?"

"Yes."

"And he told you if police found out about an affair between him and Verena, he would be arrested?"

Zanlungo agreed.

"So you had some cognition that Mr. Grant was going to be arrested, and yet you lent him your vehicle anyway?" Pamukov asked.

"Yes. He wanted to see his children."

* * *

Gail Pamukov wrapped up her cross-examination, and Eric Smith took the podium for his redirect. "Did you ever hear Stephen say anything bad about Tara's travel?" he asked.

"Quite the opposite," Zanlungo said. "He talked about the great places she traveled, like Europe."

"When Stephen first reported his wife missing, a lot of people thought he was guilty. But you stood by him. Why?" Smith asked.

"I thought he didn't do it," Zanlungo answered. "It was the worst decision of my life."

93

Lieutenant Elizabeth Darga was the next witness. She explained that police were able to obtain a search warrant after the MSP Crime Laboratory determined that the bag found by Sheila Werner on February 28 contained human blood.

After police found Tara's body parts, Darga said, she carried out a difficult task: "We notified Tara Grant's sister, and I presented her with a Polaroid photo of Tara's head for identification," she said.

Defense attorney Rabaut touched on a recurring theme during cross-examination: asking Darga if police had ever found any airplane tickets, maps, or anything else that would indicate Stephen had planned the murder and hiding of the body parts. She admitted there was no such evidence.

Sergeant Timothy Rodwell, of the Emmet County Sheriff's Office, who had helped to locate a fugitive Stephen in a Northern Michigan park, was next to take the stand. He talked about the search for Stephen in the snowy wilderness of Northern Michigan.

After several hours, Rodwell said, they began seeing footprints in the snow. Then they finally found Stephen.

"He was found hiding near a tree," he said. "He wasn't wearing any shoes."

On cross-examination, Pamukov asked, again: Had police found any plane tickets on Stephen? Did they find a map, or any other document, that would indicate Stephen had planned to kill his wife and go somewhere else? The answer was no.

Officer James Pettis, of the Charlevoix Police Department, helped the ECSO search Wilderness State Park. During his testimony, he said that during the search, he noticed footprints that seemed to go in no particular direction. At times, the footprints went in circles, he said. "We thought we were being possibly set up for an ambush," he said.

Pettis was among the officers who found Stephen huddled near a pine tree. "We told him to put his hands up, but he didn't comply. He remained where he was. Another officer and myself made physical contact and helped him stand. He wasn't wearing any shoes. He told me that he'd lost them in the snow."

Stephen's voice was slurred, Pettis said, and his hands appeared pale and waxy. As Pettis helped Stephen maintain his balance, the accused murderer repeated several times, "I couldn't do it," Pettis said.

Rabaut asked during cross-examination the same questions the defense asked every other law enforcement officer who took the stand. Pettis also verified he hadn't found evidence that Stephen was planning to skip town, or that he'd planned the murder.

Macomb County sergeant Larry King, who testified next, was among the officers who searched Stony Creek Metropark on March 5, the day after Stephen's confession, and on March 6. "There were five K-9 units, and close to one hundred people helping in the search," he said.

Stephen had drawn Kozlowski and McLean a map of where he'd hidden Tara's body parts. It turned out to be accurate, King said.

Police first found Tara's upper thigh, buried in the snow. Then her head was located underneath a log, King said. Tara's right hand, which had been severed at the wrist, was found sitting on top of the snow, unhidden. Then police found a large bone, which, King said, he thought might be a femur. He said animals had picked the bone clean. Animals also had gotten to Tara's left hand, King said. When police found it, all that was left was the bone and some tendons. A foot, severed at the ankle, was found in the snow, and then police found a lower leg inside a hollowed-out log.

Many of the body parts were found not far from heavily traveled walking paths and streets, King said. "We also found the red sled used to transport the body parts," King said. "There were saw blades nearby."

It was past 5:30 P.M. when Smith announced he had no further questions for King, and Druzinski decided to break for the day.

94

Rabaut began the fourth day of testimony with his cross-examination of Sergeant King. Under questioning, King admitted that Tara's body parts seemed to have been hidden haphazardly, and in some cases they hadn't been hidden at all. Some of the severed parts, King repeated, were found lying right atop the snow.

Deputy Kevin Silage was with King during the March 5 and March 6 searches of the Metropark. He testified that he had discovered several saw blades in the park, along with a pair of latex gloves, a knife, and a pair of scissors. Silage reiterated during cross-examination what King had said: Stephen hadn't appeared to try very hard to hide the evidence, since most of it was left right out in the open.

The prosecution called a handful of nurses and doctors who had treated Stephen at Northern Michigan Hospital. They all agreed that the patient interacted politely with hospital personnel and officers.

The prosecution's twenty-first witness was Jennifer Smiatacz, a DNA specialist with the MSP Forensic Science Division. Smiatacz said she helped process the Grant home on March 2, along with the two vehicles in the garage. She said she saw the possible presence of blood in the living room and in the wine cellar, so she dabbed the areas with a sterile cotton swab.

Smiatacz found possible bloodstains in Stephen's 2006 Jeep Commander, on the rear-door armrest, and on the passenger door of Tara's 2002 Isuzu Trooper. She also helped process Stephen's father's shop, USG Babbitt, where she swabbed two areas and collected metal shavings. The process took about ten hours, and they finally finished up at about 3:30 A.M.

Smiatacz said she later scraped the cheeks of Tara's parents for DNA analysis, adding that it takes quite a bit of skin to do the job right. Smiatacz then took samples from Tara's body parts, and from the blades used to dismember her, and sent them to the lab.

Heather Vita, supervisor of the MSP Forensic Science Division, said she tested the cheek swabs from Mary and Gerald Destrampe, and examined them against the DNA from the blood swabs taken from the Grant home and from Tara's body parts. They all matched. She said the chances of someone from the general population matching the same DNA profile were 1 in 3.7 quadrillion among Caucasians.

Testing determined that the DNA from the body parts, and from blood taken from the home and shop, were from the biological offspring of the Destrampes. However, the blood Smiatacz found on the armrest of Stephen's Jeep turned out to be Lindsey's. It was later revealed Lindsey had suffered a minor cut shortly before the murder.

Dr. Marco Scarpetta, an independent biochemist, briefly testified that the DNA taken from the body parts and blood swabs showed the odds were 1 in 2 billion that the blood and tissue analyzed at the Michigan State Police lab belonged to a child of the Destrampes.

Tobin then called to the stand Dr. Michael Johnson, who'd treated Stephen in Northern Michigan Hospital.

Dr. Johnson explained that Stephen technically didn't have frostbite when he was first arrested, although his extremities were discolored when he came to the hospital. The physician said he cleared Stephen to be interviewed by police, although he suggested they wait an hour before talking to him, to ensure he would be coherent. He said he didn't think Stephen was seriously hurt.

During Gail Pamukov's cross-examination, she asked Dr. Johnson whether he was aware that Stephen suffered from attention deficit disorder, and that he'd taken medication for it. Johnson said Stephen had disclosed that after his arrest.

Medical Examiner Daniel Spitz then took the stand and described his autopsy of Tara Grant. He said the torso, which showed early signs of decomposition, had been dismembered at the neck, shoulders, and groin. The torso was still in the plastic container when it came to his lab, he said.

In total, Spitz said, he examined thirteen different body parts, two of which were only segments of skin. The remains showed postmortem animal activity. The ME recounted his findings as the following:

- Tara's head had been dismembered between the C-6 and C-7 vertebrae. The cut was made through the front of the neck, Spitz said. Her arms were cut just below the shoulder joints, while her lower arm was separated at the elbow. Her hands were cut off at the wrists. Her lower extremities had been dismembered at the groin, knee joint, and just above the ankle, Spitz said.
- When Spitz examined Tara's head, he noted bruises on her right jaw and on the left side of her chin, abrasions on the bridge of her nose and right eyelid, and a bruise on the back of her head.

Spitz said the bruise on Tara's chin was indicative of a punch to that area.

- Spitz said there were also multiple scratches on Tara's face that he deduced were caused by animals during the weeks her head was in the park. The skin was reddish, Spitz said, because it had been exposed to the cold for several weeks.

- There were large oval-shaped contusions on Tara's lower back, a bruise on her upper chest, and a scrape on her left shoulder, Spitz said. He said all the dismemberment sites were cleanly cut, which, he said, was indicative of a serrated blade. The only exception, he said, was the right leg, which had jagged puncture wounds that fit the cutting profile of a jagged blade, he said.

- Spitz's internal examination revealed a variety of injuries, including bleeding over the chest wall that correlated with the bruise on her chest. There also was an acute fracture of the sternum. "It's not a bone that's easily broken," he said. "It would take significant compression to break that bone."

- The injuries to Tara's chin, torso, and lower back indicated there had been an altercation the night of the murder, Spitz said. He said he determined she had died by strangulation because of a vertical fracture to the thyroid cartilage. There also was bleeding in her neck muscles, which he said is also an indicator of strangulation.

Spitz said Tara likely lost consciousness in about a minute and a half. He added that it usually takes the average strangulation victim about four minutes to die from lack of oxygen to the brain.

Tara's entire body was not recovered, Spitz said. Still missing was a portion of her lower leg, between the knee and angle, her right foot, and her right arm, between the elbow and shoulder.

* * *

Things became heated during Pamukov's cross-examination as she parried with Spitz over how long it likely took Tara to die. The time element was crucial; Smith's charge of first-degree murder hinged in large part on the claim that Stephen had enough time while strangling his wife to consider what he was doing.

The defense attorney asked Spitz whether it was possible Tara died in less time than the four minutes he testified it usually takes for a strangulation victim to die. She pointed out that there had been an altercation, and asked Spitz whether the brain required more energy during a fight. Spitz agreed it did.

"The fact that Mrs. Grant's brain needed oxygen could have shortened the time it took for her to die, wouldn't you agree?" Pamukov asked. Spitz agreed, and Pamukov stated, "So you can't say how long it took for Mrs. Grant to die."

Spitz started to answer, "Well, as a general rule—" but Pamukov cut him off.

"I'm not asking for a general rule," she snapped. "You can't tell this jury how long it actually took Tara Grant to die."

"It could've taken three and a half minutes—" Spitz began, but Pamukov cut in with, "But you don't know, do you?"

"Well, I wasn't actually in the room witnessing the strangulation," Spitz shot back sarcastically. He stated again that the average time it takes to die of strangulation is four minutes.

Spitz was excused, and Druzinski brought the day's proceedings to a close.

95

Court officers, for the most part, had been professional and friendly with the media as the Grant trial wore on, but they were losing patience.

A few days earlier, a television station had mounted a hidden camera in the basement, capturing a few seconds of deputies escorting Stephen from court. After that, in an effort to provide an escape valve that might alleviate the media frenzy, court officials decided to allow camera operators to film Stephen in the basement as he was walked through the door leading to the tunnel. But officials advised against interviewing the defendant.

That didn't stop a few reporters from taking advantage of the relaxed rules. They fired questions at Stephen, sticking their microphones into his walking path, despite several requests from the officers to stop.

Lieutenant Bill Donovan assembled the media in the hallway outside the courtroom before the trial started on Friday morning and firmly reminded them to adhere to the rules.

Jeffrey Budzynowski, the Macomb County sheriff's sergeant who'd made the three-and-a-half-hour drive north to help search for Stephen on March 2, took the stand. He recounted searching the abandoned yellow getaway truck and finding the suicide note written by Stephen to his children. Budzynowski then read the letter aloud:

I know you two don't understand what happened to Mom. Maybe someday Kelly will tell you what happened. Just know that I love you both more than anything. Things kept getting worse between your mom and me, and things got physical. I ended up hitting Mom and hurting her bad. I was afraid of losing you two, so I ended up taking Mom's life in a panic. I am sorry. I know it will be hard to lose me after your mom was taken from you. I have decided to end my life. I know it is better.

While the note was being read, Stephen closed his eyes and bowed his head.

Budzynowski then testified that Stephen had asked to see his attorney after his arrest. Budzynowski said he informed Stephen that his lawyer, David Griem, had resigned from the case. "He asked, 'If I talk, will I get a deal?'" Budzynowski said. "He kept asking me, 'Do you think this was premeditated murder?' I said, 'Whoa—I don't want to talk to you about this.'"

Deputy Mark Berger, who also went up north to help with the Grant investigation, was then called to testify. He said he was assigned to guard Stephen in Northern Michigan Hospital.

"He kept asking, 'Why am I here?' and he kept asking what was going to happen to him," Berger said. "He seemed to be concerned about his safety. He said he was worried he was going to be assaulted and mistreated when he got to the Macomb County Jail."

Berger said he and Stephen watched the Detroit Red Wings play the Colorado Avalanche. During the hockey game, Berger said Stephen complained about how much money athletes make.

"His manner was very pleasant," Berger said. "He actually was pretty friendly. He really seemed anxious to talk. He kept trying to tell me things, and I told him I wasn't the one to talk about that. He said, 'You know, I can draw you a map.'"

Brian Kozlowski took the witness stand next. The detective recounted the investigation: how Stephen appeared nervous when Kozlowski and McLean visited him at his home, how Stephen retained an attorney and refused to talk to police, and how Kozlowski found Tara's torso in the garage.

After Kozlowski recounted his initial involvement in the case, up through his drive north after Stephen's capture, Smith announced he would play the recording of Stephen's three-hour confession.

Although prosecutors had released transcripts of the confession in April, this would be the first time the public would actually hear Stephen's voice describe how he strangled his wife and then dismembered her.

The jurors were provided transcripts of the confession, but the hard copies were not allowed to be entered as evidence. The transcripts were to be collected by a bailiff after the audio of the confession was played.

Bill Cataldo started the audio. Stephen was heard describing how he was naked when he began arguing with Tara the night of February 9. His voice sounded calm as he described how the argument escalated into homicidal rage. Sometimes the defendant's tone actually sounded jaunty as he talked with Kozlowski and McLean.

As Stephen told how he dismembered Tara's body in his father's shop, Alicia hung her head. Tara's mother slumped forward, and a cousin visiting from Jackson placed his hand gently on her shoulder to comfort her.

There wasn't enough time for the jury to hear the entire confession, so Druzinski called a halt to the day's proceedings, a little after 5:30 P.M. Forty-five minutes of audio remained to be played, but that would have to wait until Tuesday. The bailiff collected the transcripts from the jurors, and then they were excused.

It had been a long week.

After the day's proceedings wrapped up, Channel 4 reported on its 6:00 P.M. newscast that Stephen's visitation privileges in the Macomb County Jail had been revoked for an undisclosed infraction.

96

The tape began rolling, again, at 8:40 A.M., Tuesday. Bill Cataldo fast-forwarded over passages where Stephen talked about Tara's suspected infidelity. The same section that had been redacted when prosecutors released the transcript of the confession eight months earlier.

When the last forty-five minutes of Stephen's confession finished playing, the bailiff collected the transcripts from the jurors. Then Kozlowski took the witness stand once more.

Kozlowski said during Stephen's confession, the killer drew a map to help police locate where he'd hidden Tara's body parts, along with the sled that was used to transport the limbs.

Smith then told the jury that Stephen had left eight messages on Tara's voice mail in the days after he'd murdered her, in an effort to cover up the crime. Cataldo played audio files of the messages.

Stephen called his wife's cell phone at 2:15 A.M. on Saturday, February 10—about four hours after he murdered her—and left a message: "I think you owe me and your kids at least a . . . um . . . Just call and let me know what the hell's going on. Bye."

In another message, which Stephen left at 6:03 P.M.

that Saturday, he said, "The kids and I would like to talk to you. We're just ordering pizza for dinner, so we'll be here."

Then, on Sunday—shortly after he'd just finished dismembering Tara, according to his later confession—he placed another call to Tara's cell phone. His voice sounded angrier than it had in previous messages.

"The next time I call you, pick up your phone," he demanded. "Please—do not hit ignore. It's bullshit. It's absolute bullshit that you can't call me or your kids. Pick up your phone or call the house. Call somewhere. Call me. Call my cell. Call the kids. I know you're mad. I'm mad. Your traveling this much is not right. Just call me. Bye."

Prosecutor Smith then said he planned to play for the jury some of the interviews Stephen had given to the media during the time he claimed his wife was missing. Defense counsel Rabaut objected, claiming the interviews were hearsay statements. Smith argued that the statements of the defendant were not hearsay. Druzinski overruled Rabaut's objection, stating that the interviews were relevant to the premeditation claim made by the prosecution.

The first interview shown had been taped by Channel 7 shortly after Tara was reported missing. Stephen bawled on camera, saying, "I hope Tara walks through that door. God, please . . . call. Please. Call anyone."

The other interviews were along the same lines: Stephen crying and begging his wife to come home. In one interview with Channel 4, Stephen said Tara had been having a relationship with another man, although he didn't elaborate.

After Stephen's media interviews were played for the jury, Smith had a bailiff bring into the courtroom the red sled that had been used to transport Tara's body parts. Tara's mother and sister each shifted slightly in their seats when the sled was produced, but they showed no emotion.

Then a green Rubbermaid bin with a blue lid—the container that had been used to store Tara's torso—was entered into evidence, and a few gasps were heard in the courtroom. Smith used rubber gloves as he handled the container. He asked Kozlowski to identify it, and the detective said it was the bin that had held Tara Grant's torso.

During cross-examination, Rabaut asked, "Based upon this investigation, would you agree there is no evidence [that] would indicate Stephen Grant had a plan to do this?"

Kozlowski was quick with his answer: "No, I'm certain he planned to do it."

"Can you point to evidence that proves this?"

"Yes."

"Is it fair you located no evidence of recent purchases to dispose of the body, such as a sled or saw blades?" Rabaut asked.

"No, I couldn't do that."

"Stephen Grant tells you that the night of February ninth, he had an argument with this wife, and that they had an argument over her travel?" Rabaut stated. "And you're aware from phone records they had several conversations that day."

"Yes," the detective answered.

"And the gist of those conversations was that Tara wasn't home enough, that she didn't see the kids enough."

Kozlowski agreed that Stephen had told him he argued with Tara about her travel schedule.

Rabaut continued with his cross-examination: "And he said they argued when Tara got home. And that Tara slapped him and he lost it. He describes how she fell back and banged her head and appeared to be out of it.

"Then he said Tara used venomous words, and said, 'That's it. I'm going to take the kids.' He also described how she belittled him. She said, 'I can ruin your life,' and that's when he put his hands around her neck and started to choke her. Am I correct—you never asked him how long the choking took?" Rabaut asked.

"I never talked about that."

"And you never asked him how long the altercation lasted?"

"No."

"And he said when he knew she was dead, that he panicked," Rabaut continued. "He used that term several times, right?"

"Yes," Kozlowski said.

"He said he panicked because he didn't know what to do with her body—is that right?"

"That's what Mr. Grant said."

Rabaut then asked Kozlowski to clarify what Stephen had told him about dismembering his wife and getting rid of her body parts.

"Mr. Grant said he went to USG Babbitt . . . and it was there where he dismembered the body. And he described how he was surprised that all the body parts fit into one bin," Kozlowski said.

"He was quite efficient," the deputy added.

"He told you he'd done a bad job disposing of these parts. He actually stood in one spot, throwing the body parts," Rabaut said, emulating a throwing motion in several directions. Rabaut then produced a blue spiral notebook, which had been recovered from the Grants' bedroom. He said it was Tara's notebook. Smith objected to the notebook being introduced into the trial, claiming it was hearsay.

Druzinski asked Rabaut to explain why the writings in the notebook did not constitute hearsay, and Rabaut said it was relevant because it specifically dealt with the relationship between Stephen and Tara Grant. The notebook, Rabaut said, was titled "Goals for 2007."

The jurors were escorted out of the courtroom as the attorneys conferred with Druzinski about the admissibility of the blue notebook, along with another notebook, which had been found in Tara's car.

After the noon break, Druzinski announced that the two notebooks would not be admitted as evidence. In explaining her ruling, she revealed that the second notebook contained the letters Tara had written to her sister, husband, and parents during her self-improvement workshop.

Rabaut had said he wanted to introduce the notebooks to refute earlier witnesses who had claimed there were no problems in the marriage. But Druzinski said because the writings were all undated, there was no context to support their meaning. She also said the writing in the notebooks was hearsay.

Druzinski allowed the defense to mark the notebooks as special exhibits. Rabaut said he wanted them entered into the record for any future appellate action. The notebooks were never brought up in trial again.

With the issue of the notebooks resolved, the jury was brought back into the room, and Kozlowski again took the stand to allow Rabaut to finish his cross-examination.

"Several times during your interview, Mr. Grant started crying?" Rabaut asked.

"Yes."

"He exhibited emotion?"

"We all did," the detective said.

"When Mr. Grant stated he started choking his wife, his intent was to stop Tara from talking?"

"That's what Mr. Grant told me."

"Then later, he told you he wanted to keep from going to prison."

Kozlowski was ready with an answer: "Everything that happened that evening was his story."

"And we've went through his testimony and substantiated his story in several instances, haven't we?"

The detective agreed.

Rabaut also asked Kozlowski why he hadn't challenged any of the claims Stephen made in his confession, and Kozlowski said that wouldn't be a good interview technique. It wouldn't be smart, the detective said, to challenge a suspect while he's making a confession.

During redirect, Eric Smith cut to the chase. "Just so we're clear," he asked, "what was the very first thing the defendant asked you when you began interviewing him?"

Stephen had wanted to know the difference between first- and second-degree murder, the detective replied.

Kozlowski stepped down from the witness stand. Then, at 2:15 P.M., after calling twenty-eight witnesses in the case, Smith announced, "The prosecution rests."

97

Rabaut stood up and asked that the jury be excused. Once the jurors were out of the courtroom, he asked the court to withdraw the first-degree murder charge, arguing that the prosecution had not shown that the murder had been premeditated. He filed a motion for a directed verdict, pointing out that none of the law enforcement officers who testified ever found any evidence that Stephen had planned the murder.

Smith retorted: "The defense erroneously believes that in order to establish premeditation, you need to have a 'to do' list that ends with 'Kill my wife.'"

Druzinski denied the motion, and the jury was brought back into the room before Pamukov called the defense's first witness: Dr. Bader Cassin, who had performed a second autopsy on Tara's remains.

Cassin, who served as Washtenaw County's medical examiner, said his Macomb County counterpart, Dr. Spitz, had allowed Cassin to perform his autopsy in the Macomb County morgue.

The veteran medical examiner, who claimed to have performed about fourteen thousand autopsies in his career, said the postmortem of Tara's remains was one of the most difficult he'd ever performed, since the body had been lying around for some time and was in a state of decomposition.

Cassin agreed with Spitz that Tara had died of strangulation, and that there had been an altercation before the murder. However, Cassin said the time it took Tara to die was "irrelevant" because Stephen was in a frenzy, and he would not have had a sense of time.

Things got testy when Therese Tobin cross-examined Cassin. She asked whether Cassin had ordered toxicology or biology reports. Cassin said he hadn't, and admitted his autopsy report was "a draft."

Cassin also admitted that he based some of his opinions about the autopsy from media reports. When Tobin asked whether that was appropriate, Cassin hedged: "I would never say the media is the basis of my opinion, but every medical examiner looks at what the media says and takes it into consideration."

Tobin asked Cassin whether his boss, the Washtenaw County prosecutor, knew he formed opinions based on media reports, and Cassin shot back with, "Why shouldn't I?"

"I would submit the media is not a good source of info to base the things on," Tobin declared.

"Well, thanks a lot," Cassin responded sarcastically. "I do listen to what the media says. Sometimes they're reliable, sometimes not. Sometimes my own investigators give me information that's not reliable."

Tobin also noted that Tara's jaw injury had not been documented on Cassin's report. She also asked Cassin to show her in his report where he documented the size of any of Tara's injuries. Cassin said he hadn't noted the size of the injuries because he didn't think it was relevant. When pressed, Cassin admitted again that the report was just a draft.

"You keep referring to this report as a draft, as if it's an excuse," Tobin said. Cassin answered, "I make no excuses."

Rabaut stood up and objected that Tobin was being argumentative. The judge sustained the objection.

Tobin then asked Cassin if he thought Stephen's statement that he felt he had to kill his wife to avoid going to prison after he hit her showed clarity of mind. Cassin said he didn't believe that was what was going through Stephen's mind at the time. Tobin then asked Cassin if he was a psychologist, and Cassin said he was not.

"You didn't treat Mr. Grant?" Tobin asked. Cassin said he didn't remember treating Stephen, to which Tobin replied, "You wouldn't remember if you'd treated him?"

"I do a lot of things I don't remember," Cassin said.

"Are you testifying to this court that you don't know whether or not you've treated Mr. Grant as a psychologist?" Tobin asked.

"I've answered your questions," Cassin said.

After a short redirect by Pamukov, Cassin was excused.

Rabaut then asked for time to confer with his client. Stephen and the jury left the courtroom. After thirty-five minutes, Stephen was led back into the room, and Rabaut unexpectedly asked Druzinski to adjourn for the day. She complied.

98

Rabaut started Wednesday's proceedings by announcing Stephen would not be testifying. He said that after long discussions, Stephen agreed that the defense should rest.

Rabaut also asked Druzinski to let the jury consider a charge of voluntary manslaughter, which carried a maximum fifteen-year prison sentence. The judge agreed that evidence that a fight apparently sparked the murder could support a charge of voluntary manslaughter.

The jury was brought into the room, and then Eric Smith stood up and commenced his closing argument. "On February ninth of this year, Tara Grant had no idea what she was walking into. He was naked. He was lying in wait for her like a coiled snake."

Smith said Stephen's whole world had changed since he'd started his affair with the au pair. He said Stephen wanted a new life. "The only thing in his way was Tara. He stood face-to-face with the mother of his child and strangled every last breath from her," Smith said.

Smith portrayed Stephen as a media-hungry psychopath who enjoyed the attention killing his wife had brought him. "He's a big star. He's got the media following him. Have you ever seen a man love the microphone more?"

He then described Tara as a caring mother who juggled a demanding job and the needs of her family. He pointed out that she flew home every weekend and constantly called her children. Tara had to provide for the family, Smith explained, "because [Stephen] certainly wasn't going to do it."

Smith said Stephen must've "hated her living guts" to be able to cut her into fourteen pieces.

"Was Tara Grant having an affair? I don't know, and I don't care," Smith said. "The only thing that's important about that is he thought she was."

Smith then revealed why in the trial he'd asked Stephen's neighbor Michael Zanlungo about his conversation with Stephen Grant regarding the coyotes in Stony Creek Metropark. Smith said that the conversation, which took place less than two months before the murder, had revolved around how coyotes were eating deer carcasses in the park. Smith claimed Stephen was toying with the idea of killing Tara even then, thinking that he could dump her body in the park and let the wildlife devour the evidence.

Smith said Stephen was ready for a new relationship. He pointed out that Stephen had never flirted with his ex-girlfriend Deena Hardy until January 2007. Smith said Stephen then began flirting with his au pair, after never having approached her for sex in the six months she'd been living in his home. "He was on a mission," Smith asserted.

Stephen knew he couldn't continue his relationship with Verena and still keep his "meal ticket," Smith said, so he chose to get rid of his wife.

Smith also dismissed the "belittling nonsense"—the notion that Stephen had snapped because his wife had put him down—as a red herring. He said the defense wanted the jury to focus on things like arguments about Tara's travel schedule, and the claim that she belittled Stephen, instead of focusing on the evidence.

The murder was premeditated, Smith said, because Stephen had made a decision to shut Tara up after he'd hit her during their argument. Stephen had confessed that he was afraid he would go to jail for striking his wife, if she called the police. So, Smith said, Stephen made a conscious choice to murder her.

Smith pointed out how Stephen had covered Tara's face with a pair of underwear while he was strangling her, because, he said, he didn't want to look at her. Smith said that was another indication that Stephen was thinking clearly.

He reminded the jury how Stephen had sent a text message to Verena in the moments after the murder: *You owe me a kiss.* Smith said that disproved the defense's claim that Stephen was a downtrodden, cuckolded husband.

Smith again played the phone messages Stephen had left on Tara's cell phone after he killed her. He said the calculated decoy messages proved that Stephen wasn't panicked after the murder, as the defense claimed.

He pointed out how there was precedent in Michigan for a first-degree murder conviction in a strangulation case. He reiterated that the four minutes it likely took Tara to die gave Stephen plenty of time to contemplate his actions. Then Smith took out a stopwatch and stood silently.

After moments passed, he said softly, "Tara Grant is now unconscious." He again fell silent; the only sound in the courtroom was the whir of a ceiling heating unit, and the scratching of the court artists' pencils against their sketch pads.

Most of the jurors stared at Smith, who focused on the watch in his right hand. A few minutes into the silence, onlookers began shifting uncomfortably in their seats. When four minutes finally passed, Smith clicked off the stopwatch and said, "Tara Grant is now dead."

Smith finished his one-hour closing argument by asking the jury to "make [Stephen] pay."

99

Rabaut painted a different picture of Stephen Grant during the defense closing argument. He described Stephen as a homemaker who was involved in his children's activities. He said Stephen had a limited social life.

"He wasn't out with friends every night," the lawyer said. "He was a very lonely person." Rabaut pointed out that Alicia had testified how Stephen often would call Tara on her business trips, simply because he felt lonely.

The defense attorney said the Grants were headed in opposite directions: Tara was becoming more successful each year, while her husband dealt with the day-to-day household chores. Rabaut said Stephen felt he was in a menial role.

"He appeared to show jealousy toward Lou Troendle. There was probably jealousy because of her successful employment," Rabaut said, adding that Stephen's anger and frustration about the situation had built up over a period of time. Rabaut said Stephen felt disrespected when Tara came home the night of February 9. "She hadn't been home in a week, and he calls to her, but she's listening to [music in her headphones]."

The lawyer said after the couple started arguing, things spiraled out of control. He pointed out that Tara told her husband he was never going to see his kids again. He said Stephen reacted to her belittling words, finally snapping after years of built-up frustration and rage. That, he said, was tragic—but it was not first-degree murder.

Rabaut then downplayed Smith's dramatic tactic of silently holding a stopwatch for four minutes. "We're not talking about four minutes of looking at a stopwatch. We're talking about four minutes of passion, and anger, and frustration."

He portrayed for the jury a Stephen Grant who totally self-destructed after the murder. He stored Tara's body in the back of her Trooper for a day, because he had no plan. Then, after he dismembered her, Stephen was so bewildered about how to dispose of Tara's body parts that he stood in one spot and tossed them haphazardly in different directions. Many of the parts, as officers testified, were close to heavily traveled areas, suggesting a lack of guile on Stephen's part, the attorney implied.

Finally, Rabaut said, Stephen brought Tara's torso home to hide in the garage—of all places. It all proved, Rabaut said, that Stephen hadn't plotted the murder. "Ladies and gentlemen of the jury, there is no plan here," Rabaut said. "This is a pathetic individual, but he did not plan to kill Tara Grant."

Rabaut said Stephen's affair with Verena wasn't a motive to kill his wife. "I'm not justifying any extramarital activity. But is it understandable? Maybe."

The defense attorney dismissed Smith's claim that Stephen had been lying in wait for his wife. He said nobody would plan to strangle his wife while the couple's children slept just feet away. He said because the murder stemmed from an argument, the crime was voluntary manslaughter. He said the anger Stephen felt the night of February 9 didn't justify the crime. "But his anger does show us what the proper crime is, which is voluntary manslaughter," Rabaut said.

He finished his hour-long closing argument by stating, "The reasonable doubt in this case was overwhelming."

* * *

In his rebuttal, Smith focused again on the four minutes it likely took for Tara to die. He also ridiculed the defense's depiction of Stephen as a sad loser. "The defense is portraying this defendant as a lonely guy," Smith said. "Well, that's too damn bad. That gives you an excuse to kill your wife, for God's sake?"

After Smith's rebuttal, Druzinski gave her instructions to the jury. She told them they couldn't let sympathy or prejudice influence their opinions. And, she said, if they felt the prosecution hadn't proven the case beyond a reasonable doubt, then they must find the defendant not guilty.

She cautioned the jurors to be careful when considering the dismemberment, since Stephen wasn't on trial for that. She told the jurors they could only use the dismemberment to determine Stephen's state of mind.

Druzinski told the jurors it was up to them to determine if enough time had passed during Tara's final four minutes to allow Stephen time to contemplate his actions.

The court clerk then dismissed the four alternates, leaving a jury of six men and six women. The court broke for lunch. Then, at 1:30 P.M., the contractor, the two registered nurses, the tool salesman, and the rest of the jurors began deciding Stephen's fate.

100

Many observers predicted a quick verdict. They were wrong.

After deliberating for about an hour, the jurors asked to see the list of witnesses and evidence in the case, a copy of Stephen's three-page written confession, a transcript of Medical Examiner Daniel Spitz's testimony, along with his autopsy report, the missing persons report Stephen had filled out on February 14, three autopsy photos showing Tara's injuries, a summary of telephone records, and poster boards that had been used during the trial explaining the differences between first- and second-degree murder. It appeared from the evidence request that the jurors were focusing on the night of the murder.

Druzinski agreed to provide everything except the list of evidence and witnesses, which she said did not exist, and a copy of Spitz's testimony, which she said had not yet been prepared. Druzinski told the jurors they didn't need the poster boards because the differences in the legal charges were spelled out in the jurors' instructions they'd been provided.

101

On the second day of deliberations, jurors asked to take another look at the pictures of the injuries Stephen sustained during the fight with his wife on February 9, plus a floor plan of the Grant home.

Jurors asked again to see a transcript of Spitz's testimony, but Druzinski instructed them to rely on their memories, since it would take more than a day to transcribe the testimony. By the end of the day, the jurors had been deliberating for more than ten hours. Kelly Utykanski told reporters she was happy the jurors were taking so long to decide her brother's fate. "Someone lost their life, and another one is in the balance," she said.

As deliberations entered their third day on Friday, December 21, there was concern whether the jury would reach a verdict before the end of the day, when the holiday break would kick in. Christmas Eve was Monday, and the general consensus among the people associated with the case was that the jurors probably wouldn't want the case hanging over their heads during the holidays.

However, because it was taking so long for them to agree on a verdict, there remained a chance they would still be deliberating by the end of the day. And it was clear that the media, prosecutors, defense attorneys, and Tara's family were hoping things would wrap up by the end of the day. The trial had been a long, exhausting process, and most people said they were ready for it to come to an end.

At about 9:30 A.M., the jurors asked to listen to audio of Stephen's three-hour confession for the second time. The jurors wanted to hear several parts of the confession, so Druzinski instructed a bailiff to pass out copies of the confession transcript to the jurors. The judge told them to each close the transcripts when they'd heard the part of the confession they were interested in.

About forty minutes into the confession, as Stephen talked about sleeping with his au pair, one of the jurors, a middle-aged man in a plaid shirt, was the first to close his transcript. By the time an hour had passed, eleven of the jurors had closed their transcripts, but one woman asked Druzinski if she could listen again to Stephen telling about the night of the murder. In all, jurors listened to about ninety minutes of the confession before breaking for lunch. Deliberations would pick up at one-thirty in the afternoon.

During lunch, Lieutenant Donovan announced that a reporter had been handcuffed after trying to talk to a juror in a nearby restaurant. Speculation ran rampant about who the offending reporter was, and members of the media began a head count to see who wasn't accounted for. But the search for the guilty reporter abruptly ended at about 2:30 P.M., when the word came down: the jury had reached a verdict.

102

An edgy drone of conversation buzzed through the packed courtroom. Attorneys on both sides of the aisle cracked forced, nervous jokes, which fell flat. The murmur halted abruptly when Judge Druzinski entered the courtroom. "All rise!"

Everything seemed to be moving in slow motion, in a vacuum of anxious silence. Stephen's face was ashen as he shuffled into the courtroom. He sat stiffly at the defense table and watched the jurors file into the jury box. Their somber faces revealed no clues.

Druzinski's voice broke the stillness: "I understand the jury has reached a verdict?".

"We have, Your Honor," jury foreman Gary Hafner declared. In his hand was a small, folded piece of paper. He handed it to the bailiff, who gave it to Druzinski. The judge glanced impassively at the verdict, then returned it to the bailiff, who handed it back to Hafner.

The simple black-and-white clock on the starboard wall appeared to be stuck at one minute past three. Gail Pamukov put her hand reassuringly on Stephen Grant's back. They exchanged a brief glance.

Finally the foreman spoke: "We find the defendant, Stephen Grant, guilty of the count of second-degree murder."

There was a long moment of stunned silence. Mary

Destrampe gently squeezed her daughter's arm. Stephen leaned in and whispered something to his attorneys. A few people shot surprised looks at each other from across the room, while others nodded, affirming their predictions of a second-degree verdict.

Druzinski set the sentencing date for February 21; then Stephen was led out of the room. He mouthed something to his sister as he hobbled away.

The hallway outside the courtroom was a madhouse. A line of cameramen trained their lenses on the door, while behind them reporters dashed from one direction to the other, trying to secure interviews with the principals as they left the court. Local television stations broke into their regular programming with news of the Grant verdict, and the TV reporters gave their live reports in the corridor amid the swirl of activity. Several onlookers hung around the hallway and checked out the show.

After about ten minutes, court spokesman Phil Frame announced Eric Smith would soon give a press conference in the media room. All the seats in the small anteroom had already been taken, so some reporters and photographers sat on the floor, while others crowded, shoulder to shoulder, in the doorway. Eric Smith, Therese Tobin, and Bill Cataldo appeared grim as they moved to the podium.

"I thought from day one that this was a first-degree murder case," Smith said archly. "He certainly had time to reflect. The fact that he's sleeping with his au pair the night before, and the night after, I thought made it first-degree murder. I think there's premeditation all over this case. But I'm the prosecutor and not the jury. All you can do is put it in their hands."

Smith said he spoke briefly with the jurors after the verdict. "They asked me to clarify the definition of premeditation. When I told them, half of them pointed at the other half and said, 'See, I told you so.'

"If I never hear the name Stephen Grant again, I'll be happy," Smith said. "It's time for him to go away. He's had his fifteen minutes of fame, and it's time to put him behind us."

Then Gail Pamukov briefly addressed the media. She looked weary, as did Stephen Rabaut, who stood silently by her side.

"We believe that the right result was achieved," she said. "But as we said from the very beginning—there are no winners here today. We offer our condolences to the family, and I hope they can get on with their lives."

Alicia Standerfer next took the podium, flanked by her mother and husband. Alicia had been able to publicly hold her emotions in check throughout the whole case. But now she broke down, openly sobbing as she tried to speak.

"We thank God this horrific nightmare is over with the conviction of Stephen Grant," she said. "The cold-blooded murder of Tara has altered our family forever. I made a promise to Tara that I would see that justice was served, so no matter how hard it was—every single day, to sit there and hear, again and again, how it happened—it needed to be done."

A reporter asked Alicia if she was happy with the verdict. "No," she said grimly. "I'm very disappointed.

"My family will forever be influenced by this tragedy, but we will recover, I guarantee you of that," she said. "I will personally serve as my sister's voice the best way I know how. I love you, big sis."

Alicia hugged her mother and Erik, and then they walked out of the room.

* * *

Kelly Utykansi took the podium next, with her husband, Chris, at her side. She said she was happy with the verdict. "Obviously, we wanted him punished and we felt that manslaughter would have been a slap on the wrist," she said.

When asked about her relationship with Tara's family, Kelly said, "We never had a strained relationship before this, so I would hope things would work themselves out in the future."

Kelly also said she thought the murder was not premeditated. "I couldn't see him sitting around all day thinking about murdering someone.

"He was a normal person."

103

Jury foreman Gary Hafner said the jurors wanted to convict Stephen of first-degree murder. But, he said, that would have been going against the judge's instructions. "It's not like we didn't try to find a reason to convict him of first-degree murder," Hafner, a thirty-nine-year-old tool salesman from Warren, said a few months after the verdict. "I wanted him to go to jail for the rest of his life, and we spent hours arguing over the definition of premeditation. In the end, we just didn't think the murder was premeditated."

"A lot of the jurors thought it was premeditated because he got into a confrontation with Tara, knowing he could cause bodily harm. We went around and around on that one bullet point. I didn't agree with them. There were three of us who held out for second-degree [murder], and the rest of them eventually came over to our side.

"This was a horrible murder, but the evidence didn't show that Stephen Grant planned to kill his wife. I think it just happened. He got mad during an argument and snapped. That's not premeditation. And even though cutting her up was horrible, that had nothing to do with first- or second-degree [charges]."

Hafner said people who knew he was on the jury harassed him for coming up with a second-degree verdict.

"I have a few coworkers who keep asking, 'How could you not give him first-degree murder?' I don't think a lot of people realize how little difference there is between first and second degree. People don't know the guidelines the judge gives you," Hafner said.

"I don't mind people's opinions. It's when someone comes up to you and gets right in your face, screaming, 'What are you thinking?' First of all, I tell them to back off. There's no need to get that angry about it. Even my wife said some people were aggressive with her about the verdict. This case was very emotional for a lot of people."

Hafner had high praise for Judge Druzinski. "I thought she did an awesome job," he said. "She ran a tight courtroom."

Legal experts said Stephen Grant could be sentenced to a range of eighteen years to life, but most predicted he would be an old man before he ever got a chance for parole. Druzinski had a reputation of handing down tough sentences.

The judge would assess the sentence by taking into account twenty different "offense variables" in the *Michigan Sentencing Guidelines Manual.* Druzinski would assess points for each variable that applied to the crime. The variables included "intent to kill," "degree of physical injury," "sadism, torture or excessive brutality," and "family members' serious psychological injury."

Bill Shelhart, a Mount Clemens attorney who'd argued several cases before Druzinski, predicted a tough sentence. "She's a fair judge, but she has no qualms about sentencing on the harsher side of the scale," he said.

Because of Michigan's truth in sentencing laws, Stephen Grant would have to serve his minimum sentence before being eligible for parole. "The people of Macomb County don't have to lose sleep thinking Stephen Grant will come back to hurt them," said Sterling Heights attorney Charlie

Langton, who attended the trial from the beginning as a correspondent for Channel 2. "He's not getting out of prison any time soon."

A few hours after Stephen Grant was convicted of second-degree murder, deputies at the Macomb County Jail told him he was being put into an observation cell, which meant he would be on suicide watch.

Police later revealed that Stephen loudly complained about being moved to the secure cell. "Why should I kill myself, since I just hit the lottery at court today?" he reportedly shouted as he was being led to his new lodgings.

104

In most trials, there is a lull between the reading of the verdict and the sentencing. But with the Grant case, some of the most amazing twists and turns were still to come.

The first order of business was to figure out whether Alicia or Kelly would get custody of Lindsey and Ian. Relations between the two women had grown progressively worse, to the point where they didn't bother pretending to get along, as they once had.

Two weeks after the trial ended, on Wednesday, January 2, 2008, a hearing was held regarding visitation of the Grant children. It was merely a procedural hearing to deal with motions that had been filed, but an angry Judge Foster used the occasion to vent.

The judge was livid because someone had leaked to the media a report written by Brian Bethel, the counselor in Ohio who was treating Lindsey and Ian. In the report, Bethel wrote that Lindsey was having *nightmares, intrusive recollections of being told of her mother's death [and] irrational worries that her aunt [Alicia] would die.*

Bethel also recommended in his report that Kelly should not have unsupervised visits with the children, because, he wrote, *Lindsey's nightmares have increased in frequency and intensity after the current supervised visitation.*

Foster was furious about the leak. "Someone violated

this court's order that no pleadings or communications would be given to the press," the judge said. "I see quotes in the paper from some pseudopsychologist in Ohio. I find that unacceptable, and I realize this person can't be trusted. But, given that the person who provided this information won't be testifying in this case, I can't do anything about it."

Then, in an unusual decision, Foster ruled that the next day's termination hearing, in which Stephen Grant's parental rights would be decided, would be closed to the public. "Because adoption hearings are closed to the public, I believe anything leading up to the adoption should also be closed," Foster said. "Details will be coming out about the adoptive parents, and my concern is for the children."

Longtime attorneys said it was the first time they'd ever heard of a judge banning the public from a parental rights hearing. Legal analysts also explained that Stephen had a right to a trial at the next day's hearing, and he could ask for six jurors to determine whether his parental rights should be revoked. But because Stephen was now a convicted murderer, attorneys said, it would be futile for him to try to keep his parental rights to Lindsey and Ian.

The only question was, would the kids go to Alicia or Kelly?

Later that afternoon, rumors surfaced that the Standerfers and Utykanskis were meeting in Foster's chambers, a day ahead of schedule.

Court spokesman Frame acknowledged that a hearing was indeed in progress. He said the meeting had hurriedly been set up because Stephen Grant had voluntarily surrendered his parental rights earlier that afternoon.

Now that Stephen had given up his rights, the Standerfers and the Utykanskis were meeting with a mediator in an attempt to work out a deal on the custody of Lindsey and Ian, Frame said.

Word about the impromptu meeting spread quickly, and by late afternoon, a handful of reporters, photographers, and cameramen were staked out in the hallway outside Foster's fourth-floor courtroom. A handwritten sign hanging on Foster's outer door bore the message *Courtroom closed. Hearing in process.*

A few reporters ventured past the outer doors on the pretense of getting their coats from the rack in the nook just outside the courtroom. They peeked through the narrow windows in the second set of doors and saw that the courtroom was empty except for a handful of deputies and attorneys, who were sitting in the empty courtroom chatting. The hearing on the Grant children was being held in the judge's chambers, one of the deputies explained.

At about 3:30 P.M., a woman, with a teased bleached-blond hairdo, walked out of an elevator car, carrying two bouquets of mixed flowers. "Is this where they're doing the thing for the Grant kids?" she asked the assembled media.

One of the reporters told her it was, and the woman was directed toward the deputies in the courtroom. She gave the flowers to one of the officers and spoke with him briefly before walking back into the hallway, where the reporters were waiting for her.

The woman, who would only give her name as "Rebecca," said she asked the deputy to give the bouquets to the Standerfers and Utykanskis. "I don't know either side of this," the woman told reporters, "but I thought I'd bring some flowers to help. It's sad what's happening to those poor kids.

"No more questions," she said over her shoulder as she hurried toward the elevators.

* * *

Finally, at about 5:00 P.M., Alicia, Kelly, and their attorneys emerged from the hearing, looking drained.

Michael Smith, Alicia's attorney in the custody matter, announced that an adoption deal had been reached. But, he said, the terms of the adoption were confidential because of Judge Foster's gag order.

"This was more difficult than you will ever know," Alicia said.

Kelly's eyes welled with tears as she talked about the eight-month custody battle. "Alicia's right," she said. "Nobody knows how tough this was, unless they were in there."

Although Judge Foster had ordered the parties not to discuss the custody agreement with the media, several news organizations the next day reported that Alicia had been given primary custody of the children, with Kelly getting visitation rights.

The reports turned out to be true. Lindsey and Ian would live with Alicia in Ohio.

105

Alicia's attorney Patrick Simasko announced on January 9, 2008, that Stephen would be making the first payment on the $50 million he owed from the wrongful-death lawsuit he lost in May. The payment would be a paltry $24.71—the amount Simasko had garnisheed from Stephen's jail account.

"I guess you could call this symbolic, to the extent that we certainly didn't expect there to be fifty million dollars in his account," Simasko said.

Simasko added that Alicia wanted him to garnishee whatever money Stephen accrued in his future prison accounts. "We're going to do whatever we can to make sure his assets are collected," he said.

It was clear: Alicia was going to do whatever she could to make Stephen pay for murdering her sister.

On February 5, 2008, prosecutors revealed that two of Michigan's most notorious murderers had been secretly communicating in the Macomb County Jail. Prosecutors released twenty notes Stephen had clandestinely written to other inmates in the facility. In a bizarre twist, most of the letters had been written to Jennifer Kukla, the woman who had fatally stabbed her two young daughters on Super Bowl Sunday, a week before Tara's murder.

The notes, which were passed back and forth by trustees, were written from June to October 2007, while Kukla was still incarcerated in the county jail. In October, after her first-degree murder conviction, Kukla was sent to the Huron Valley Correctional Facility in Ypsilanti to serve out her life's sentence.

Prosecutors also released notes Stephen had written to another female inmate, Crystal Conklin, a twenty-seven-year-old Warren woman who was in jail awaiting trial on charges she fatally beat her two-year-old son. Additionally, they made public police reports that explained how investigators found out about the letters. Also released were audio files of the calls Stephen had placed to Tara's cell phone in the days after he killed her.

The voice mails had already been played in court, but for the first time the public got a chance to actually hear Stephen's angry voice as he left messages to the woman he'd just murdered, chiding her because she hadn't called her kids.

I still laugh when I remember your one note, Stephen wrote to Kukla in one of his letters. *You asked "are you scared of me?" (LOL) You are too nice to be scared of. I just wish we could arrange a rendezvous in the closet one of these days.*

Stephen wrote that he missed his wife. *You are the 1st person to ask if I miss Tara,* he wrote to his fellow murderer. *She, for the last 13 years, has been the one I went to with my problems and now I don't have that person to ask for advice.* He added a sad face at the end of the sentence.

In another letter to Kukla, Stephen appeared to brag about his celebrity status. *Ask the other ladies if they know "Steve Grant,"* he wrote. *They probably do.*

Stephen also wrote that he was keeping a journal for his children, *so when they are older, they can hear about where they really came from, from two people who loved them and each other.*

* * *

Police had found out about Stephen's letters on November 28, the day after jury selection in his trial began, when an assistant Macomb County prosecutor phoned sheriff's detectives to inform them that a woman identifying herself as "J.C." was being interviewed on radio station 95.5 FM, claiming to have knowledge about notes Stephen had been passing to other inmates in jail.

Sergeant Grammatico tuned in to the station and heard the last few minutes of the interview. He then contacted the radio station's program manager, who provided him with J.C.'s telephone number.

Grammatico called J.C., who had served a jail sentence the previous summer after being arrested for a probation violation. She said she worked passing out food in the mental-health ward, where women and men are housed separately. J.C. told the detective she passed notes back and forth between Stephen and Kukla by hiding them underneath food trays.

After talking to J.C., Grammatico and fellow detective Jason Abro interviewed Kukla in prison. She told them she wrote to Stephen, at first pretending to be a girl named Sarah. *"Everybody on our side wanted to find out what he would say about his crime,* Kukla said, according to Grammatico's report.

Kukla told Grammatico and Abro that she had given the letters to her father. When the detectives visited Kukla's father, he gave them the notes. The detectives then turned them over to prosecutors.

106

Despite the surprising news about Stephen's letters to Kukla, it wasn't as big a bombshell as it normally would have been, because one of the biggest political scandals in Detroit's three-hundred-year history dominated the headlines.

The *Detroit Free Press* uncovered racy text messages sent between Mayor Kwame Kilpatrick and his chief of staff, Christine Beatty. The messages were printed on the paper's front page on January 26, setting off a firestorm that lasted months and resulted in the mayor being removed from office and jailed after pleading guilty to obstruction of justice.

The text messages, sent on city-owned BlackBerry smartphones, proved Kilpatrick and Beatty had lied under oath earlier that year during a federal whistleblower lawsuit, in which former Detroit police officers Gary Brown and Harold Nelthorpe claimed they were fired for investigating wrongdoing committed by the mayor. The city eventually settled the lawsuit and paid the officers $8.4 million.

One of the allegations Brown and Nelthorpe were investigating at the time of their firing was a rumor that the mayor had held a wild party at the Manoogian Mansion, Detroit's mayoral residence. There allegedly were several strippers at the party.

According to the story, the mayor's wife, Carlita, came home and beat up one of the strippers with a baseball bat, sending her to the hospital. It was alleged that the mayor's bodyguards accompanied the stripper to the hospital, where she was treated for her wounds.

At the time of his firing, Brown also was looking into reports that Kilpatrick's bodyguards were regularly dispatched to stand guard outside hotel rooms while the mayor and his chief of staff, Beatty, had sex.

During the whistle-blower trial, both Kilpatrick and Beatty denied having an affair. The text messages, in which they explicitly discussed former sexual encounters, showed they lied under oath.

It was a huge story—one that would culminate in the ouster and jailing of both Kilpatrick and Beatty—but when the audio files of Stephen's taped jailhouse conversations with his sister were released to the media on February 6, they hit Metro Detroit like a sledgehammer. For one day at least, the Grant saga was again the biggest story in Metro Detroit.

The recordings of Stephen's jailhouse conversations were never brought up in trial, and they had no bearing on the jury's verdict. But in the court of public opinion, the conversations had a major impact. Dozens of readers called and e-mailed newspapers, aghast at the way Stephen and Kelly had guffawed about the murder.

In addition to the crude jokes, Stephen and his sister also discussed trying to craft a book and movie deal about the case in a way that would allow them to keep the proceeds, rather than turning the profits over to Tara's estate.

"The problem is, if I write a book now, I'd get fucked in court," Stephen said.

Kelly suggested Stephen dictate the book to her so she could keep the proceeds from a book or a "Lifetime movie," she said, referring to the women-oriented cable television network.

Stephen gave Kelly the name and phone number of a Beverly Hills entertainment attorney that he said could help them get their book and movie deal. The attorney was the friend of a friend, Stephen explained.

Stephen then speculated about who would portray him in a movie. "I want Adrien Brody. He looks like me," Stephen said of the actor who won an Oscar for his role in *The Pianist*.

"I don't think he'll do a Lifetime movie," Kelly said.

"But that's who I want," Stephen insisted.

As Stephen and his sister talked, they were obviously aware they were being taped. Whenever they began to speak of Tara's suspected affairs, they wrote messages back and forth to avoid being recorded. A few times, they wrote out a list of five men and ventured guesses about which ones had slept with Tara.

It was a recurring theme.

Alicia said shortly after the audio was released that she'd already heard the conversations between Stephen and Kelly. And, she added, she wasn't surprised.

"This only reveals what kind of people we're dealing with," she said. "Stephen never liked me, and I never liked him from the start. Obviously, he doesn't have a conscience. He's the type of person who only cares about himself, and that's so evident on the tapes."

Regarding Kelly, Alicia said, "I knew who she was, from what Tara told me, and my gut impression from when I first met her hasn't changed."

Prosecutors vowed to use the taped conversations to try to persuade Judge Druzinski to exceed the minimum-sentencing guidelines of eighteen to thirty-one years.

"These conversations demonstrate an obvious lack of remorse for his crime," Bill Cataldo said.

* * *

Stephen's attorneys filed a presentence memorandum on February 14, 2008, asking Judge Druzinski to ignore a recommendation by the Macomb County Probation Department to sentence Stephen Grant to nineteen to thirty-one years. Rabaut and Pamukov asked instead for a sentence of fifteen to twenty-five years.

Steven Rabaut said the memo was intended as a preemptive strike against the prosecution's expected request for Druzinski to exceed sentencing guidelines.

107

Prosecutors dropped one of the case's biggest bomb-shells when they filed their forty-page sentencing brief on Friday, February 15, 2008: Lindsey and Ian had witnessed their mother's murder, Smith said.

In early January 2008, the prosecutor's office learned Lindsey Grant, 7-year-old daughter of Tara Grant, disclosed on Christmas Day that she and younger brother Ian witnessed the fight between her parents. She then described, in detail, how they watched their father kill their mother, Eric Smith wrote in his brief.

Alicia confirmed the report. "We sensed from the very beginning that the kids had seen something that night," she said. "I know how the house is laid out, and I know how loud Stephen's voice carries when he's yelling. I always thought the kids might have woke up and saw something that night."

In his sentencing brief, Smith asked Judge Druzinski to sentence Stephen to fifty to eighty years in prison. Because the judge had to weigh the impact of Stephen's crime in her sentencing decision, Smith asked her to consider the fact that Lindsey and Ian had seen the killing. *Stephen Grant's two small children witnessed a life-changing event, the murder of their mother, and their future psychological harm has been established,* Smith wrote.

Kelly questioned the veracity of the revelation. "Alicia is

saying that the kids just mentioned it. [Stephen] refutes that, because it competes with what his confession states," Kelly told Fox 2 TV correspondent Charlie Langton.

February 21, 2008, sentencing day, started out cold and windy, as it had been for the past week, with temperatures in the low teens. There were ten television trucks parked on Main Street outside the courthouse that morning. Inside, thirty-four members of the press milled around the hallway outside Druzinski's courtroom.

Mary Destrampe was with a group of nine relatives. They were allowed into the courtroom by Sergeant David Abbott. The rest of the public and media were allowed inside a few minutes later. The benches filled up quickly, and deputies brought in nine chairs to accommodate the overflow. They weren't enough. All told, sixty-six people crammed into the small courtroom. Among them were thirteen members of the media, including two sketch artists.

Druzinski came into the room at 8:54 A.M. Then Stephen was led in, once again wearing a blue prison jumpsuit, with his hands and feet manacled. His hair had grown shaggy and curly, and with a bit more gray than there was before his trial. He blinked several times as he was led into the courtroom.

Then the judge began the proceedings with a stern warning. "This case has generated some very strong feelings and reactions," she said. "I want to caution people against outbursts or misbehavior. Should this occur, they will be arrested and charged with contempt of court."

Stephen Rabaut then announced he had an issue with the presentence report. "I have one comment that deals with the suggestion there was a major rules violation that Mr. Grant was in possession of gambling paraphernalia in the Macomb County Jail," Rabaut said. "Mr. Grant takes exception to that."

Eric Smith rebutted, "But the defendant was cited for having gambling paraphernalia, which is a major rules violation, and as a result, his visits were restricted from October fifth to October twenty-third."

"I'm satisfied from the report that it's correct, and I won't be making any changes," Judge Druzinski said.

Rabaut then stated that the probation department had erred by assessing points to Offense Variable 7, which pertains to sadism or torture. "The guidelines are clear. Any abuse had to occur prior to anybody dying. I think when the court looks through this trial, it's clear that an altercation occurred between the two. The opinion of two medical examiners showed that the victim lost consciousness within fifteen to twenty seconds. This was not an aggravated circumstance where the victim was tortured. This was an altercation," Rabaut said. "I ask the court to rescore the guidelines."

Smith was ready with his argument. "The victim was treated with extensive brutality," he said. "If all we were alleging was that she had injuries on her neck, we'd agree. But her injuries were extensive." Smith went on to list Tara's injuries observed by Dr. Spitz in his autopsy report: blunt-force injuries to the shoulder, chest, and lower back, as well as contusions on her jaw, right hand, and right eyelid.

Smith also said Tara had a broken sternum. "Dr. Spitz said it takes extensive force to break that bone. This beating was prolonged, prior to her being strangled," Smith said. "And the variable talks about sadism. We believe it was sadistic when he cut her body into fourteen pieces."

Rabaut interjected that it would be inappropriate for the judge to consider the dismemberment, since it occurred *after* the death, and wasn't one of the offense variables the judge had to consider before assessing her sentence.

But the judge declined to take away the fifty points the

probation department had assessed for sadism and torture. "The defense's position has no merit," she said.
"The statute doesn't require that the victim has to experience torture. Fifty points may be assessed for sadism,
and the defendant inflicted extreme humiliation on the
victim. He felt superior to her, and put her in her place.
He even put a pair of underwear on her face so he
wouldn't have to look at her."

Lou Troendle was first to address the court before sentencing. Troendle, who interviewed Tara when she first
applied for her job, said she made a strong impact. "I
clearly remember fourteen years ago when Tara came
into our office for an interview," Troendle said. "First impressions are everything, and she impressed.

"She was open, honest, intelligent, and willing to learn,"
he said. "She proved to be willing and dedicated. She did
whatever it took to get the job done. She grew from a marketing specialist, to business development, to a position
in management. Tara only asked for two things—respect
and equal opportunity. She was a woman working in a
man's world.

"Her most recent accomplishment was being accepted
into our company's LEAP program, which is for our employees who are on the fast track. Only fifteen or twenty
people are accepted into this program out of a company
of twenty-five thousand people," Troendle said.

"Any business manager must balance family and career,"
he said. "Her family—especially her children—was always
at the front of her mind. It's true she loved her career,
but she loved her family more.

"Tara looked forward to the day when her children
would grow up so she could show them all the places she
traveled," Troendle said. "I've heard it said that time
heals all wounds. However, this is one wound that won't
be healed."

* * *

Erik Standerfer was next. Throughout the case, he had remained in the background, allowing his wife to do most of the talking. But for the first time, he bared his feelings, reading aloud his eloquent statement, which he said he'd spent hours preparing. Erik explained Lindsey and Ian were traumatized by the murder, and called them *"the living victims of this tragedy."*

"Their entire security blanket, including their parents, friends, school, house and neighborhood, were immediately stolen from them," he said. *"Our effort to give them a security blanket and chance at a normal life through the adoption process over the past year has been nothing short of horrific as well for my family. Our family still deals with this tragedy daily, and it will influence our lives and her children's lives forever."*

Erik said his wife and Tara talked often on the telephone. *"Whether Tara realized it, I will never know for sure, but Alicia looked up to her big sister tremendously. We celebrated each of our children's births together, with Tara in the birthing room only minutes after our daughter was born,"* Erik read. *"As a mother, she did many little things for Lindsey and Ian, like calling daily while traveling for business, leaving cards on their pillows for no other reason than to say she loved them prior to leaving for work, or planning birthday parties for her children.*

"As we sorted and organized their belongings in the months following Tara's murder, we came across many hand-written cards from Tara addressed to Lindsey and Ian, along with many others, still unwritten, which Tara no doubt intended for future use.

"I believe the horror of leaving her children was the last thought that went through Tara's mind that fateful night," Erik read.

"Tara would sort and save clothes for our children just like many other families take time to do, marking them in containers

as 'girls' clothes' or 'boys' clothes' intended for use years later," Erik said. *"Just like the one that Stephen Grant has now made famous by storing Tara's torso in it.*

"I often wonder what, if anything, went through the killer's mind as he removed the now-infamous 'boys' clothes' from that container, which were likely destined for my house and ulti- mately my own son," he read aloud.

"Alicia and I never lived in the same town as Tara and Stephen, but it was clear to me as her brother-in-law and close relative that she was a special person and had a passion for life. Away from Stephen, Tara was a very different person. Stephen was her Achilles' heel, one that ultimately brought her to this darkest point of our lives."

Erik described an incident at their home a few years ear- lier, when Stephen was putting the Standerfers' eighteen- month-old son to bed. Erik said Stephen was screaming at the child. *"I had to kick him out of my son's room as he force- fully tried to get him to lay in his crib,"* he read. *"Even my eighteen-month-old son recognized Stephen was a monster.*

"From the first moment I met Stephen at the funeral for Tara's grandmother in 1994, I knew he was trouble. He showed up and introduced himself to the family and Tara's boyfriend—yes, Tara's boyfriend at the time as well.

"The day Alicia and I arrived at Tara's house in February after she went 'missing' roughly thirteen years later was no dif- ferent," Erik stated. *"I knew immediately as we walked up the driveway to their home for the first time following her disap- pearance that something was terribly wrong with the situation. Of course, I had no idea it would take the turn it did in early March.*

"I will never forget Stephen met us in the driveway that day and it became immediately obvious that Stephen knew it was a waste of time to look for Tara. Never once did he lift a finger to look for Tara, and his tears were immediately recognizable as fake and on demand."

* * *

"We celebrated the births of our children, winter holidays, and other fun times together, but typically there was some type of controversy that involved Stephen, resulting in the fun coming to an abrupt halt," Erik continued. "We learned after Tara's death that Stephen could not pay their bills on time.

"When Tara was alive, Stephen would routinely belittle Tara and her mother, and acted as if he were 'Mr. Mom,' in his words. Stephen did sports activities with the kids, but he was no Mr. Mom. They had an au pair in the house at his request from the moment their second child was born.

"I often watched silently as he manipulated Tara, her mother, and later their kids, often lying and verbally overpowering them to make them believe he was superior," Erik read aloud.

"Lindsey has described to Alicia and I in detail what she witnessed that terrible night," Erik went on. "Lindsey became overwhelmed with fear and guilt the night of December 25, 2007. After nine months in our house, Lindsey shared a secret that was eating her up from within.

"She provided a chilling, detailed account of the tragedy as seen first hand, through her own eyes," Erik said. "Based on her description, Lindsey supports the fact that Stephen conducted a calculated, thorough beating and ultimate killing of Tara.

"It was absolutely brutal to listen to Lindsey describe that night, watching her dad scream directly into her mother's ear to 'quit looking at me!'

"I have sat and listened for several hours as Lindsey described the mental abuse he inflicted on Tara and the children over the years. I have listened as Lindsey described the night Tara was killed—what she saw, what she felt, what she heard, what she tried to do to make it stop—and it is nothing short of terrifying.

"My wife and I began to weep as she described checking her mother's still-warm eyelids to see if she was dead or alive after Stephen left the room. How she observed undetected as her father rolled her mother's lifeless body to the door.

"I truly believe Lindsey was scared for her own life."

* * *

Mary Destrampe was next to say her piece. She asked the judge if she could speak directly to Stephen.

"Technically, you're not supposed to speak to the defendant, although, I assure you, he is in the courtroom, and he will hear you," Druzinski said.

Then Mary began her address. "We accepted Stephen into our family, with the understanding that he would treat our daughter right," she said. "He obviously betrayed our trust. He betrayed everyone.

"In this very courtroom, he turned to me and said, 'I am so sorry,'" Mary continued. "How can he tell me he's sorry for squeezing the life from our daughter? He showed no remorse. Instead, he joked about her remains.

"I will never forget February thirteenth, when Stephen said Tara was missing. He was crying and playing to my emotions, like he always did.

"Stephen was demeaning to our daughter, even in death. He used me. He used my friends, my family, his friends, and the media."

Mary then turned and glared at Stephen. "Stephen Christopher Grant, you are without remorse," she said. "I cannot forgive you. You will live with your actions the rest of your life. Stephen, I hope you live the rest of your life alone."

Alicia followed her mother to the courtroom podium. As she read her statement, her voice cracked several times, and a few people were seen weeping in the courtroom.

"Tara had a beauty that could light up a room," Alicia read aloud. *"By now, it should be clear to the world that Tara was trapped in a verbally abusive, controlling relationship that ended in the destruction of her life.*

"On Christmas Day, much to our horror, Lindsey told us she

witnessed the murder. She said she saw her father choke, as she put it, her mother; but she also heard her take her last breath."

Alicia then handed the bailiff two pictures that had been drawn by Lindsey, and asked the judge to look at them.

"One of the pictures was of Tara's burial," Alicia explained. *"Lindsey placed her father under a rock.*

"The other picture states, 'My dad thinks he has power.'"

"Stephen took pride in causing pain," Alicia continued. *"He's not a kind man; he's a master manipulator and a psychopath. He has such a need for control that he cut my sister's body into fourteen pieces."*

Alicia broke down crying as she talked about how tough the past year had been on her. But she said it was nothing like what Tara endured. *"My sister lived under the control and manipulation of her husband for years."*

She said she was horrified when she heard jailhouse conversations between Stephen and his sister in which they joked about the crime and its aftermath. *"I listened to him and his sister snickering about releasing purple balloons at her funeral,"* Alicia acknowledged.

Kelly chewed her gum vigorously and stared straight ahead as Alicia discussed the taped conversations in the Macomb County Jail visiting room. *"These conversations give an insight into the sadistic nature of Stephen Grant. This man does not possess a conscience. I believe in my heart the only thing he is remorseful about is that he got caught."*

"I've learned the hard way that we often take for granted our loved ones," Alicia noted. *"I can never replace the relationship I had with my sister."*

Alicia said as she drove home from Tara's March 26 funeral, she reflexively started to call her sister's cell phone number. *"I often used to call my sister when I traveled.*

No less than three times I took out my cell phone and began to dial Tara, only to realize there was no one to pick up on the other end. I never felt so alone in my life."

Alicia said Stephen manipulated her sister into keeping Tara apart from her. *"In hindsight I realize driving a wedge between relatives is all a part of domestic violence."*

She explained that Tara had been mentally abused by her husband, who was jealous of her success. *"In my opinion, Stephen Grant realized Tara had exceeded him as a person, and as a professional. He could no longer control her.*

"He's not worthy of being called human," she said. *"And I'm going to take it one step further: Stephen Grant is Satan in the flesh."*

Stephen stared straight ahead, displaying no emotion.

"I think God has a master plan," Alicia observed. *"I believe He recognized the kids were living in a horrific home, and He decided to get them out of that situation, even if it meant sacrificing Tara's life. They suffered years of mental abuse. He ripped the innocence from his children."*

After Alicia was finished speaking, she asked the judge for permission to play a four-minute video. The presentation, which was taken from a tribute uploaded to the Web site Taralynngrant.com, flashed pictures of Tara, accompanied by a song from country artist Carrie Underwood, "Don't Forget to Remember Me."

During the tribute, several people in the courtroom wept.

108

Eric Smith then pleaded for the judge to hand down the toughest possible sentence. "There's a time for compassion and forgiveness," Smith said. "This is not the time. We ask on behalf of the one person who can't be heard from—Tara Grant—that you banish Stephen Grant and the evil of his legacy from our society forever."

When it was Rabaut's turn to address the court, he questioned the validity of reports that the Grant children watched their father kill their mother. "Mr. Smith seems to be relying very heavily on the revelation that these children purportedly had witnessed the murder," he said. "What's most bothering about this is that Brian Bethel, who is the children's therapist, sent me a letter on January twenty-eighth indicating that it was reported by Lindsey on May 21, 2007, that she'd seen the murder. Then, on December sixth, Ian made a similar statement.

"It's bothersome that this was not reported sooner," he said, and asked Druzinski to refrain from considering the reports that the children had witnessed the murder. "Mr. Grant would be entitled to an evidentiary hearing so it could be determined how these children were able to describe the events—whether they actually witnessed it, or by other means.

"What's disturbing to me is that we have eyewitnesses to the murder supposedly, and that it may have been known months earlier," Rabaut said. "Had this information come forward, maybe all of us in this courtroom would have had more accurate information."

Druzinski asked Rabaut if his client wished to address the court. "At the advice of counsel, he has elected not to make a statement," Rabaut said.

There was a moment of silence, and several people in the courtroom shifted in their seats, waiting for the moment of truth. Druzinski began speaking in a measured tone.

"I could sentence the defendant up to life, but he would be eligible for parole in fifteen years, and the court does not believe he should be eligible for parole in fifteen years."

"My second option is an indeterminate sentence," she said. "That is a sentence for a term of years. Under this scheme, he's not eligible for parole until he's served his minimum sentence."

Druzinski then handed down the sentence prosecutors had asked for: fifty to eighty years. Stephen wouldn't be eligible for parole until 2058. The judge also ordered Stephen to pay $41,063 in court fees.

Stephen didn't so much as twitch. Neither did his attorneys.

"This matter was an exceptional case," Druzinski said, explaining the tough sentence. "The psychological effects to the children are mind-numbing to this court. They are afraid of their father and don't want to see him again.

"Because of this very public trial, caused in large part by the defendant's media attention, they will hear the brutal details of their mother's death at the hands of their father. There is no love like that of a parent for a child," Druzinski said. "It is said no child should die before the parent—but especially not at the hands of their father.

"The court is satisfied that the upward departure in sentencing is warranted because of the demonic, manipulative, and barbaric actions in this case," the judge said. "This case has keenly grabbed this court's attention like no other case before it."

Druzinski then reminded Stephen Grant he had forty-five days to file an appeal. And then, with a rap of her gavel, the judge brought the Grant trial to a close.

109

The media crowded into the small room next to the courtroom in anticipation of the postsentencing press conferences. Alicia was first to take the podium. She stood next to her mother and husband—all of them looked exhausted.

"I think what my family just endured was one of the most difficult times of our life, reading to the judge how much Tara is missed. The sentence reflects Stephen's natural life, and our family is so grateful for that. Lindsey and Ian will never have to see their father. They won't have to see his hurtful ways. That definitely sits well with us," Alicia said.

Alicia described the events of the past year as "a horrific nightmare that I'm not sure I've woken up from. It's still not quite sunk in. To describe this past year as a roller coaster wouldn't even come close. I hope there's a lesson learned with my sister's death, and that domestic violence doesn't know boundaries. It doesn't know age. It doesn't know race. It doesn't know sex."

Alicia described her sister's family as a "classic American family" with two kids, a nice home, and two jobs. "Yet she was taken from us by his hands," she said.

"Steve had a manipulative way about him. . . . I could tell you so many stories," Alicia said. "He was demeaning, narcissistic. He really relished in seeing controversy. He put Tara down in ways that I've never seen before—never heard before. He manipulated my mom.

"He drove a wedge between Tara and me. I can tell you the exact day it happened. I don't want to go into it, but he tried to keep us apart. A wedge was driven, and at that point in time, Tara didn't open up to me like she'd done before. She didn't share personal aspects of her and Stephen's relationship after that.

"Erik and I decided not to push Tara to open up to us because we still wanted an open avenue," she said. "We didn't want to cut off what relationship we did have. I'm regretful I didn't try harder to get her to open up. But, like everyone says, hindsight is twenty-twenty.

"I would like to have a few minutes face-to-face with that man, and I probably will still want that in the future," Alicia said. "But if that were to ever happen, I wouldn't believe a word he said. He's so much of a coward that he doesn't look me in the eye in the courtroom," she said.

When a reporter asked Alicia if she was concerned about Stephen coming after her if he'd gotten a light sentence, she said, "There is no doubt in my mind that I was target number one."

Another reporter asked Alicia whether she suspected Lindsey and Ian had seen anything the night of the murder.

"You know, I think my husband and I both had suspicions right from the start," she said. "Obviously, we knew the layout of Tara's house, and we knew how Steve carried his voice. There was no doubt in my mind that at the very least the kids had to have heard something.

"You know, obviously, hearing Lindsey describe, detail by detail by detail, what she saw that night was unbelievable. I don't think anything could have prepared me for hearing those words come out of her mouth," she said.

"As adults, we know how difficult it is to bear the burden of something, even a little secret, let alone something as enormous as what she was carrying around," Alicia said. "So I think at this point, she does feel relieved, and obviously being able to tell her that her father is going to be in prison for a minimum of fifty years, I think that will put her even more at ease."

A reporter asked Alicia if the stiff sentence brought closure to the family.

"This is closure for another chapter," she said. "For myself, I don't know that I'm ever going to have full closure. He'll be eighty-eight when he is eligible for parole. That definitely puts me at ease for the sake of the kids and my family. And we all feel the same. It resonated very well when the judge handed down the sentence."

Then Erik took some questions. A reporter asked him to clarify his earlier story about when Stephen tried to put Erik's son to bed.

"It turned into a disaster, if you will," he said. "My son was scared to death of him."

Mary was asked if she wished to speak to Stephen.

"I have no desire to," she said. "Stephen could never tell me anything that would make me forgive him for what he's done to our family. I'm absolutely pleased with the sentence. I prayed for this day."

Mary said she glared at Stephen in court earlier in the day as she walked back to her seat after addressing the court. "I wanted to make him realize how this affected me and my family," she said. "It was the last thing that he saw of me."

Eric Smith appeared pleased as he took the podium. "Today justice was served," he said. "This sentence banishes the evil of his legacy from our society forever. And for that, we are forever grateful."

A reporter asked Smith to explain how he told Druzinski about the Grant children seeing the murder.

"It went to the judge through our sentencing memorandum," Smith answered. "And then, subsequent to that, we had letters from Erik and Alicia indicating when Lindsey told them about this, and also a letter from the therapist. So they told them that on Christmas Day, Lindsey told Eric and Alicia what she witnessed.

"And sometime after that, in the beginning of January, Erik and Alicia came up here indicating they had to talk to us about something, which we thought was a little odd, until they sat down and told us exactly what it was. And that certainly changed the scope of our sentencing memorandum a little bit right then."

Smith was asked why the information about the children witnessing the crime hadn't come out during the trial.

"We found out about it in January," he explained. "The police department found out about it in January. So that's why it didn't come out in trial."

Would Smith have still charged Stephen with first-degree murder if he'd been told the Grant children had witnessed the murder?

"Let's not forget what these two kids have been through," Smith said. "So before we would have ever thought of using them as witnesses in this case, boy, we would have put a lot of thought and effort into that.

"Just standing here now without knowing the exact details of what they said and what they saw, I seriously doubt we would ever put them through what they would have to go through in court, testifying about the murder of their mother, in front of their father in a courtroom. I sincerely doubt we would ever do that.

"And if that meant the difference between first and second degree, I think we would have erred on the side of second degree and relied on the judge to do her job—which, by the way, she did a phenomenal job, made a record that is beyond reproach," he said. "Any one of the reasons that she gave are substantial and compelling—compelling reasons to exceed the guidelines. It was just what we wanted, fifty to eighty years."

Smith said he wasn't surprised that Stephen stayed mute throughout the trial. "Alicia thought he was going to testify because, as all of you know in this room, Steve likes to talk. And as we know from listening to his fifty to sixty hours of tapes, that he's still talking. But I thought he would not [address the court].

"It's one thing to talk when you're back at the jail, when it's he and his sister. But when you know every person in the courtroom hates you, and everything you're going to say is going to be torn apart, I think he probably saw the writing on the wall and knew that no matter what he said—false pleas for remorse—I don't think the judge was going to buy that. And you saw what she said. I don't think she would have bought anything he had to say.

"So, no, it didn't surprise me. But I would like to have heard him. I would have liked to hear what he had to say."

A reporter asked, "Would you have wanted more than fifty years?"

"More than fifty years? We would like life in prison without parole," Smith said. "But having said that, fifty to eighty years is essentially the rest of his life behind bars. He's thirty-eight right now. That means he would be eighty-eight when he's up for parole—not when he's released, that's up for parole. And I'll be ninety-one at that time. So someone will wheel me in and I'll object to that parole.

"So we're very pleased with the sentence of the judge and very pleased with the record she made," Smith said. "I don't think this case is ever coming back."

* * *

That evening, the Standerfers had a celebratory dinner at Madison's, a popular bar and restaurant in downtown Mount Clemens known for its delicious hamburgers and cream of mushroom soup. Lindsey and Ian were there, Alicia said; the family had been staying in a hotel for the past few days before the sentencing, she explained.

Alicia also said the adoption papers had gone through, and she was now officially Lindsey and Ian's new mother. "It's going to be a challenge for all of us," Alicia said. "But I'll raise my sister's children as if they're my own."

Epilogue

On Friday the thirteenth, two days before Father's Day, 2008, a man phoned the St. Clair County Sheriff's Office at 1:40 P.M. to report a suicide. The dispatcher asked whose suicide he was reporting, and the caller said it was his own. The man dictated an address and hung up.

A deputy was immediately sent to Connors Road in Emmett, a small town about fifty miles northeast of downtown Detroit. As the officer was exiting his vehicle, he heard a gunshot; it came from the garage behind the house.

William "Al" Grant was sprawled on the concrete floor. A rifle lay nearby.

"We're asking the media not to come to the funeral," Kelly said the next day. Her dad was cremated after a private service.

Bryan Buero, owner of Trio Maintenance, a landscaping company located in the same industrial complex as USG Babbitt, said he was "floored" when he heard of Grant's suicide. "It's a shame," he said. "He was a good man. He didn't deserve all that stuff that happened to his family.

"He got really quiet after the Tara Grant thing happened," Buero said. "He spent more time to himself after that. He didn't go out of his way to talk to me any more. I would go to him often to make sure everything was OK with him, and see if he needed any help. He'd say everything was fine. But I could tell something was different. He just wasn't the same man."

Prisoner #674421 will remain in an isolated unit for the first few years of his incarceration in the Bellamy Creek Correctional Facility, said Michigan Department of Corrections spokesman Russ Marlan.

The redbrick men's prison—the state's newest lockup— is located on Bluewater Highway in Ionia, Michigan, amid pastoral countryside in the southwest region of the state.

Stephen Grant fancied himself a celebrity during the search for his wife, and later when he bragged that inmates in the Macomb County Jail wanted his autograph. But his high profile would be a detriment in prison, Marlan said.

"Prisoners get television, and they get newspapers, and they're aware of what's going on in the world," Marlan said. "I'm sure most of them know who Stephen Grant is. We don't want a prisoner to harm him in order to make a name for himself, which prisoners will often do to elevate their status. So we'll keep him in a segregated area for the first few years."

The battle between Alicia Standerfer and Kelly Utykanski continued to rage long after Stephen's criminal case wrapped up. In September 2008, Kelly's attorneys called Alicia into court to explain why Alicia wasn't allowing Kelly's side of the family to visit Lindsey and Ian, as had been ordered in the adoption settlement.

On September 4, the two sides met for more than three hours in a private conference with juvenile court referee John J. Kennedy. Alicia and Kelly left without talking to the press. It was later revealed that Alicia was censured by the judge for not allowing visits to Stephen's side of the family.

Alicia has vowed that Stephen Grant will never see his children again.

Acknowledgments

The authors extend special thanks to Macomb County sheriff Mark Hackel and his staff, including Captain Anthony Wickersham, Lieutenant Elizabeth Darga, Sergeant Pam McLean, Sergeant Brian Kozlowski, Sergeant Larry King, spokesman John Cwikla, and Deputy William Hughes; Macomb County prosecutor Eric Smith and assistant prosecutors Bill Cataldo and Therese Tobin; *Detroit News* editor Kelley Root and the staff of the Macomb Bureau; *Detroit News* photo editors Jan Lovell and Robert Houlihan; photojournalist Todd McInturf; Tom Gromak; Sergeant Tim Rodwell, Emmet County Sheriff's Office; Officer James Pettis, Charlevoix Police Department; Robin Launderville and Sue Scott, Gardens of Rest cemetery; Carl Carlson, Delta County Chief Deputy Registrar. Most of all, love and thanks to our families and friends for their patience, understanding, and picking up the slack while we were busy with "the book."